C0-ATC-465

The Library

COLBY JUNIOR COLLEGE

An Interpretation of PARADISE REGAINED
and SAMSON AGONISTES

by *ARNOLD STEIN*

HEROIC
KNOWLEDGE

UNIVERSITY OF MINNESOTA PRESS, Minneapolis

PR
3565
S75

© Copyright 1957 by the University of Minnesota

ALL RIGHTS RESERVED

Printed at the North Central Publishing Company, St. Paul

Library of Congress Catalog Card Number: 57-8035

PUBLISHED IN GREAT BRITAIN, INDIA, AND PAKISTAN BY
THE OXFORD UNIVERSITY PRESS, LONDON, BOMBAY, AND KARACHI

The text used for all quotations from Paradise Regained *and* Samson
Agonistes *is* Milton's Complete Poems, *edited by Frank A. Patterson,
copyright 1930 by Mr. Patterson. These quotations are reprinted by
permission of Appleton-Century-Crofts, Inc.*

38532

TO

Robert Mark Estrich

AND THE MEMORY OF

William Hildreth

PREFACE

THIRTEEN consecutive essays which call themselves an interpretation have laid claim to certain perquisites and liberties, but they must also accept a certain range of responsibility. They have to represent an author's considered judgment of what he thinks most important to emphasize and elucidate. If he proceeds by essays, as I prefer, rather than by formal chapters, he is nonetheless accountable for his choice of what he engages in the poems. But he ought under no circumstances call his critical work a definitive study. One may make a definitive study of all the known facts, but not a definitive study of the meaning or beauty of a work of art. To do so, one would have to immobilize history and, what is as impossible, arrogate to oneself all the perspectives, insight, knowledge, sensibility of one's contemporaries. All criticism is incomplete. It may even represent less than the author's full knowledge and interest.

Criticism is no exact science. Literary reality retreats from our fixed grasp, retreats and renews itself, waiting for us to renew ourselves. At its most fortunate, criticism points (as Eliot says). It suggests and opens up; if it gets between the unprepared reader and his individual, immediate response to the work, it does not stay there, but like a capsule gently dissolves to do its intended office. It does not coerce; it does not insist on knowing everything. A critical interpretation is, or should be, one self-consistent and orderly demonstration of individual response. We may judge an interpretation by its originality-and-truth, by its depth, by the comprehensiveness of its grasp of the important, by its balance of immediate insight and conceptual grip on the whole. But we may not expect it either to settle or to engage all possibilities.

Most of the best critical writing of our age has cultivated a cool neutral style, the better to demonstrate the formal, intellectual properties of literature, and the better to dissociate itself from the aims and manners of a previous age. But there is no one ideal criticism or critical method, though there are many examples of good-better-best and bad-worse-worst. And every choice of method is a choice of limitations, bringing in the inevitable train of what one will not do, possibly cannot do. I have taken some chances, with my eyes open, being of age. I have tried to cultivate objectivity, but I have not tried to train out of the writing my personal response to the developments I describe. No esthetic fact can be demonstrated to the blind, deaf, or unfeeling. An honest enthusiasm of response, if it is not foolish or ignorant or self-loving, can both record the esthetic facts and prepare an imaginative capacity for seeing the facts to be responded to. The critic may choose to be a propagandist (in the good sense), wanting to stimulate the individual response of the reader's thoughts and feelings. And this can be done, I hope, without lapsing into the errors of the old-fashioned "appreciation."

For the most part I have tried to demonstate rather than to argue, and have (except in some notes) avoided engaging the established critical problems separately; but have instead trusted that a fresh critical interpretation of the poems would come to terms with the major problems while in motion, as part of a developing grasp of the integrated working of the poems. Criticism, as I understand the office, is no ordinary argument and cannot proceed so. If we debate at every turn we see then only what has been seen, or what the argument produces for us by a method which in its form of discourse departs dangerously from the internal laws of what we study, the work of art.

I had some other plans of attack for my treatment of *Samson*

Agonistes. My own approach to that poem — in some ways that are probably no longer quite discernible — has been through *Paradise Regained.* For some reason I had to come to terms with the more difficult and less available poem before I could see many of the things that interested me most in *Samson Agonistes.* Some of the exploration of issues in *Paradise Regained* was intended also to help solve problems in *Samson Agonistes.* I have referred to a few of these connections in the text, and I shall make some further brief comments in my Postscript. But when I came to the actual writing I found that I was no longer engaged by the desire to work out many of the relevant similarities and differences which had been part of my own preparation. The materials, partly formed, are still there in the text. Though not developed, they have often provided important assistance to me; I hope they may prove occasionally suggestive to others.

I have also had to abandon my plans for treating the styles of the poems, particularly that of *Samson Agonistes.* I found myself too engrossed in working out the structural details of the drama in terms of its moral development to pause for the long (and necessarily slower) demonstrations of stylistic and textural qualities. For though I have read, thought about, and taught this poem for years, in the heat of finally stating my views in written words new and better insights pressed themselves upon me and dictated both the shape of my exposition and the tempo. In confining my attention chiefly to interpreting the dramatic structure of *Samson Agonistes,* I have but followed in my own way the precedent established by my chief twentieth-century predecessors: Jebb, Tupper, Baum, Curry, Hanford, Clark, Tillyard, Grierson, Parker, Bush, Woodhouse, Krouse, Allen, Watkins.

My basic orientation toward Milton is probably not different from the lines laid down or followed by Hanford, Hughes, Bush, Woodhouse, Parker, Allen. But there are some inevitable differences in detail and emphasis. I cannot personally associate myself with Christian humanism, for Christian thinking and feeling are available to me only through my efforts at historical imagination. Besides, being younger than they I have also been exposed to some different interests. Some of my reading has gone in different directions, and we have read the same books at different times and with different eyes. The Milton they have given us cannot be quite the same Milton who is emerging to my contemporaries. He will not be the same Milton to my juniors. How could it be otherwise? And who would want to deny each age its immediate and individual claim on a great poet?

My view of history implies an intimate collaboration between present and past. As God (according to a theological concept which does not contradict the spirit of *Paradise Regained* and *Samson Agonistes*) works through individuals rooted in their present, so does history. We regain the past not as pure gift, nor even by merely making conscientious efforts; but only by giving something of ourselves and our insights as individuals living in a present. We have to know and feel what the questions ought to be before we can hope for significant answers. Some of my predecessors have used their concepts of Milton's Christian humanism to solve relations between his personal thought and his art in ways that do not quite satisfy me. Milton's moral art suffers not inconsiderable losses from too peremptory a translation. When we reduce his poems to their moral paradigms, we not only sacrifice "subtleties," which some admirers might be willing to spare, but we damage the paradigm itself — we distort through omission, and through hasty substituting of abstract formulas (however good or true) for the rich circumstantial endowing of ideas with imaginative life.

I have reserved for a Postscript, which some readers may want to read now, further comments on assumptions that underlie this book.

I have some general debts to acknowledge: to my students, for their constant contribution, by now largely anonymous, toward sharpening issues for me; to scholars from whom I have learned both by agreement and disagreement. I wish particularly to thank A. S. P. Woodhouse for some comments on the organization of my historical essay on the virtues. I am indebted to John Crowe Ransom through a correspondence of many years, frequently

touching on Milton. One cannot live as a member of an academic
community without acquiring, if one is lucky, many large obligations. Glenn H. Leggett and James W. Hall have heard or read
parts of the manuscript and made comments. By now I cannot
remember who said what, but I wish to express my gratitude to
the following friends for conversations extending over several
years: to John Verrall on music, to John B. McDiarmid on ancient philosophy, to Theodore Roethke on poetry and related
matters.

My chief personal debt is to my wife. I have drawn freely on her
judgment and learning.

I wish to thank the American Academy in Rome, and its library
staff, for many courtesies; and the Fund for the Advancement of
Education for a year free to read at large and think. My essay on
"The Kingdoms of the World" is reprinted from *E.L.H.* I am
grateful to the editors, and particularly to Don Cameron Allen.

A. S.

Seattle, Washington
February 1957

CONTENTS

PARADISE REGAINED

SOME PROBLEMS AND SOLUTIONS

THE theme is most formidable, even for a poet truly fascinated by what's difficult, and with a great talent to indulge. And this poet is no experimenting youth flushed with inspiration He is writing a special kind of a major poem he intends to stand beside an epic and a tragedy — both notable for ambitious themes difficult to realize poetically. The theme of *Paradise Regained* is the most difficult — not only for what it requires doing but for what it forbids, and Milton accepts fully the poetic challenge of the limitations imposed by his theme. For this is a poet with a great sense of structure and decorum, with his own conscious mastery of form, an intimate and practiced awareness of his own talents, a long and self-examining experience with the great poetry of the known world, and with intense, "heroic" preparations for adding to this poetry his own poetic things unattempted, his own poetic deeds above heroic. I conclude, not from biographical but poetic facts, that he must have known what he was up against, and relished it. The *Paradise Lost* and *Samson Agonistes* of a Milton may at worst be glorious failures; but a *Paradise Regained*, even of a Milton, runs the pressing risk of being a mere failure, another of the long list of poems patiently prescribing piety to almost no readers, fit or unfit. And I guess that Milton knew this too, and relished the risk as a necessary part of his triumph.

The theme declares that the protagonist is to be tried fully,

3 .

through *all* temptation, and is to be proved by merit as well as history "the undoubted Son of God." And this high enterprise is to be accomplished, not by acting but by a special kind of not-acting, by a special kind of conquering weakness, "By Humiliation and strong Sufferance." The hero our drama gives us is a *perfect man*, a legitimate subject for poetry but extremely difficult to present in dramatic action. A perfect divine hero would be more difficult, in fact impossible, and a semi-divine hero would be less difficult, for he would not need to be perfect. By the techncial rules of this drama, which *are* observed, the protagonist is free to fail, but historically, and by God's prefatory, providential word, he is destined to win — a calculated embarrassment for any drama, and a weakness that must be turned to strength.

By the rules of the dramatic fiction he is to be presented only as man, though perfect; he is not "divine" until the proof of the drama has run its calculated course. Here, to be sure, Milton's personal convictions can help support the rules of the drama, but only by proper poetic invention, which may support but may not usurp; for the rules become laws once they are chosen, and Milton has chosen promptly and unequivocally. But still the hero as man cannot be quite stripped of history, not even in a fiction — at least not by a poet with a long sense of decorum and tradition (in poetry anyway); for Milton is determined to be original by bettering tradition decisively, not by violating it ingeniously. And so the protagonist, though man, must accept some of the poetic consequences of his divine history. He may not *feel* with the interesting freedom of historical common man; the drama of his consciousness may not be explored as if he were a mere tragic hero. And a certain necessary "religious decorum" must be maintained, as a flexible but absolutely limiting negative, in order not to offend.

The secular hero without flaws has proved no irresistible subject for fiction. The heroine is more possible, for by common assent what she must do can be limited. She is free to feel truly, to love, to sacrifice; she is not required to think truly, at least not through any difficult and sustained course of action. The perfect religious hero has many of the fictional advantages of the perfect heroine.

He ought to be a man of feeling, who expresses perfection in the quality of his love, in its imaginative sensitivity, in depth, in fullness. His wisdom, if it is called for, ought to be expressed by the completeness of its simplicity. But Milton's religious hero is of a stature more ambitious. (The drama of feeling is for another stage. This is the drama of knowledge.) He is, though man, required to play the *role* of a god in a cosmic contest against the *external* forces of evil. His wisdom is perforce simple since it *is* wisdom — which Milton would have regarded as redundance, not paradox. But this hero may not rest in the pure sweetness of his simplicity; he may not answer argument with love. He has a course of action to prepare, and the simplicity which is private wisdom is required to answer publicly the subtle and complex arguments that evil will advance, and answer them fully and clearly, on their own chosen grounds. The intellectual scope of simplicity is here to be demonstrated, and that is no task to trifle with for two thousand lines.

So our hero must argue and display the convincing superiority of his wisdom. He must wisely reject temptations that do not tempt him. The major action has to be negative. Austere and unmoved Good must resist and frustrate passionate Evil, which has to be endowed with the plausibility and interest of complex human personality, endowed even with some measure of pathos; and with arguments that are not straws but have an ancient hold on human minds and hearts, arguments that will reverberate attractively when quickened.

How is a dramatic poem to be constructed on this theme and with these necessary limitations? How is the poet to create any sense of immediacy? The decorum he has accepted will not permit him any free use of stylistic tricks to conjure up the credible magic of present. (He can do something in the skirmishes, and he will, but not on the main battle line.) And with his perfect hero, and the drama of debate, how is he to enlist the reader's involvement? And if he does not need the high dramatic feelings of pity and terror, how is he to get the lowest common necessity of plain narrative interest?

He has learned lessons from *Comus* to be sure, but one of the most surprising lessons is how to make things much harder for himself, and to get along with less, even less than the little of *Comus*. (This is not unprecedented in the history of an artist, but it is far from common; and it ought to have made Milton technically more interesting to the twentieth century, if it had been observed.) The stage is more limited than in *Comus*, for we are never allowed to forget that it is really the mind of the hero. We have some hymning, but no pretty songs, or girls, or almost-Elizabethan poetry. There are fewer extras for "human interest," fewer characters, less stage-movement, or shift in tempo or expectation — only a single protagonist to be tried through *all* temptation, verbally, by a single antagonist. If we think of the Book of Job, as Milton did, we must be impressed with the poetic advantages of a hero who can feel and suffer, who has wife and friends and children and possessions to enlarge the stage of his feelings with their significant reflections. If we think of a poem like George Herbert's "The Sacrifice," with its one sustained theme and most limited stage, we can see that that virtuoso achievement is of a different kind, and however difficult, of a less difficult kind. For the theme has the advantage of being more limited, and it can be developed lyrically, with much cunning modulation of the dissonances and intensities. The stage and theme are static, but the dynamic variations can roam the world and universe with their ranging exploration of single and multiple ironies. There is no lack of room, or angle, for human involvement, for the movement of human feeling.

This is enough, though but a sketch, to indicate the handicaps Milton chose, and deliberately increased, for this poem. But perhaps one thing more ought to be noted, his matching the handicaps with the high claim of the title and introduction. The kind old poet in the rich autumn of his years, so obligingly bringing to fruition the quick hint of his pupil Ellwood, and amending a lack in *Paradise Lost* with a sequel not before thought of! He is very gentle and generous to the simple Ellwood, but he confronts the reader with an amazing humor, a literary joke of unprecedented dimensions. *Paradise Regained* is the real epic, not *Paradise Lost*! That

6

entertaining poem is sung about "the happy garden" — a felicitous expression to describe his "early pastoral," the Virgilian apprentice-work he is about to graduate from.

> I who e're while the happy Garden sung,
> By one mans disobedience lost, now sing
> Recover'd Paradise to all mankind,
> By one mans firm obedience fully tri'd
> Through all temptation, and the Tempter foil'd
> In all his wiles, defeated and repuls't,
> And Eden rais'd in the wast Wilderness.

Now the theme of *Paradise Regained* is higher, formally; and according to the criteria of Scriptures, which are to dominate all other standards in the poem, whether political, ethical, or meta-physical, this "brief" epic on a biblical model ought to be more exalted than the epic on a classical model. But the formal priority does not quite cover the whole situation, and to insist on it so at the outset is to fling down a challenge — from Milton, we can surmise, it is not without some irony. For formal priority is one thing, but the relative classification of *Paradise Lost* cultivates the incongru-ous deliberately. To the embarrassing difficulties already inherent in the theme and treatment, the poet prefixes this challenge of comparison. Now we are to have the real epic — "hoc opus, hic labor est." And this announcement, with a remarkable difference, echoes the famous lines, perhaps not apocryphal, that signalize with sincere modesty Virgil's transition to epic:

> Ille ego, qui quondam gracili modulatus avena
> carmen, et egressus silvis vicina coegi
> ut quamvis avido parerent arva colono,
> gratum opus agricolis, at nunc horrentia Martis
> arma virumque cano.

This has been the easy and pleasant part of the critical task, mak-ing the inventory of an artist's prearranged difficulties.[1] How did Milton solve the problems he accepted and prepared and flaunted? A moderately full answer will take most of a book. The fine points are so fine, and so firm in the structure and significant, that they cannot be dealt with summarily, in isolation. What I shall attempt now is a kind of rough sketch, to be filled in later. Some of my exposition I intend as preface, to indicate the special terms of this drama; some points will indicate, if broadly, Milton's elected solutions. I shall try to present the main directions a full answer must take, but I shall try not to raise the kind of point that will not serve here as useful prefatory hint.

Milton's technical solution is very bold. He shifts much of the dramatic weight to Satan and his anguished consciousness. The tempter finds himself tempted, and has to play a double role.[2] On the other side the perfect man who cannot be moved has a traditional symbolic role that is rich in potential movement for all imperfect men; in the bridging of this gap Milton does not neglect his opportunities. The weakness that is proved strength is both the formal theme of the drama and the permeating conceptual form. I shall need to return to these large matters.

Some mythic business ought first to be noticed. The drama is domestic and individual, like tragedy, with the great stage set in one man's moral consciousness. But the hero is now assigned a task that the old stories assign to a god, that of the ancient cosmogonical battle against external forces of evil, darkness, chaos, to create real order and the beginning of time. Or rather to re-create what has already been created (in a previous drama), to renew time and order in a private ritual all men depend on and can participate in. It is a *re*-creation, though it is new and one essential stage in an ordained, progressive (circular) scheme. But original creation could not be participated in, and this can be; so in this sense our drama is a ritual. To borrow Eliade's phrase, it is an "imitation of the cosmogonic gesture." If we participate in the purifying conflict we assist in the transforming of "speckled" time to mythical time: "Through repetition of the cosmogonic act, concrete time . . . is projected into mythical time, *in illo tempore* when the foundation of the world occurred."[3] If the poem affects us as ritual, if we feel the time of this once-upon-a-time, if the old pattern moves us at all, Milton will have solved some of the problem of his unmoved hero. (Needless to say, the big pattern does not swallow up the small, concrete patterns in which the individual reader's moral consciousness may participate.)

8

In this, the second stage of the mythic world-conflict, the son is champion of the father. And he is champion of the people, also, taking on (though in this drama *preparing* to take on) suffering, even guilt, to rescue mankind. The venture into the wilderness is a quest, or voyage, or soul-journey, through dangerous and besetting difficulties and labyrinthine ways, toward the "center" of being, the goal of self-realization, the passage of the human to the divine. The monsters are familiar and domesticated, because they are the new, domesticated appearances of the same old monsters. Yet the movement here, since Milton is also modern and sophisticated in his use of myth, is not external but internal and self-willed. We have no physical journeys into the underworld but instead a kind of double acceptance of death — the passion to come later, and the philosophical "way of death" in the process of being designed before our eyes. Finally, the Eden to be raised in the wasteland of the desert will be the consecrated ground of a new beginning, the new symbolic center for a new world.

The mythic patterns help support the poem certainly, but the detailed structure must depend on other patterns, less deep no doubt in the human psyche, but also more available for the immediate stresses and strains in the quick turns and counter-turns of a dramatic action. Milton could count on an accepted and continuous tradition of "significant temptation." For instance, according to Origen (*Contra Celsum*, I, 61), who did not invent this, Herod was instigated by the devil, who plotted against Jesus from the beginning. Men did not wrestle only against flesh and blood. The presidents of the public games did not allow "accidental attacks" — these were intended to test men, to exercise or manifest their faith or patience, or to teach them the humility of their weakness. Thoughts originated from inside or from outside men by the agency of Satan or by good angels. And readers saw more than political morality couched in St. Paul's phrases, "principalities," "powers," "the rulers of the darkness of this world." [4]

There are established rules for the contest and these give Satan no physical power directly. God does not allow man "to be tempted above that ye are able." (I Cor., 10, 13.) And every true believer

9

ought to quote John, 19, 11: "Thou couldest have no power *at all* against me, except it were given thee from above." Satan cannot use physical torture or brainwashing. Nor would he want to, we may suppose; for he is playing for ultimate stakes and not for a merely immediate and material power — with the released victim able, as now, to recant, and however thoroughly humiliated, not absolutely corrupted because not self-corrupted. Satan aims always at a purer and final victory, not at another demonstration of the old fact that the flesh is weak.

A long temptation is a grueling affair. Even brainwashing apparently takes a long time, a lot of concentrated effort, with teams of operators working over one victim, and having to check the effectiveness of their instruction by frequent academic tests. The process here, when it covers all the classic bases for human temptation (and clearly includes the formal parallel of the second Adam), must be long and concentrated, most susceptible to an excruciating narrowness and dullness — especially when the protagonist has one main line of defense (he has others, but they *must* be secondary): a singleness of faith in the will of God, a perfect "passivity."

Milton accepts the narrowness and exploits the length, to miss no possible fine turn. But he also enriches. Although the dialectical drama holds absolutely true to the special conditions and to its unique protagonist, there is constant symbolic relevance for Everyman. And besides, every turn of the intellectual action is an intellectual form of the most basic kind of physical drama — pursuit, trap, and escape. Excitement cannot doze when the stakes are the highest possible and a single wrong move means ruin. And although the physical level of the drama is always uppermost and transparent, underneath are the fascinating implications, packed down intricately, but inviting the mind to penetrate and to follow them out into patterns that relate to still other patterns.

It is not enough for the protagonist to refuse offers; he must answer, and fully. Milton's own belief in reason is heroic, and he could not be interested in a hero prevented by his drama from giving full expression to the dignity and responsibility of the human mind — not even in a drama of salvation, which is a highly specialized business, fiercely exclusive, and bound to a particular revelation that must ignore or scorn as irrelevant to the main and single economy of salvation many other kinds of human interest, and knowledge, and wisdom. But this does not mean that the hero must merely offer superior rebuttals, or even that he must confine himself to astute description of the trap he refuses to enter. The physical drama reminds one of a perilous interview between Raskolnikov and the detective who casually draws the conversation over sudden pitfalls. Milton can add something to the basic device. For the hunter is also hunted, and the answers not only expose the intentions of Satan, but they undermine his pitfalls and play cat-and-mouse with his motives, checkmating or taunting the secret motive still several removes from sight.

Though this exercise in the wilderness is, formally, for the purpose of laying down the first rudiments of the "great warfare," it is in Milton's mind the most important preparation for war, the preliminary self-conquest of the successful soldier or captain of men (as for instance Cromwell).[5] It is a preparation hardly to be distinguished from war, and for Satan it is the actual war. In his campaign he always has, like any good strategist, two objectives — the big one, and a more limited, secondary objective.[6] There is the total victory of successful corruption; but, failing that, there is always a lesser aim — to find out, *is* this the real Son of God, and so to find out *when* the prophecy will come to pass, which leads inevitably to *how*, and its special symbolic terms. Satan is the vehicle of an extraordinary, torturing irony: he offers a surface of specific, comprehensive, *assured* temptations which cannot cover his own inner, tremulous uncertainties.

There is patristic tradition for Satan's doubts, and Milton is able to extend this amazingly as part of the central structure of his fiction, with a fine and biting psychological realism that makes for both immediate and sustaining interest. "Thou thyself subjected to torture. . . . Seeing these things, thou wast in utter perplexity," as Ignatius writes in his *Epistle to the Philippians*.[7] Nor would Milton have had to look far to find hints for irony. "Perfect love

11

casteth out fear; because fear hath torment." (I John, 4, 18.) Satan is dogged by fear.

But Milton needs no instruction in irony. He relishes it and believes in it as a mode of intellectual discourse and of art. He has the precedent of Scripture to show "what force of teaching there is sometimes in laughter . . . of answering 'a fool according to his folly'"—and so to teach both the fool and hearers. He knows what Cicero and Seneca have to say, and Horace:

> Jesting decides great things
> Stronglier and better oft than earnest can.

And he likes the words of Sophocles' Electra:

> 'Tis you that say it, not I; you do the deeds,
> And your ungodly deeds find me the words.[8]

There was precedent available for interpreting some of Christ's ambiguous answers as intended to "outwit" hostile questioners, and something of that occurs in our drama, though Satan is seldom only outwitted. His persistence and patience—for this is a competition in patience too—make a grim kind of comic pattern. One is reminded of the famous self-justification of Aristippus after Dionysius I of Syracuse spat in his face: he must expect to be splashed sometimes when landing a big fish. Patience, though traditionally an austere virtue, had its pleasurable side too. According to Tertullian's psychological analysis,[9] an adversary loses his enjoyment if you are not pained, and his loss will pain him and pleasure you. (This fits our case of course, but I mention Tertullian's treatise chiefly to indicate how much richer Milton's concept is; for in his concept of moral drama heroic knowledge is a necessary achievement of the hero, and patience is no simple virtue able to stand alone.)

Satan does all the acting and "refluxing" around Christ as a still point, and this structural irony of imbalance is Milton's radical and deliberate intention. For this is only the immediate impression. The quiet *actio*, not *reactio*, of Christ's mind disposing of Satan's proposing, and maintaining his vision even in apparent suspension, more than holds the balance. One motion of the drama is a return of the protagonist to the source of being. And Satan's motion is parallel, in his drive toward source and definition — not his real source but the one he has chosen, willed: the port of worst. He would be at the worst, and in his drive for willed certainty he reminds us of Macbeth forcing the witches to tell him. Just as the torture of knowledge is appropriate to Satan, so is the torture of time, for he is the arch opportunist, the violator and manager of time. And his *timing*, though exquisitely shrewd, is always essentially wrong.

These are points that need further exploring, but they must serve as part of this rough preliminary sketch of Milton's technical solutions. We come now to a basic consideration, Milton's use of the symbolism traditional and potential in the role of his perfect man. The hero may seem, superficially, to be static, but the symbolism quickly establishes itself as in motion and to be revealed in its fullness under the forward pressure of action. The full meaning is a prime source of Satan's rich perplexity and what he will do to relieve himself of that burden. We hear him brooding early about the prophecy of his doom and trying to translate God's metaphorical language into prose literalness. He shows the same naiveté, though more intense and subject to a continuous irony, that Adam displays after his fall. But Adam receives angelic instruction about the nature of divine language:

> Dream not of thir fight,
> As of a Duel, or the local wounds
> Of head or heel.

And the naive chiliastic Apostles, who make up part of the human audience of *Paradise Regained*, will presumably have been instructed on the subject of Christ's real kingdom, and related points. But Satan must struggle toward a kind of instruction more appropriate for him.

It is most convenient to start from Milton's prose description "Of the Office of the Mediator," in Chapter XV of the *Christian Doctrine*. He is (1) prophet. And the "manner of administering" is both external ("the promulgation of divine truth") and internal ("the illumination of the understanding"). He is (2) priest, and

13

this function is fulfilled by sacrifice and intercession. He is (3) king, and made so by God the Father. He "governs and preserves chiefly by an inward law and spiritual power." In his description of the kingly function Milton can be most emphatically Miltonic. The pre-eminence of Christ's kingdom and the divine laws on which it is founded are manifested so: "He governs not the bodies of men alone, as the civil magistrate, but their minds and consciences, and that not by force and fleshly weapons, but by what the world esteems the weakest of all instruments. Hence external force ought never to be employed in the administration of the kingdom of Christ, which is the church." Satan will ignorantly fix on the aspect of the kingly function that he can understand. But while he is tempting so, the function most important for *Paradise Regained* will be exercised, that of prophet in its two aspects; and for the symbolic drama the more important aspect will be the internal "illumination of the understanding." [10]

In the early angelic chorus we hear that "The Father knows the Son." This is the other side of the Son's implied obligation, to "know" the Father. The vanquishing "by wisdom" will be, as it were, a by-product of the primal knowledge — as the social benefits achieved by the philosopher-king may be expected to be less his direct aim than the results of his vision of the Good. The emphasis, very squarely, is on symbolic "illumination" — on the knowledge and self-knowledge Christ will demonstrate in the action of the drama, while he is demonstrating his mastery and full control of that knowledge; and this will provide illumination for the individual mind, by the great lesson of the great *exemplum*. The Saviour is to "recure" Adam's death, as Adam is told at the end of *Paradise Lost,* "Not by destroying Satan, but his works," in Adam and the children of Adam.

Christ is Illuminator of the individual seeking to know himself. Origen provides a basic text for this harmonizing of biblical and Greek anthropologies: "The mind bears a certain relationship to God, of whom the mind itself is an intellectual image, and by means of this it may come to knowledge of the nature of the divine, especially if it be purified and separated from bodily matter." (*De*

14

Principiis, I, i, 7.) This is close to Milton's working concept, though
in Milton we may expect to find no approval of the separation from
"bodily matter"; his doctrine is purer Greek, as I understand it,
and purer Hebrew, and is content with the superiority of the mind.
The Christ of this poem hungers, thirsts, dreams, apparently without conscious volition; he plans and conjectures consciously. But
everything is under the control of his major illumination, and
illuminates. He is a pattern of knowledge and virtue. As Origen
argues against Celsus, Christ is "the pattern of the most virtuous
life," and so to be related to the ideal of the Greek tradition. (I,
68.) We are presented with an imitation of God that has roots in
Greek rationalistic ethics, though the controlling metaphor is the
biblical one of man's being created in God's image. The true image
is revealed by the unfolding of mind, by what Kierkegaard calls
"becoming what you are" — if I may borrow Kierkegaard's fine
phrase, without all the associations of the strenuousness of "sub-
jectivity." It is a process of symbolic illumination related to T. S.
Eliot's, "To arrive where you are. . . . And know the place for the
first time." [11]

Milton has described the interesting subject of poetry as "what-
soever hath passion or admiration in all the changes of that which
is called fortune from without, or the wily subtleties and refluxes
of man's thoughts from within." (III, 238–39.) There *are* some fine
motions within Christ, but these cannot be part of the immediate
dramatic effect, and they yield themselves to perception only after
many other patterns of movement have been seen. Elsewhere we
have an Adam and his other self, Eve, as well as the Satan without.
We have the two Samsons, and his conscience between, as well
as the outside tempters. But most of the "wily subtleties and refluxes" of this poem must be provided by Satan, and by the symbolic role of the Saviour. To compensate for the restricted motion
of the drama of the mind, there is the released motion of what the
successful Saviour will mean to a waiting world. To compensate
for our knowledge of the destined outcome, the symbol of a potentially unsuccessful Saviour is transferred to the consciousness of

15

Everyman — to *his* liability to these temptations, vicariously experienced, with the possibility of defeat personal and immediate.

But the chief burden of immediacy is shifted, with brilliant results, to Satan, who also has symbolic chores to run. He is a diminished antagonist. In *Paradise Lost* he knew that the moral issue was whether good was to come from evil, but then he represented cosmic evil and now he is more nearly domestic. He is intensely interesting of course; he has made some unfortunate gains in personality; he is always formidable, at least to Everyman. But he is fascinatingly wrong, essentially inept. For all his dazzling footwork, he has a kind of monomania: all his temptations are in terms of *power*. Whether he offers kingdoms of the world, or mind, or spirit, he can think of only one bait for the knowledge he wants. He has been diminished, we may interpolate, by his own empire (usurped) of the world, and that makes a fine argument hidden from him. As antagonist and stage director he will have rich opportunities for producing dramatic action.

THE VIRTUES

THIS essay will attempt to sketch some of the background of Milton's moral scheme for the poem. That the leading ideas are Platonic is a fact so long taken for granted that it may be practically neglected in ambitious interpretations of the poem. I want to insist on the fact again, for purposes of critical emphasis. But I must warn the reader not to expect a full, or strictly methodical, exposition of the Platonic elements in the poem. What I am presenting here is not a complete argument, and is more exploratory than methodical. Nor shall I draw many of my points directly from the poem itself, or press their application to the poem, though such an omission will certainly lessen the immediate persuasiveness of my views. But my present purpose is to provide a background which will help open the way for a fuller interpretation of the poem. I do not expect the reader to be quite convinced by a preparatory argument, however final it may have to sound in order to be said at all. I shall be content if he finds the approach suggestive, and if it opens his mind to new ways of seeing the poem.

My underlying assumption, to be demonstrated in later essays, is that *Paradise Regained* is a dramatic definition of "heroic knowledge," not of heroic rejection; and that the contest is a preparation for *acting transcendence in the world*, by uniting intuitive knowledge with proved intellectual and moral discipline. If I am right, the familiar formulas of repressive negativism, allegorical self-punishment, "quasi-allegory" of the church, allegory of world-flesh-devil — these will not, I believe, provide the best insights for understanding the poem.

Since my argument is exploratory, perhaps it will be helpful if I anticipate the general plan of my subject. The virtue I am most concerned with is temperance, which is of central importance in the poem but cannot be understood without exploring the connections with other virtues. First, I shall sketch some general background. Second, I shall look more closely at Milton's concept of temperance, and at the problem of its relationship to other virtues, particularly to the virtue of piety. Third, I shall offer a reinterpretation of magnanimity and its connection with temperance. Finally, I shall examine a special relationship between temperance and justice.

Let us begin with the familiar definitions from Book IV of the *Republic*:

And so we call an individual brave in virtue of this spirited part of his nature, when, in spite of pain or pleasure, it holds fast to the injunctions of reason about what he ought or ought not be afraid of.

And wise in virtue of that small part which rules and issues these injunctions, possessing as it does the knowledge of what is good for each of the three elements and for all of them in common.

And, again, temperate by reason of the unanimity and concord of all three, when there is no internal conflict between the ruling element and its two subjects [the spirited and appetitive], but all are agreed that reason should be ruler.

Our principle that the born shoemaker or carpenter had better stick to his trade turns out to have been an adumbration of justice; and that is why it has helped us. But in reality justice, though evidently analogous to this principle, is not a matter of external behaviour, but of the inward self and of attending to all that is, in the fullest sense, a man's proper concern.

The virtues are inseparable. For Milton this is not a fact to be learned as a careful student of Plato; it is a commanding insight. For the moment let us regard this as self-evident, along with the superior importance of wisdom, and consider more closely what is involved in the virtue of temperance. This virtue will have a special importance in *Paradise Regained*, as will the virtue of justice in *Samson Agonistes*.

The early Socratic definition of *sophrosyne* associates the virtue with the sane, the balanced, the wholesome. The virtue is related no doubt to the Apollonian tradition, probably reinforced by the Pythagorean doctrine of limit. There are physical overtones, with health considered as a kind of harmony; and there is the analogy of "healthy thinking." The virtue also comprehends a proper modesty. In still another sense it means control of the appetites, but easy and graceful control; for some things, if they can be done decently at all, are to be done readily and quickly. This is pre-eminently the virtue of the disciplined life. In the *Republic* temperance is to be understood as self-mastery, the subordination of lower faculties to higher. In politics the virtue is like a harmony pervading and uniting all parts of the whole in agreement. The metaphor of harmony is almost inescapable in considering temperance; one may perhaps even surmise that the metaphor preceded the name.[1]

The later development of the concept of temperance would make an interesting history by itself. Under Stoic influence and its repressive effects, temperance tends to become restricted to an exaggeration of but one of its possible characteristics, the virtue Comus aptly calls "lean and sallow Abstinence." It is easy to see how this happened, since the Stoics regarded intemperance as the fountain of all disorders.[2] Early Christianity, having to deal with an active concept of evil and the consequent separation of will from intellect, makes temperance into a virtue that is the chief guardian of the moral threshold. The qualities of temperance as an achieved effect become completely subordinated to the negative, preventive qualities of the virtue. The seeds of sin proceed far, as Origen says, if we have not "resisted the first movements to intemperance." He speaks of the "natural movements, as those of covetousness, or of anger, or of sorrow, or of all those generally which through the vice of intemperance exceed the natural bounds of moderation." And St. Augustine, in his thumbnail sketch of the virtues, which are for him authentic testimony of the presence and power of evil, describes "that temperance which suppresses the lusts of the flesh, and curbs them from carrying the mind away into mischief." [3]

We shall need to return to this attitude, but first let us look briefly at some "new" virtues that Milton must either take into account or obviously ignore. Already in the *Gorgias* (508) it is reported that sages say the universe is held together by communion and friendship. The influence of Judaism, and the identification of the Ten Commandments with the classical virtues, lead Philo to introduce faith as a primary intellectual virtue (along with piety), and humanity as a primary moral virtue (along with justice). A single quotation from *The Special Laws* can serve as a kind of landmark:

> For each of the ten pronouncements separately and all in common incite and exhort us to wisdom and justice and godliness and the rest of the company of virtues, with good thoughts and intentions combining wholesome words, and with words actions of true worth, that so the soul with every part of its being attuned may be an instrument making harmonious music . . . Of the queen of the virtues, piety or holiness, we have spoken earlier and also of wisdom and temperance. [4]

The unity of the commandments is like the Platonic unity of the virtues; the ideal is the psychological integrity of thought, word, and deed; the result is the harmony associated with Platonic temperance. Intention is part of the integrity, but perhaps with a conscious side glance at the intention required by Hebrew law, and at the Stoic emphasis on forethought and assent. For Philo's virtue of faith there is, according to Professor Wolfson, no real precedent in Greek philosophy. But there is the great watershed of Abraham's experience and the proverbial fear of God as the beginning of wisdom. Philo, who relates faith to justice toward God, is following the example of Greek philosophy, which relates piety to justice and to justice toward God. One last virtue still needs mentioning at this point, for our future reference. That is *Simcha,* the joy that comes from the faithful performance of the law; it is probably to be associated here with the attunement of the soul in harmony.[5]

Before finally coming to Milton's views I want to pause on Cicero's interesting and influential handbook presentation of the virtues in *De Officiis*. The "new" virtue of humanity receives a long exposition that is commensurate with its new importance. Even more significant is the way it becomes involved in other virtues. The excesses of fortitude, for instance, are associated less with defects of wisdom than with defects of justice, and justice is considered chiefly under the aspect of the community. (I, 19.) In summing up, Cicero identifies justice with *communitas*; for those duties are closer to nature (*aptiora*) which depend on *communitas* than are those which depend on *cognitio*. (I, 43.) The reasoning back of this is feeble and casually amateurish, but what interests us is the gap between this kind of diluted Platonism and Milton's return to the pure source. As a Roman concerned with the duty of citizens, Cicero stresses the social aspects of the virtues. His Stoic ideal of nature, which is part of Milton's eclecticism too, makes it possible for him to give precedence to *communitas* — just what a Milton would deny even in the flush of his revolutionary zeal. *Communitas*, which spills over into charity, liberality, kindness, is obviously snubbed by the scheme of *Paradise Regained*. For the time being, it is enough to note this.

Cicero's treatment of temperance is more relevant to our interest, for it both diverges from Plato and extends implications. The virtue "embraces" the other three and binds them together in a sort of harmony. It is characterized by propriety, decorum of action, by self-control; and it gives a kind of grace to life (*ornatus vitae*). It is more separable theoretically than practically. But Plato's master metaphor of harmony is here much diluted. The emphasis falls on the harmony (consistency) within man's nature that distinguishes him from animal nature. Temperance is linked with a kind of human transcendent nobility (to be connected with the social aspects of magnanimity, justice, generosity, liberality, etc.), and this must be displayed with an ethical pedantry that reminds one of Milton's Mammon ("Our greatness will appear / Then most

conspicuous"): "ut . . . appareat cum specie quadam liberali."
(I, 27–28.) Self-control must be part of our prepared appearance
in any course of action: "ut caveamus, ut ea, quae pertinent ad
liberalem speciem et dignitatem moderata sint." The Stoic harmony and self-control of temperance become "the science of doing
the right thing at the right time" — with an obliging eye on "considerateness" and "the approval of those among whom we live."
The order of actions that constitutes our lives shall make a harmony
(public) "as fitting in the parts as a finished oration." (I, 39–40.)

The Renaissance owes something to Cicero for this bridging of
art and life, for his practical formulation of the link between temperance and the decorum of style and form. It is implicit and explicit in Plato but not spelled out. Yet even here, Cicero's concept
of decorum is a practical, workmanlike one, with the rhetorician's
eye never removed from the calculated effect on a large audience.
Decorum harmonizes parts in the whole harmony of beauty, "by
order, consistency, and self-control of all our words and deeds."
But the result is no grand masterpiece; for it is too dependent on
a considerateness (*verecundia*) for public opinion, and this is a
kind of negative nephew (bidding us not offend) of a negative
justice (bidding us not injure). (I, 28.)

Following the Stoic path Cicero identifies temperance with
"complete subjection of all the passions," and he piously regrets
the anger allowed by Peripatetics. (I, 27, 25.) From this concept of
temperance Milton, following one Christian tradition, completely
diverges. The temperance of his perfect man is not passionless. It
is easy to see why, for all its otherworldliness, early Christianity
should have left some allowable place for anger without sin. A
passage from the very naive *Life of Porphyry Bishop of Gaza* by
Mark the Deacon interestingly connects temperance with apathy,
and excludes anger but allows a saintly kind of indignation. Porphyry had so completely mastered the flesh that one would have
supposed his sickness to be "not in his own but another man's
body." He was gentle and meek: "exceeding temperate, so that he
was delivered utterly from all passions, knowing not anger, remembering not evil, letting not the sun go down upon his wrath, having

all his passions dead, save only that indignation which he stirred up against the enemies of the faith." [6]

Porphyry is a little amusing (and not only here), but the problem is real enough. Biblical man is committed to an overpowering sense of the otherness of God and to the riskiness of any desire but the desire of God's will, for which there is no easy blueprint. And extreme Neoplatonists like Proclus could speak of the need not merely to master desire but to root it out — which may have given Meister Eckhart his hint for rooting out everything that was not God.[7] It is a problem never long absent from T. S. Eliot's consciousness: "Teach us to care and not to care"; "For hope would be hope for the wrong thing . . . But the faith and the love and the hope are all in the waiting." [8] The Stoics made their acknowledgments in their wariness concerning human wishes and prayers. They were not without some evasive resourcefulness, as when Seneca, denying the usefulness of emotion, denied the name of emotion to a feeling regulated by reason.[9]

The problem is a classical one for christology, but our concern, luckily, can be casual. Clement of Alexandria, teaching that the Logos became man, made this distinction: "having assumed the flesh, which is by nature passible, the Logos trained it to the habit of impassibility." And so Christ was "entirely incapable of suffering and inaccessible to any emotion." He was the great example of how the body can be "deified into apathy." If Clement is influenced by what R. V. Sellers [10] calls "the essentially Greek enlightenment and knowledge of God," Milton's "Greek" is different, less puritanical, and perhaps (if we may believe some modern reinterpretations of Greek philosophy and religion) closer to the essential. At any rate, Milton deliberately avoids this kind of solution; and with it the need for an embarrassing explanation like Clement's, that Christ ate, not for the body, but lest his companions should think him a phantom.

Milton wants and needs the Socratic notion of "training," but he does not need to carry it to apathy. He deliberately endows his hero with emotions and a full, Platonic tripartite soul. The desert is no place, nor is this an occasion, for being Socratically at ease in Zion. Yet Milton's Christ may fairly be described as behaving with sober, easy grace, attentive to the business at hand, but not stiff or tense. His control is both internal and external. He is, one should observe, *witty*; and that notable quality, along with the ease and grace, links him with an ideal hero of Renaissance Neoplatonism. Given a context encouraging the more severe interpretation of temperance, this recovery of the old idea of easy, disciplined grace is surely remarkable. We must be obliged to Satan for saying it best, and, incidentally, giving us a fine Platonic version of that integrity which makes the style the man:

> I see thou know'st what is of use to know,
> What best to say canst say, to do canst do;
> Thy actions to thy words accord, thy words
> To thy large heart give utterance due, thy heart
> Conteins of good, wise, just, the perfect shape. (III, 7ff)

Had Milton on his way to Venice stopped in Ravenna to see San Vitale, the great thousand-year-old mosaic would have shown him what he did not need to have shown him, a figure of Christ whose graceful majesty links the religious thought of Palestine with the art and philosophy of Greece. Or he might have seen paintings like Piero della Francesca's figure of the baptism, not a philosopher-king, but with a dignified natural ease of beautiful body bespeaking temperance to one who could read. Florence was full of the physical ideal, though it also had its share of lean, prim-mouthed ladies pouring a long thin stream of water to illustrate the virtue. Raphael's beautiful allegory of the virtues, done for the Vatican, was true Renaissance Greek, with perhaps less dignity than grace, but a marvel of grace. Milton, however, had Plato open for him.

Temperance is for Milton primarily the virtue of self-mastery, discipline. It is a guardian of the threshold, as in the Christian tradition, but it is also the achieved effect. It binds all virtues together into that inner "integrity of life" which is the foundation of "real and substantial liberty."[11]

For there is not that thing in the world of more grave and urgent importance throughout the whole life of man, than is discipline

. . . all the movements and turnings of human occasions are moved to and fro as upon the axle of discipline . . . she is that which with her musical chords preserves and holds all the parts thereof together . . . if any visible shape can be given to divine things, the very visible shape and image of virtue, whereby she is not only seen in the regular gestures and motions of her heavenly paces as she walks, but also makes the harmony of her voice audible to mortal ears. (III, 184–85.)

This is a very large claim for temperance, under the name of discipline — a large claim even for a virtue endowed with a special *unitive* function always associated with the high concept of harmony. Milton here extends the virtue to take over some of the qualities of the Idea of Beauty recorded in Socrates' vision in the *Phaedrus*. As befits a poet's vision, Discipline-Temperance-Beauty is not only visible on earth as well as in heaven, but audible too. And the vision of temperance is related to the vision of the Good, which is to be identified with the "new" virtue of piety.

In his early autobiographical soliloquy Jesus holds the "winning words" that "conquer willing hearts" to be "more humane, more heavenly." This unqualified apposition of humane and heavenly is entirely deliberate. Spelled out in prose we have it thus: Plato's advice was

that to such laws as were of principal moment, there should be used as an induction some well-tempered discourse, showing how good, how gainful, how happy it must needs be to live according to honesty and justice, which being uttered with those native colors and graces of speech, as true eloquence, the daughter of virtue, can best bestow upon her mother's praises, would so incite, and in a manner, charm the multitude into the love of that which is really good as to embrace it ever after, not of custom and awe, which most men do, but of choice and purpose, with true and constant delight. (III, 181.)

The induction is a turning of the soul in the right direction, which is piety; it embraces free choice, purpose, and a family relationship of genesis, a metaphor derived from the metaphor of harmony; and the effect is that of true delight (*Simcha*), which expresses the harmony of temperance in the larger harmony of all the virtues, in the largest harmony of God's justice.

The basic Platonic distinction from Book VII of the *Republic* is followed, that the true education of the soul is not from the implanting of "science" but from turning the soul in the right direction, "the way it ought to be." Poetic gifts can contribute to both piety and temperance. These gifts, "though most abuse" (now Milton is echoing the judgment of the *Timaeus,* 47D, as still up-to-date), nevertheless do have power over the virtues, to sow seeds, and "to allay the perturbations of the mind, and set the affections in right tune." (III, 238.) Here the harmony is not the achieved effect of virtue, but the necessary beginning. Without this beginning, which is a kind of psychological preparation for vision, there would seem to be no basis, as there seems to be none in Plato, for any acts of wisdom, whether private or public. But it is plain that the temperance here associated with piety has a more fundamental and positive function than the Christian temperance which is chiefly the guardian of the moral threshold.

Let us more narrowly consider what Milton means by piety. It is, first, a prologue, an initial orientation of the soul. If the wise Plato proposed his "induction," then of course that "better and more ancient authority than any heathen writer," Moses,

knowing how vain it was to write laws to men whose hearts were not first seasoned with the knowledge of God and of his works, began from the book of Genesis, as a prologue to his laws; which *Josephus* right well hath noted. That the nation of the Jews, reading therein the universal goodness of God to all creatures in the Creation, and his peculiar favor to them in his election of *Abraham,* their ancestor, from whom they could derive so many blessings upon themselves, might be moved to obey sincerely by knowing so good a reason of their obedience. (III, 181f)

This is the Platonic vision heightened by the true knowledge of creation and of God's love for man; it is the basis of the true religion which is, for Milton, the basis of all the values of human life. This is where one begins, whence everything truly desirable follows. Piety is the beginning of wisdom, the turning of the soul to God — whether the heart first be seasoned with fear, or love, or what Milton prefers, knowledge of the reason for love.

Piety is also, it follows, the end of wisdom. After such a begin-

ning what else would be possible? Piety as the end of wisdom, and
the relating of the end to the beginning, will be the subject of the
whole dramatic process of the poem. But let us confine our attention, now, to piety as the beginning of wisdom. Piety is not only
the cause, with other virtues, of real liberty (VIII, 241), it is the
one essential cause; and if anyone should think the ideal abstract
and remote, the results of the violation are remarkably concrete.
This is how they were depicted for the citizen-colleagues of Cromwell:

Unless by real and sincere piety towards God and men, not idle
and wordy, but efficacious, operative piety, you drive from your
minds superstition, which originates in an ignorance of true and
substantial religion, you will not want those who will sit upon your
backs and upon your necks, as if you were beasts of burden; who,
though you are the victors in the war, will sell you, though by no
military auction, as their plunder to the highest bidder; and will
make an excellent market of your ignorance and superstition.[12]

This is the answer, though but prose, which underlies Christ's replies to the temptations of the power of wealth, kingdom, mind.

In summary, then, we may say that the basic scheme of the
virtues in this poem is the familiar Platonic one of wisdom, temperance, justice, fortitude. There are some accretions, as the as-
similation of wisdom to piety, and the extended significance of
temperance. We must return to the concept of wisdom, and to the
interrelationship of the virtues. We shall need to say something
further on the subject of joy. The "new" virtue of kindness (*communitas*), however, has no positive function in this drama. It is the
bold bait of Satan's initial trap of the stones, and it is one of the
scorned baits of the trap of kingdom.

Fortitude plays an entirely minor role. Satan, with his inept timing, directly tries fear only at the desperate end. But a Miltonic
hero who has demonstrated secure control of the other virtues cannot find the trial of courage a major one. Neither could a Platonic
hero, it seems plain. Fortitude, however necessary a link in the
schematic chain, or the dramatic demonstration, is clearly a smaller
link. Though no virtue can stand independently, this is the most
dependent, the closest to being a merely executive virtue. It is the

virtue most easily disparaged by followers of Plato, less wise and temperate than the master. Milton does not disparage fortitude, but he uses the test cunningly as a kind of easy hinge on which to turn his drama into its final and positive stage. Morally the trial of courage is anticlimax, though for poetic drama it is something else. The trial for Samson is less trial than opportunity, and comes as a kind of stimulating grace. This is more fitting for the drama of an athlete than for the drama of our perfect man, but the timing of the trial is significantly similar, and perhaps it is enough merely to note this now.

At this point we had better admit that identifying the basic scheme of the virtues does not solve all the problems of relationship. If we forget Milton for a moment and think only of Plato, we may see that he finds it necessary to do some shuffling of his virtues. In the *Republic* justice has a place of special importance. In the *Laws*, which emphasizes the union of different and complementary elements in a second-class state, temperance has a special importance. Without harmony, in the individual or the state, wisdom cannot practically work. And self-control is thus a prior condition (as in the Christian recognition and over-recognition), though it is also a necessary effect. Similarly, justice plays a dominant role in *Samson Agonistes*, and temperance in *Paradise Regained*. When virtues are inseparable some shifting of emphasis is not disruptive. Indeed, perhaps one may say, though with more enthusiasm than scrupulousness of assent, that the boundaries which separate inseparable virtues must necessarily reflect the higher idea of unity to which they are bound.

Or perhaps one should just flatly say that, for whatever reason, we may see in Plato's definitions both shifts in emphasis and some overlapping. The self-mastery of temperance is the subordination of lower to higher. If training does not tune up the spirited elements of the soul, allaying their wildness by "harmony and rhythm," these elements with the naturally insatiable appetites will try to usurp dominion, "thus turning the whole of life upside down." But justice, we find, also brings into tune the parts of a man's nature. And justice in the soul is like health in the body, which is a simile for temperance too. And, further, justice establishes "the elements concerned in their natural relations of control and subordination" — which is the function also of temperance.[13]

In Christian tradition this concept of subordination, within the microcosm and macrocosm, becomes dominantly an aspect of justice. But Milton, we have seen, reappropriates this concept, though not exclusively, to temperance. And he further extends the range of temperance significantly. As a poet, of course, he is not bound to any single system of unified self-consistent extensiveness, with every part of his work at once a defense and extension of every other part. That his whole work has a unity of vision is unchallengeable, but it is not a unity which must present and defend itself like a philosopher's. The vision which is most comprehensive is that of the big epic; the other two major poems present visions which are, not less profound, but more specialized, reflecting with the uncompromising truth of poetry, the special conditions of their poems.

What of other virtues, like the Christian magnanimity which Professor Hughes [14] interprets as the moral key to the poem? If this is a drama of knowledge, as I think, then no concept of magnanimity, however aggrandized, can support the full weight of the theme.

In this matter, as in some others, the example of Spenser is likely to be misleading. In Spenser's moral drama temperance is a mean between two extremes; particularly, it "can measure out a mean" between pleasure and pain (as in *F.Q.*, II, i, 58).

Milton's imagination, and I include his moral imagination too, seems relatively untouched by Aristotle. There are some Aristotelian influences — how could it be otherwise? — but they are more important around the edges and in the prose. In Aristotle temperance-moderation is not the great Platonic principle of harmony. It seems more related to practical reason, Aristotle's *prudence*, than to *wisdom*. As an insight it is, no more than Plato's, initially or primarily or exclusively, ethical. But it does not seem to be primarily metaphyical, as Plato's is. Rather, it seems derived, perhaps transferred, from an insight in physics, related to a Heraclitean tension, and a tension certainly true to human experience. Perhaps there may not be much ultimate difference in philosophy. I am not capable of saying. But the difference for poetry, for this poem anyway, is unmistakable.

What is the case for magnanimity, so obviously important in Spenser? Professor Hughes aptly cites Renaissance extensions of the concept and Milton's own definition from the *Christian Doctrine*. "*Magnanimity* is shown," says Milton, "when, in seeking or avoiding, the acceptance or refusal of riches, advantages, or honors, we are actuated by a regard to our own dignity, rightly understood." (II, 9.) Among examples given is that of Christ "rejecting the empire of the world."

But in the prose treatise, we should observe, Milton's attitude toward the virtues is not the same as in his poetic drama of salvation. Minor definitions tend to be brief, even hurried. And, more important, the virtues are splintered, in an effort to cover all cases. (Temperance is merely the virtue prescribing bounds to the desire for bodily gratification.) But poetic vision, and especially the vision of this poem, works in the opposite way, to draw multiplicity into unity. For instance, in the poem, where the wisdom is Platonic, it does not need to be split into wisdom-prudence, and then into sincerity, promptitude, constancy. Nor do we need the convention of definition by opposites — and opposites which are not always those which the logical Aristotle could respect, for Milton is here at the mercy of religious tradition; and it is hard to see how he could well have avoided this, though it ought to have given him grief. In the poem Satan can furnish the opposites, with no pretense to a fixed apparatus of logic, but with much better definitions resulting.

Back of this definition of magnanimity, which Milton calls a "special virtue" connected with the duty of man toward himself, is the general virtue of "righteousness towards ourselves." (II, 8.) This properly precedes man's love for his neighbor, and follows his love for God. "Righteousness towards ourselves consists in a proper method of self-government." This must mean, if we have learned to understand Milton, that the virtue is to be associated with discipline, and so with temperance. What he says further makes this certain. It is the virtue from which, "as from a fountain," the special virtues derive. It includes, first, "the entire regulation of the internal affections," and, secondly, "the discriminating pursuit of external good, and the resistance to, or patient endurance of, external evil." Hence magnanimity: which is temperance united to wisdom. It cannot be any mere, ascetic contempt for the world; nor can it be any grandiose, or madcap, daffing the world aside to "bid it pass."

The "dignity, rightly understood" reminds us of the difficulty in separating the virtues; for temperance-wisdom here clearly requires the traditional associations of justice, the proper self-esteem which is a man's great and "proper concern," since it is both the differentiating principle of his individuality and the principle which binds his private world properly to the world outside. Fortitude may seem to be the only major virtue not adumbrated in the definition of magnanimity now being considered. Yet traditionally fortitude was often associated with magnanimity, and it provided a welcome example of a human virtue transcending, by means of physical action, the merely human. It was the achievement "splendidissimum videri, quod animo magno elatoque humanasque res despiciente factum sit." [15] (It is not a long step from this formula of Cicero's to the virtue Professor Hughes describes.) Milton sometimes thinks of magnanimity in connection with courage, but he always thinks of true courage as the Platonic virtue which is informed by understanding. And this observation takes us back, again, to that fountain of *disciplined discrimination* from which magnanimity must derive — whether it is the heroic rising above superstitions by the common people of England, or the incredible intellectual candor of the Queen of Sweden, or "the composed magnanimity of the Italian," or Cromwell's preferring to be father of his country rather than king.[16] The patience which is the trial of the fortitude of saints may demonstrate a kind of magnanimity, but the virtue is pre-eminently the brave understanding and maintaining of individual dignity, the "discriminating pursuit" of external good and the consequent "patient endurance" of external evil.[17]

Perhaps the most important advice Raphael gives Adam is this:

> Oft times nothing profits more
> Then self-esteem, grounded on just and right
> Well manag'd.

It is a master-cue, for Adam to miss and the second Adam and Samson to take. It is the recognizable signal of righteousness-toward-self, that intellectual love mediating between God and one's neighbor. It requires temperate self-attunement for the wisdom of recognition and understanding; it requires justice for the proper understanding of the whole order and the proper recognition of one's individual place in that order; it requires temperance, again, for the disciplined managing of one's precarious and dynamic individuality in a stable vision of order and justice; it requires the implied presence of fortitude, whenever that virtue may be needed.

When Christ "patiently" replies to Satan that it has been thought nobler to give a kingdom, and "more magnanimous" to lay down than to assume (II, 481ff), he is not openly defining his central moral position. The fact that Milton in his prose treatise cites this as an example of magnanimity may help elucidate the passage, but it provides us with no complete interpretation of either the passage or the poem. Satan has been offering riches as the readiest means to kingdom and to "greatness." The answer "patiently" but shrewdly examines the limitations of wealth for gaining and keeping dominion. Christ then proceeds to glance, in anticipation of future developments, at the true nature of ordinary kingship and its responsibilities, and at the true nature of his own extraordinary kingship (here implied): which is leadership in the way of truth, governing the inner man, "To know, and knowing worship God aright." (This is the beginning and end of wisdom, which we have identified as the virtue of piety.) His final comment is the one on magnanimity, introduced by a casual, provocative "besides." The comment applies, and mockingly does not apply, to his own kingship. He will, we know, lay down mere rule over the bodies of men (no honor for his dignity, rightly understood), but he *will* assume rule over the "inner man." The seeking and avoiding are both in accord with the prose definition of magnanimity if we remember what is back of it, the larger concept of righteousness toward self — but it will take the whole drama to release the full implications. Furthermore, Christ will "give" a kingdom, though not in any way that Satan can understand (which is part of the deliberate enigma of the "besides" on magnanimity). This will be no ordinary kingdom for which there is any adequate model; nor is there any adequate model of magnanimity for either the giving or the laying down of this kingdom.

It is hard to see how the magnanimity of Milton's Christ relates to the Renaissance fusion, described by Professor Hughes, of the active and the contemplative ideals in the name of the active type. Here as everywhere in Milton, though nowhere else carried to so great a length and height, thought is prior to action, is a preparation for, and implies action.[18] The emphasis is important, and to be referred to causes of which magnanimity is an effect. It is a virtue, however noble, splintered from the nobler virtue of temperance.

The ultimate cause is knowledge and the ultimate knowledge is the knowledge of God. In this drama we have the two competing theories of knowledge.[19] Satan is the great empiric, the advocate of knowledge for power, knowledge derived externally from the impressions on sense, and worked up into patterns of practical reason reflecting human experience in the world, and among men. Christ's theory is the Platonic one of pure thought inaccessible to the senses, with judgment more important than perception. The *Theaetetus* (186D) states the basic distinction: "Then knowledge does not consist in impressions of sense, but in reasoning about them; in that only, and not in the mere impression, truth and being can be attained." Subject is more important than ordinary object; not that the two cannot meet, but that the stability of reason is prior to all *becoming* and division. The higher judgment, light from above reflected by the Logos in the soul, self-consciousness, unity of the self — these are the true bases for knowledge. And the wis-

33

38532

dom which is a vision of the highest good is reinforced by the allied and inseparable intuitions of temperance, justice, and fortitude, and by their executive functions. Temperance, as the special virtue of discipline, purges; and by its positive vision orders and unifies the self into a proper balance of selfless response to vision, which determines, by self, the true self. The condition of purification is self-knowledge. Recovery of self by knowledge is the recovery of being which was never absent. The Christ of *Paradise Regained* is the great *exemplum* of this doctrine of Plotinus. He is more, but we must learn to see this much at least.

Finally, I have one last extension of temperance to explore. It is a special relationship between temperance and justice. Philo, we saw, related faith to justice toward God. Faith in the performance of God's just law brings, before and since Philo, *Simcha* — joy. Among the great precedents from Scripture (texts widely commented upon) are the following: "Thy word was unto me the joy and rejoicing of mine heart" (Jeremiah, 15, 16); and from the ninth Psalm: "the statutes of the Lord are right, rejoicing the heart: the commandment of the Lord is pure, enlightening the eyes"; and many lines from the one hundred and nineteenth Psalm. We find something of this also in Colossians 1, 11: "strengthened with all might, according to his glorious power, unto all patience and long-suffering with joyfulness." The concept is not without a kind of parallel in Greek thought. Andronicus of Rhodes associated thanksgiving with justice.[20] Delight in the discovery of order, implicit in Aristotle's great tenet of the pleasure in learning, is perhaps not irrelevant, in spite of the emphasis on discovery. And the same may be said for the philosopher's rational insight, defined in the *Philebus* as the highest pleasure. The emphasis on discovery, at least in the matter of joy, is perhaps not important if the beginning of wisdom is not blocked from the end.

The expression of joy in justice unites with the idea of religious, or philosophical, liberty, that turning of soul in the true direction, from which all order derives. The turning to order and the full, free expression of that order constitute the harmony of temperance. John Smith's eloquent discourse on "The Excellency and Nobleness of True Religion" presents an attitude very frequently expressed by Milton, an attitude which, though not obvious in *Paradise Regained*, it is ruinous not to recognize. I quote at length:

Religion is no sullen Stoicism or oppressing Melancholy, it is no enthralling tyranny exercised over those noble and vivacious affections of Love and Delight . . . but it is full of a vigorous and masculine delight and joy . . .

The most generous Freedom can never be took in its full and just dimensions and proportion, but then when all the Powers of the Soul exercise and spend themselves in the most large and ample manner upon the Infinite and Essential Goodness, as upon their own most proper Object . . .

Nor does he [God] charge any Duty upon man without consulting first of all with his *Goodness*: which being the Original and adequate Object of a Good man's Will and affections, it must needs be that all the issues and effluxes of it be entertain'd with an answerable complacency and cheerfulness. This is the hinge upon which all true Religion turns, the proper Centre about which it moves; which taking a fast and sure hold of an innate and correspondent Principle in the Soul of man, raiseth it up . . .[21]

This is the positive view of *Paradise Regained*, which does not contradict the view of *Paradise Lost*, that man was made "to delight . . . and delight to Reason joyn'd." Even in the exercise of crucial moral choice this remains true. A prolonged drama of choice, and particularly when the stakes are as high as in this drama, must inevitably draw close to the ascetic. Yet in Milton's treatment the ascetic does not dominate but is carefully contained. There is no rejecting of the natural world in hate. What is rejected is the perverted natural world, or the natural world threatening to pervert — to pervert true order and the true basis of man's possible joy in the free exercise of his functions: which exercise connects the harmony of his being with the harmony of the largest justice. Christ demonstrates, and conveys, in the free and graceful exercise of his faculties a joy that expresses the union of temperance and justice, and the larger symbolic unity of being. His actions form a solo, exemplary voice which *answers* and *renews* the "perfect Diapason." The poet's joy in the performance is properly sober and subtle but it is permeating.[22]

35

PREPARATIONS AND THE FIRST ENCOUNTER

MILTON is a great master of structural prolepsis. Under the stylized postures and movements of antagonist and protagonist there are often slight, unstylized, "natural" movements, so swift as to be barely perceptible sometimes, but every exciting. We shall try to mark these. And under the stylized movements, or as part of them, there are often movements which anticipate gestures still to come; these give a special quality to the structural development, and create a kind of movement that is very important in a poem composed of a series of formal confrontations.

The poem begins with seven introductions, all proleptic, extending for three hundred lines. First, there is the poet's looking backward to *Paradise Lost*, to the theme of this poem, and to the outcome. Second, there is the address to the Muse, further defining the theme, and also the style and its range, the significant "highth or depth of natures bounds." Third, the episode of the Baptist, whose voice is more awful than the sound of trumpet, further anticipates the deeds "Above Heroic" and introduces the problem of kingdom by his announcement of "Heavens Kingdom nigh at hand." The "private" humanity of the protagonist is here introduced, and we have the first of three versions of the baptism: "Heaven open'd, and in likeness of a Dove / The Spirit descended."

Fourth, there is the episode of Satan's "consistory," which ends in the formal decision to subvert by fraud. In the course of Satan's speech many of the specific terms of the contest are revealed. Most important is the nature of Satan's doubt and *his* understanding of the issues. First, there is his baffled wonder at the meaning of God's metaphorical prophecy, the meaning of "wound" and "head" and "Son." Though the primary objective of the formal temptations will be to subvert, even then, and still more in the shrewd sparring between formal attempts, the secondary objective will be to "know." Dramatically, the secondary objective will prove to be the more important. The authentic voice and the visible testimony of heaven may be conclusive enough so that "Thenceforth the Nations may not doubt"; it is not conclusive enough for Satan's doubt. His version of the baptism is revealing, and anticipatory:

> I saw
> The Prophet do him reverence, on him rising
> Out of the water, Heav'n above the Clouds
> Unfold her Crystal Dores, thence on his head
> A perfect Dove descend, what e're it meant.

His version is the most circumstantial of the three. He does not know what it means, and, interestingly, he sees not symbol but literal object, no "likeness" but a perfect dove. We are here given an important clue to Satan's mind and its range of knowledge.

This episode introduces the theme of time, which will provide some of the richest ironies in the poem. There is the familiar time, "as the years of men," by which Satan's reign is measured, and by which his followers must measure their immediate indulgence of fear and grief — "but no time was then." There is also God's time, the psalmist's thousand years as a day. Satan's images reveal the conceptual knowledge of this time as circular:

> And now too soon for us the circling hours
> This dreaded time have compast.

This is part of the grand circle, proceeding from original creation to the final return of all uncorrupted being to God, when God shall be all in all. Christ's role is of course to enter, or re-enter, this grand circle, and to renew man's relationship with the grand circle by a kind of re-creation that will redeem time by bringing man back into concord with God's time. But Satan sees, or tries to see, the circle as a smaller independent circle of destiny, against which "something sudden" may be opposed. This is another version of his agony over symbol and knowledge.

Finally, this episode introduces Satan's idea of kingdom. That idea is based on his own rule and possession of the "fair Empire won of Earth and Air." Again we see the constricting literalism of Satan's mind. What will God "not do to advance his Son?" The crowd at the baptism was there to do Jesus "honour as their King"; the opposition of fraud must be sudden,

> E're in the head of Nations he appear
> Their King, their Leader, and Supream in Earth.

The fifth introduction is provided by the second group of spectators to this drama, God and the angels. This further defines the *real* terms of the contest and the issue. It introduces the significant analogy of Job; it emphasizes the special meaning of "weakness"; it names the hero a perfect man, but requires him to "earn" salvation and his high title of "Son" as a man, "by merit." The angelic chorus may be considered another introduction, for it advances the important stipulation of vanquishing by wisdom, and it makes the point that the Father knows the Son. This last implies a reciprocal obligation of knowledge, to be fulfilled by the hero's action of mind in the evolving drama.

Finally, there is the major introduction of the hero's "musing" walk into the wilderness. It comes as autobiographical disclosure; it is human, sincere, and revealing. The soliloquy for the most part looks backward in time, but anticipates in important ways the temptations to come. In one sense Christ is revealing a human mind potentially susceptible to Satan's offers, but it is misleading to think that hints are being dropped to anticipate the psychological clairvoyance with which Satan will project as temptations parts of Christ's own mind. It is more accurate to observe that Christ, in his own developing progress toward knowledge, though the reasoning has not been tested by action, has already passed beyond the range of what will be offered.

The pattern of mind and aspirations presented in the soliloquy will not significantly change in the development of the poem; but our understanding of the pattern, and presumably the hero's, will change and develop. We may distinguish in the soliloquy four stages of knowledge. The first two stages are briefly presented:

> When I was yet a child, no childish play
> To me was pleasing, all my mind was set
> Serious to learn and know, and thence to do
> What might be publick good; my self I thought
> Born to that end, born to promote all truth,
> All righteous things: therefore above my years,
> The Law of God I read, and found it sweet,
> Made it my whole delight, and in it grew. . . .

The first response is the desire to learn-know-do. The beginning and the end of the poem touch here, for the hero will not be budged from this identification of knowledge and action. Wisdom must work in the world and search for what "might be" public good: this is a basic proposition to be explored and fully defined by the drama. The initial statement is followed by an apparent apposition, which relates knowledge and public good to the promotion of truth and righteous things. This, though the definition is now deliberately casual, already anticipates what will become a clear identification. The child's first consciousness of having been born to that end represents, in Milton's view, the intuitive response of all elevated humanity. The difference for us to mark will be in the metaphorical and literal fulfillment of that end, symbolically common to all humanity but special to this protagonist.

The first response is intuitive, then, the desire to learn and know and do. The second response is discursive and disciplined, the study of the law (wherein man may verify the intuitive). In the increase of his knowledge he grew. The discipline of reason is here related, as elsewhere in Milton, to the harmony-justice of "delight." This order of intuition followed by discipline is basic in Milton; we must get it straight if we are to understand the development of the poem to the climactic temptation of the kingdom of the mind.

Next, we are presented with a third fundamental stage of consciousness. This is the aspiration of the knowing-doing-promoting to fulfill specific ends: the heroic acts which will begin by freeing Israel and end by freeing truth and restoring equity all over the world. (We shall return to this third stage in a moment and try to identify it in the pattern.) The fourth stage redefines public good in terms of knowledge. It is more humane, more heavenly, to conquer by persuasion: which reasserts the bridge between intuitive and discursive, between the truth of righteous things and real public good, which is to be sought rather through the action of reason than through the action of force.

The first stage, then, is intuitive, the beginning of wisdom pointing to the end of acting in the world. The second stage is discursive, looking back toward the intuitive. The third is again intuitive, but based on a human, a social, orientation. The end of its wisdom is to effect on earth one human kingdom of truth and justice by the human discipline of force. But the beginning of this wisdom does not go all the way back to the beginning. As intuition it is unconvincing; we may perhaps regard it as a kind of human substitution, a special turn, by analogy, of the first stage. (I associate this with Samson's second marriage, where he presumed a logical rationalization of intuition.) We shall do well to bear this third stage in mind during the temptations, for Satan will provide rich opportunities for misconstruing intuition.

The fourth stage returns to the original intuition, but has the support of a fuller human discipline of reason and intellectual experience. Force is rejected as not proper to the original humane-heavenly intuition of wisdom; the progress of the poem will further define the reasons for that rejection; it is enough to note now that the discipline of force is a derivative extension of reason, and not connate; one may add that for Milton force as a principle violates reason, and is not even "practical." Force has a final but minor office, to be sure. It sweeps up, both in the state and the universe (the Last Judgment), the small but certain residue of evil. The fourth stage is the final one, though it will take the whole poem to define the specific terms, not now prematurely conceived as in the third stage. (For instance, as part of the *experienced* return to original intuition, the discursive discipline of persuasion moves toward inspiration.) What follows is not a further stage. Knowledge offered by the Mother serves a special individual illumination for self-knowledge, and provides a perspective, an insight, for the inspired study of the law and the prophets. From this, another collaboration of the intuitive and the discursive, comes the anticipation, now loosely related, of death, promised kingdom, redemption for mankind.

This, then, is the major anticipation of the major introduction. Most important is the preliminary sketch of the four stages. The pattern may be considered as symbolic, of the elevated human mind in general and of this hero's mind in particular; but the development of dramatic action will be required for full definition. The rest of the soliloquy raises the theme of time again, the time "prefixt" for which Christ was waiting, and the recognition after the scene of the baptism that the time was now "full." This, the third description of the scene, again preserves the image: "The Spirit descended on me like a Dove." And, finally, the last comment on knowledge:

> And now by some strong motion I am led
> Into this wilderness, to what intent
> I learn not yet, perhaps I need not know;
> For what concerns my knowledge God reveals.

This I assume to be a version of the intelligence of the fourth stage supported by the experience of the preceding stages. The discursive discipline of learning is not rejected but kept in reserve. The statement is that of a man who has *learned* to recognize and to trust primary intuitive knowledge. We have been given some insight into the process of the learning, and so can affirm that the confident statement is not without some verification by the discipline of experience, and not without some discipline of active discursive reasoning. The statement augurs ill for the tempter's chances, and re-emphasizes the basic conflict in their approach to and concept of knowledge.

There follow forty days of unmolested meditation. We know the subject but the details are "not reveal'd" — no more than the circumstances of nightly habitation. That the withdrawal constitutes an initiatory purification and preparation, a descent into the self, we may assume — a preparation that looks forward to a real return to the source of existence, as far beyond the immediate barrage of tests that Satan is due to present as beyond the mere physical return strangely underlined for contrast:

> The way he came not having mark'd, return
> Was difficult, by humane steps untrod.

The emphasis here is physical and literal; one may suspect (given the context) a suggestion of metaphorical similarity, between the difficulty of the real return and what is here noted as difficult, unmarked, and without human precedent. As metaphor, this would be a submerged and subtle version of the traditional metaphor of mystic experience that T. S. Eliot treats as a theme for variations:

> In order to arrive at what you do not know
> You must go by a way which is the way of ignorance.

> ❊ ❊ ❊ ❊ ❊ ❊ ❊ ❊ ❊ ❊ ❊

> In order to arrive at what you are not
> You must go through the way in which you are not.
> And what you do not know is the only thing you know.

> ❊ ❊ ❊ ❊ ❊ ❊ ❊ ❊ ❊ ❊ ❊

> And where you are is where you are not. ["East Coker," III]

We come now to the first formal temptation, that of turning the stones into bread:

> So shalt thou save thy self and us relieve
> With Food, whereof we wretched seldom taste.

The technique and some of the issues anticipate, as we might well expect, the later temptations (especially the last); but what is entirely surprising is the radical difference of this temptation. The antagonist has tried to get everything staked on one first casual card, to win as preamble. It is a bold, ambitious, deadly thrust, a measured, knockout punch from a hand apparently making a persuasive rhetorical gesture against the air. After the long introduction, which has prepared us for a long contest, the sudden brush, abrupt and possibly final, catches the reader unprepared; in the immediate heightening of his sense of the dangerous excitement potential in the contest, he is, by the most physical of dramatic means, made to identify himself with the protagonist. After Satan has failed he will settle down to the long pull, to hard, thorough work. He will explore all possible shifts and variety of tempo, all levels, angles, directions, intensities. But the effects of this initial movement, in its impetus and in its individual quality, will carry through and be part of the dramatic consciousness of the reader; and it will be integrated into the final repose of the *form* of the poem only with the last temptation.

Successful evasion by the right kind of refusal requires that there be no gap between wisdom and prudence, between meditation and practical action. Forty days of solitary thought on past and future must not leave Jesus exposed to the present. Human eyes must not be so dazzled by any intuition of being as to be blinded by the sudden proposition of a moment in time; they must be able to recognize evil, whether by intuition or by a discipline of discursive inference hardly less swift than intuition.

Our analysis, of necessity, tends to separate what is clearly inseparable; an important part of Satan's effort and Christ's reply is to demonstrate the sure integrity of the hero's self-knowledge, which will not be distracted from its proper end. The mind fixed in piety on its proper end, "actively" recognizing its relationship to that end and "passively" resting in that relationship, possesses an essential perception to which all other perceptions can be referred, and so instantly tested. The true ear will recognize a false sound, because it does not sound true. The pious mind will recognize impious suggestion.

The answer Jesus gives show quick penetration to the heart of the issue: excessive trust in the material and distrust in God. But it is by no means a simple, unambiguous answer. It leaves Satan almost where he was, except that he is now informed, though not usefully, by one kind of failure, and must temporarily go on the defensive while he looks for another opening. His disguise has been penetrated, and so he proffers a long, ingenious defense of his identity. But the identity of the hero, which he hoped to learn in one of several possible ways, he learns only in terms of the knowledge he has already himself expressed, the revelation of the baptism. And he hears this in a form that could hardly have given him comfort: "Knowing who I am, as I know who thou art." The reference to our fathers who were fed here with manna, and the forty days of Moses and Elijah — that is a good, pious, impractical, traditionally oblique answer, which tells him and does not tell him. "The same I now" — that helps even less. And interestingly skirted is the question of what Jesus is doing in the desert to enjoy such preferential historical treatment.

Satan's defense is an impressive display of footwork and sparring, and something more. It can hardly be intended as mere self-justification. The skill exhibited in defense is, perhaps deliberately, excessive, and so dazzling that it astonishes the reader and impresses him far more with the exorbitant, dangerous display than with the defense itself. So brazen and brilliant is the skill that it cannot but be provocative, and this is surely part of Satan's intention. But he is also preparing a kind of reason for the long attendance which now seems necessary. Since he *knows*, he says, that Jesus has been declared the Son of God, and since (I translate the irony) evil is not pure and thus indifferent to good, naturally he wants to hear wisdom and "behold thy God-like deeds." He has a business relationship with man (and so may have something to offer?); he is no foe, and presents as a kind of proof (and seductive skill) a piece of pure sincerity:

> This wounds me most (what can it less) that Man, Man fall'n shall be restor'd, I never more.

This last is really the most impressive exhibition, though not obvious, of virtuoso skill. We shall see more of this; for Satan will use sincerity as he traditionally uses flattery, to soften up an opponent. (That this is not merely a rhetorical device and completely in his control had better be stated now for future reference.) The general purpose may be to promote confidence, or confusion, but Satan is also most specifically fishing where a major obsession lies, in the pool of time.

The answer accepts the challenge of the provocative skill and the ironic insults, and does so with deliberately humiliating effect.

In one way Christ is humorless; he ignores the skillful flourishes of Satan's art but cuts through them with devastating efficiency and force, and with an unblinking eye on the embarrassing facts. It is a crushing commentary on Satan's art and wit. Blunt truth disregards the ceremony of footwork, and is remorseless in the corner — as Samson would have been to Harapha.

The humorless is not unproductive of comedy in this way, but Jesus also attacks directly with ridicule and indirectly with irony. He answers "sternly," a harsh drubbing for a hypocrite the ridiculousness of whose position is held up for unsparing analysis. Nor does Jesus lack rhetoric to make the idea felt:

> As a poor miserable captive thrall
> Comes to the place where he before had sat
> Among the Prime in Splendour, now depos'd,
> Ejected, emptyed, gaz'd, unpityed, shun'd,
> A spectacle of ruin or of scorn.

And he more than matches the art of Satan's irony when he taunts him on the subject of oracles. What Satan's mind requires is the blunt literal truth, and all his fantastic ingenuity of art is a tormented expression of that simple passion, which his mind is impotent to receive. But the oracles of Satan's inspiration have provided dark, ambiguous, deluding answers — no doubt a projection of one fixed quality of Satan's mind. And Satan before the "living Oracle" that God has now sent into the world is incapable of learning the unambiguous truth — "And not well understood as good not known." Is he not in the case of those who have consulted him

> To flye or follow what concern'd him most,
> And run not sooner to his fatal snare?

This is immediate irony, which Satan can feel. What is beyond his compass is the symbolism of the "living Oracle" which is to be the source of all requisite truth "In pious Hearts, an inward Oracle." There Christ is telling him what he wants to know, but not in a form which can satisfy his impious heart. The pattern is a basic one, so rich dramatically that all repetition will seem variation and will illuminate like exploratory invention.

45

The subtle antagonist returns an "Answer smooth," and curbs his anger and disdain. This will be a trial of his fortitude also, a kind of competition in patience. In what follows there is less virtuoso display of skill but there is no less skill. He adopts the plausible voice of fallen humanity, and makes it sound humbly earnest in its admission of human weakness. As master of the world's wisdom he emphasizes the division between thought and action, between the pure idea and the impure human effort — and so justifies his own present "ministry" and prepares for the continuous argument he will present. He is obsequiously respectful of the idea, but "Hard are the ways of truth, and rough to walk." There are, however, two sharply aggressive blows, barely disguised — the general reference to God's suffering of evil, and the specific reference, in parenthesis, to Christ's lack of human following, "since no man comes." The calm reply he receives cuts again to the heart of the matter. Christ *knows* (unlike Satan), and refers his knowledge to God:

> I bid not or forbid; do as thou find'st
> Permission from above; thou canst not more.

SATAN'S BANQUET

Book II begins like Book I, with a series of introductions extending, once more, for three hundred lines. The effects, however, are almost entirely different from those in Book I. These introductions are not intense. They do not anticipate with brilliant concentration the major lines of development. Instead, they are part of a complete shift in tempo. The first two of these introductions are leisurely, almost digressive, as they bring in the third audience of the drama, the human audience.

We can see already, though better from the vantage point of the whole poem, that Milton is managing the rhythm of his action with deliberate variety. (We may work on the assumption that the variety is part of a total form and not merely a spinning out, by shrewd delays, of a thin action.) If we look back, we see that the earlier introductions were moving in a steady line toward the first encounter and beyond. Besides, they were taut with potential symbolic action. The first encounter was impressively energetic, and promising. The contest was finally joined and could be counted on to go through to an end. But now we have a pause, a delay, an excursion that the poet apparently feels he can afford. If we look ahead we see that, once the direct action begins again, it will continue unbroken, except by small pauses and imaginative excursions, until the major pause which precedes the final temptation on the tower.

The first introduction emphasizes the human aspect of Christ's symbolic role, what his victory or defeat will mean to the waiting world of men. The geography, as the time, is local. The search and the lament are the natural expression of plain fishermen — though that expression is projected against a background of "plain" history which includes Moses, Elijah, and prophecies of the Messiah. But that background works as historical and human fact. This whole passage, in style and focus, deliberately interrupts the lofty emphasis on the cosmic issue to assert the significance of the private and domestic. True, the vision of this human audience is too local, and naively chiliastic; their comment does not interpret the issue correctly, but it does serve the larger dramatic clarification. Interestingly, their local emphasis on "kingdom," and on the historical climacteric apparently at hand, runs parallel to some of Satan's attempts to solve the cosmic domestically. But the fishermen are simple and well-meaning, like the disciples after the Resurrection, and many Christians and Jews since, in their expecting a literal restoration of the kingdom to Israel. The drama will redefine the concept of kingdom, by going beyond the limits of this innocence of expectation, and beyond the similar limits of Satan's non-innocence. But this human expectation will remain as a kind of literal mark or measure that will be extended and illuminated, without any passing of moral judgment, by Christ's symbolic demonstration. In their simple innocence the plain fishermen cannot see the scope of the problem, but in the individual effort they make, in their search, in their discipline of patience and hope, they display the same essential piety as the hero of the poem.

The second introduction presents the Mother Mary cast mostly in a domestic role. She is a mother and entirely human, almost free of the evocative religious feelings frequently attached to her. The barest minimum of feeling is admitted from the inevitable associations of the *Pietà*. She reviews domestic history; her version is in part parallel to her son's autobiographical soliloquy, but it is much humbler. She does, however, reinforce with significant epithets a view we have already had of his preparation for the heroic role: his life has been, for "many years," she says, "Private, unactive, calm, contemplative." Knowing more than the fisherman, she anticipates some "great purpose" in his absence, but she asserts the same essential piety of patience.[1]

We return briefly, as a narrative reminder, to the hero meanwhile "tracing" the desert as he meditates, "Into himself descended." This is a reminder, a necessary mechanical link before the leisurely narrative excursion about to occur. It reminds us, more significantly, of the major dramatic problem of the relationship between thought and action, for the hero is contemplating the whole scope of his "great work to come":

How to begin, how to accomplish best
His end of being on Earth, and mission high.

Most important of all, this reminds us of the essential problem, that of *knowing*. We have not seen enough to face the issue yet, but we ought at least note this, for it is one of the great cues of the poem. Barely stated, the point is this: we ought to look for a center of knowing in the relationship between the depth of descent and the height of transcendence.[2]

We may now turn to more entertaining matters. The second council of Satan's "peers" is a lively one, introducing what may appear to be a fresh comic spirit into a poem remarkable for its concentrated austerity. But this impression is only partly right. The effect is perhaps less that of comic relief than of imaginative relief. The stage, as we have already seen it prepared, and in part acted upon in the first book, is one for "divine comedy." Or, if the assertion seems too strong, one may say that such comedy has seemed, at the very least, an important element in the drama. The mind and attitudes displayed in the first speech of "the old Serpent doubting" should recall some of the effects in the first book, though here the comic demonstration is perhaps more relaxed, and it is fuller. The stage is for the moment completely occupied by the potentates of evil, and this accounts for some of the apparent freshness of the comic feeling. There *is* a relaxation in tension, made possible by the interruption of the contest and by the loosening effect, in style and focus, that marked the introduction of the human audience. The mind of evil expressing itself in the present

49

scene maintains the point of view and tone of the book thus far —
it is an evil concerned with the local and domestic aspects of the
great issue. This comic expression is, admittedly, something new
in its degree of emphasis, but I want to insist on the effect of the
staging. Milton does not present the scene for relief, in the usual
dramatic sense of that word. The poem does not particularly need
that kind of variation now. Rather, the scene is at once an extension
of the human and domestic in the preceding scenes, a re-quicken-
ing and full extension on an unshared stage of comic lines already
laid down on a shared stage, and it is an important preparation for
comic developments to come.

What is new is the imaginative relief, the way the poem seems
to slip out of the rigid bounds of its absolute drama. It is imaginatively surprising — as one would count on being surprised if privileged to eavesdrop on the most private thoughts of towering public
figures in a moment of recess between the acts of a great public drama. Suddenly we have ordinary human feelings expressed,
ordinary but impure and not expected. Belial advising the bait of
women convinces the reader completely — of Belial's feelings. It is
an impressive dramatic speech, for Belial's account of the amorous
arts deliciously projects his own response to those arts, and may
strike some echoes from the reader's actual, or imagined, experience. The spectacle of Belial publicly tempting himself, even if it
stopped there, would be funny in *this* drama of unsuccessful temptation. But we are also furnished with the charming development
of Satan rising as advocate to defend the elevated virtue of his
opponent.

The answer suddenly floods the established boundaries of the
drama with illicit exotic materials. Satan, using an authentic license
of dramatic decorum, bootlegs the heady imaginative stuff of
pagan myth, the amorous escapades of the gods. But Satan — and
this is fascinating comedy — is morally on the "right" side in this
matter. He turns into a kind of legal officer to seize the imaginative
contraband he brought in. And he judges the case too. It is Belial
who is guilty of the damage done to the reputation of pagan gods;
Belial and his cohorts did the roaming, lurking, waylaying, coup-

ling, and then covered up the historical truth-at-the-source by
starting the fine fables which blame the gods. It is a delightful
piece of mythological debunking by a puritanical Satan. Later,
when he needs an example from myth, he is as proper as any ra-
tionalist poet in an age of enlightenment; he illustrates and dis-
owns: "so Fables tell."

These imaginative materials are of course "new" and surprising,
but as one looks back one sees that they are not completely without
precedent. They are surprising because they are unexpected, but
they are more significantly surprising, and esthetically satisfying,
because one recognizes that they are *right* in their introduction,
that they fulfill a structural expectation, though in an unexpected
way. The imaginative excursion gives Satan a fine comic opportunity to display himself, and properly to throw out such stuff from
the drama — after we have had a leisurely chance to taste that
comic cake. That is surprising and right, for Satan, and for the
structure of the poem. (Incidentally, Milton has managed with
perfect propriety to introduce the touchiest aspect of a temptation
of the "flesh"; it was difficult enough in handling Adam's drama;
but now the problem is beautifully solved by having Belial pro-
pose and Satan, whose judgment in such dark matters ought to be
absolutely authoritative, dispose.) The structural expectation is
this: Belial and Satan are extending the human emphasis which
has been the distinguishing mark of this book thus far. The courts
and regal chambers, and the varied rural scenes of Belial's business — these are parallel in effect to the concentration on local
geography in the section dealing with the fishermen. This is the
effect, which is in its way also human and domestic in emphasis,
granted some necessary differences between the movements of
plain, pious men and the movements of a devil whose taste for
debauchery is cultivated and, one may suppose, aristocratic. The
devils share and quote the same local-universal history of Scripture; Satan's references to mythology and to Alexander and Scipio
Africanus extend the history but reinforce the human emphasis.
The historical figure of Solomon is entirely human in Satan's presentation, which is that of a rationalistic historian stripping a leg-

endary hero of his aura by concentrating on certain "hard" facts which reduce the heroic to the experientially familiar and common.

If we look ahead, even a little, we can see the further structural relevance of this scene. The "new" imaginative materials, introduced and rejected by Satan, return as part of the seduction of the banquet scene. And there will be other imaginative diversions from the hard core of the real drama. More important is the self which Satan here displays. We have seen it before, but not so clearly; we are now being prepared for the major, sustained demonstration of self to be dramatized in the temptations.

That self, one may say, is "human." The term is of course not precise, but we have a rough standard to go by. Back of this Satan we may have an idea of Evil, and it is not entirely misleading to remember the dramatizing of that idea in *Paradise Lost* — if we remember this as a standard, and do not confuse the characters as interchangeable. Besides, we have a standard — mythic, philosophical, and literary — for the role of cosmic evil engaged in a universal conflict. But we have already seen signs that in this, the second stage of the conflict, cosmic evil has become recognizably more domestic in character. And now that the stage has been entirely human for a while, and Satan has spoken at length from that stage, we can see it more clearly.

> *Belial,* in much uneven scale thou weigh'st
> All others by thy self.

Is this the voice of cosmic evil recognizing a lesser evil which acts inadequately because of an inadequate self? Will Satan's estimate of Christ's aspirations reflect Satan's mind or Christ's? This much at least is clear: to the extent that Satan underestimates Christ's transcendence, his evil is more domestic than the evil which tempted Eve. And Satan, for all his histrionic talents, cannot avoid — these are the inescapable terms of the drama — judging Christ by himself, Satan. Finally, that is all he has. And that self is human, domestic evil, trying to make the most of the sphere of activity still left it.

The debunking, rationalistic mind which Satan reveals is fascinating, and familiar. It seems able to dissolve anything — but itself, its fears, and the belief in power. It is a middle-aged and lesser version of the Satanic mind, still fiercely committed to transcendence, if a lesser transcendence, and still a little embarrassed over the vulgar trick of the apple and Adam's accidental fall by his wife's "allurement." The antagonist has his own austere discipline of temperance, his subordination of the low and superordination of the high. He despises the low temptations of the "world." He is frankly contemptuous of Solomon, living "at ease" and content with mere honor, wealth, and the enjoyment of his "State." Most important, he despises beauty:

> for Beauty stands
> In the admiration only of weak minds
> Led captive; cease to admire, and all her Plumes
> Fall flat and shrink into a trivial toy,
> At every sudden slighting quite abasht.

But his brilliant image of beauty becomes a richly reflecting image of himself, and the trivial toys which have "more shew / Of worth." His transcendence, faced with real transcendence, has its "female pride deject." He has been describing himself more than he realizes — as befits a character on a human stage.[3]

We return to the desert and the hero, who is still descended into himself, "from shade to shade," still wandering the woody "maze." The images are those of profound, labyrinthine self-search, but the depths of the meditation are not expressed. We have not seen any thoughts, it is worth remembering, as deep as those of the auto-biographical soliloquy, and those were perhaps symbolic of a profound intellectual pattern, but certainly not spelled out. There was a demonstration of profundity in the first encounter with Satan; but that was, rather, a demonstration of profundity in action, the answer to an immediate proposition by a mind able to deal authoritatively with the immediate because that mind was composed in depth. The dramatic impression of depth was, I think, self-evident. And perhaps one may begin legitimately to wonder whether the images of descent and self-search are not part of the careful arranging, the setting of the stage of mind: on which stage one may expect to see acted out the results of depth, or rather the dramatic process of discovering depth. At any rate, the isolated meditation tells us little directly. In the present scene we get some discriminating footnotes, which are very Miltonic, emphasizing the fact that the body is not in any way being damaged by this long fast. The pain of hunger is felt, but the mind's faculties are being neither strengthened ascetically nor weakened materially as a result.

The emphasis of the scene is also human — hunger expresses itself naturally in a dream of food. Milton handles the little episode beautifully, with consummate religious and artistic tact. It is an image of perfect temperance, in which the unconscious has been so thoroughly permeated by the conscious that even the dreams are pure. (To the twentieth century this may seem the chief miracle of the poem; the seventeenth century may have remembered Zeno on the purity of dreams as a test of virtue achieved; I do not think that Milton's handling of his fiction requires the support of the latter or is subject to the criticism of the former.) The senses *can* be deceived, but what they produce of their own volition in the unconscious of the perfect man is the illusion of modestly banqueting with Elijah or Daniel. We are being prepared, of course, for the conscious illusion, labeled "no dream," of Satan's banquet, and for the "real illusion" of Satan's storm. And Satan may also be the contriver — there is a strong suggestion of this — of the pleasant valley which Christ sees in the distance and finds attractive. It seems to be a kind of mirage in the desert, a daylight dream viewed from the indeterminate distance of a high hilltop, but with this quite strange, apparently impossible detail: "With chaunt of tuneful Birds, resounding loud."

Now for the formal temptation of the banquet. In its most obvious aspect it is a temptation of the flesh. But it is introduced by Satan's renewal of the theme of distrust. It also involves deception, and is to be associated, in more than a transitional way, with the glories of the world. I do not doubt that these considerations are part of Milton's scheme. But I think his plan is too subtle and comprehensive to be content with a simple progression, one at a time, of flesh-world-devil. I regard Elizabeth Pope's book highly, but I think she has over-systematized her materials.[4] Similarly, Howard Schultz's contribution goes much too far in restricting the poem to a point-for-point identification with an allegory of the church.[5] My own interpretation can, I hope, accommodate what is valid in other interpretations, but in a concept of Milton's form which is more flexible and comprehensive. Let us consider the scene from the viewpoints we have been following.

First, a relevant consideration is the continued emphasis on the human. In its most obvious aspect, as temptation of the flesh, this is the lowest stage of the drama of knowledge. Satan is, on this level, appealing to the judgment chiefly through appetite, and apparently attempting to subvert the true disciplinary order of temperance. Satan generally follows an old, experientially tested, ascending scale of temptations. But the appetite appealed to is not merely animal. It is not even, one may say, merely human. The whole scale now is different in range from the one used on Eve; its lower range is higher (though the forbidden fruit itself naturally appealed to mere appetite), and its higher range is lower. The temptation of bread, if it had not been linked with a high order of transcendence, might have been merely human. But even Belial's suggestion, it is worth noting, is put in terms of a transcendent kind of voluptuousness. The women are beautiful as the noon sky, and seem like goddesses; their virgin majesty is mild, sweet, but terrible; like magnets, they attract the hardest iron.

Granted, then, that Satan's appeal at the lowest level goes beyond any direct appeal to the human need for food. It quickly crosses that boundary after which basic need becomes what our age calls conspicuous consumption, that inexpensively produced model of transcendence for the soul of modest resources. Why? Why does Satan not begin at the actual bottom of the scale? He has announced the intention, as one of his possible next moves, of trying the protagonist's "constancy" with

> that which only seems to satisfie
> Lawful desires of Nature, not beyond.

It was traditional that in a natural desire, as the desire for eating, man could go wrong without the agency of the devil; so Satan

55

seems to be surrendering that possibility for inconspicuousness. But why should Satan begin again even this low, at what is the upper range of the lowest level of temptation? He has already sampled the temper of the hero's mind and virtue. One would not ordinarily expect, either from the demonstration of the first encounter or from the report to the devils, that low temptations had much chance of success.

The scene itself should provide us with some possible answers, for traces of Satan's consciousness ought to be in a scene which he has staged and partly directed. Though the formal announcement of the drama prescribed a full course through "all" temptation, we cannot legitimately transfer this intelligence to Satan's motives. One may postulate in evil an allegorical compulsiveness to go through all the appointed motions, and this may be relevant, though Satan has already exhibited at least some free choice and rejected Belial. Or one may suggest the psychological experience of evil, which knows how surprising, and sometimes not very elevated, are the weaknesses of the exalted in spirit. But that would be for the audience to whisper cues to the players, or to the playwright himself. We must perhaps look for another kind of reason for the particular lowness of the temptation. Perhaps we can find it in considering the transcendent nature of this appeal to the flesh. Is Satan carried away by an Iago-like enthusiasm for his creation, so that he goes beyond the bounds of nature without meaning to?[6] Or does he actually think that the more lavish his banquet is, the harder it tickles all the senses, the more attractive it will be to this hero? Or is the excess directed not alone toward having the gift accepted but toward alternative goals? If we follow the hint of this last possibility, I think we may come closest to interpreting Satan's motives.

First, the emphasis on the excess of the scene is extraordinary. The sensuous presentation is gorgeous and evocative. History, myth, and literature are imperiously ransacked by the Miltonic imagination working at the top of its form, fusing the kind of splendid image that would shine in the world of *Paradise Lost*. In the desert it is astounding. Nor is Belial's low transcendence quite excluded from the scene. There are, not to miss any possibilities, the beautiful stripling youths as cupbearers. And discreetly arranging themselves in the background, with a Botticelli-like lyricism uniting a beautiful moment with history:

> distant more
> Under the Trees now trip'd, now solemn stood
> Nymphs of *Diana's* train, and *Naiades*
> With fruits and flowers from *Amalthea's* horn,
> And Ladies of th' *Hesperides,* that seem'd
> Fairer than feign'd of old, or fabl'd since
> Of Fairy Damsels met in Forest wide
> By Knights of *Logres,* or of *Lyones,*
> *Lancelot,* or *Pelleas,* or *Pellenore.*

The "regal" dinner itself is harshly contrasted with "that crude Apple that diverted Eve." And the reception of the offer also emphasizes the excess of the "pompous Delicacies" and their irrelevance to hunger. However possible of casuistical debate Satan's introductory moral red herrings may be, the actual banquet is not debatable; it insists on being *wrong.*

The scene is comic in a way that the first temptation was not, though the high irony and the exchanges of wit have much in common. But the first temptation was sudden, deadly, and possible in its presentation. This is more leisurely, and far less likely to succeed, because of the heightened incongruity of the excess. The scene carries over some of the comic relaxation of tension that marked the second conference of the devils — and, incidentally, carries over some of the same illicit imaginative materials, which are not less incongruous for being presented under the authority of a firm offer. So we may say, then, that the comic incongruity of excess is emphasized by the presentation itself, and by our sense of the total drama, of which this is but a local episode, and by the response of the protagonist, which only notes the obvious. And so we can see an additional comic element: the offer is provocative, not only in fact and presentation, but in the assumed tone of the offerer, in his gestures and presence, in his taunting insistence on the certain identity of the protagonist. "Hast thou not right to all Created things?" Ought they not tender their service, not "stay till bid" (unlike those stones?)? "Nature asham'd" has prepared this table in the wilderness: "To treat thee as beseems, and as her Lord / With honour." "What doubts the Son of God to sit and eat?" "What doubt'st thou Son of God? sit down and eat."

And so the effrontery of the proposition is emphasized by the effrontery of the manner, by the taunting assertion of identity, and by the strongly implied challenge that if he *is* the Son of God (not deserted and unregarded) he will not doubt his right to these things. The manner, as well as the proposition, is replied to — "temperately." This epithet describes the whole discriminating discipline of the hero, and not his abstention from food, or luxurious food. Jesus accepts now the assertion of identity as he accepted it in the first encounter, in terms of the Satanic knowledge already expressed: [7]

> Said'st thou not that to all things I had right?
> And who withholds my pow'r that right to use?

The answer is an insulting reminder that Satan's hypocrisy has already received full treatment; besides, there is a fresh and direct insult for the new occasion: "Why should'st thou then obtrude this diligence?" But Christ in his answer to Satan reveals nothing useful.

I raised the question before of a possible compulsiveness in evil. It is a pertinent question, but of the sort which must be kept in its proper place, or else it will preclude other questions which may be important though less final. Satan's mind, as it acts, "refluxes," and evolves, provides the best perspective for interpreting the drama; and that mind is fully developed by action, symbol, and image; it is made dramatically immediate, as the hero's mind, by the terms of the drama, cannot be. But this emphasis on Satan as a dramatic character does not exclude the possibility of a compulsiveness in evil; rather, the emphasis asserts that the inflexible logic of sin must express itself, according to the laws of artistic form, *through* the flexible logic of character, *through* the imaginative logic of drama. Satan may have *had* to appeal to the flesh, and may have *had* to make that appeal transcendent, because of something essential in the general character of evil which is brought out by this particular drama. But the transcendence, at least, is consistent with Satan's character and uncertainties and with our interpretation of Satan's limited objective possible to obtain through provocation. One may attribute to a character of demonstrated subtlety some complex skill at turning the weakness of split, multiple motives into the potential strength of a complicated trap able to evoke more than one profitable response.[8]

Evil as it acts in this poem seems intent both on trying everything that may succeed and on doing so according to a scale that apparently leads from low to high. What reasons may account for the scale? Should we say that evil seems to be obeying some kind of economic-moral law of efficiency, and is committed to corrupting at the lowest level possible? May we recognize also a psychological-moral law of efficiency, by which a possible step omitted cannot be returned to with the same initial chance of success? That is, if a big and undisguised human desire is rejected with full consciousness and control, a smaller desire, even if not previously attempted, has lost whatever original attraction it may have had. If the situation remains the same, the high bid refused must be followed by a higher, not a lower, bid; the price of a man's soul, if not accepted and not withdrawn, can only go up. (There is always the possibility, of course, that surprise may deceive consciousness and control; we should note, also, that the big temptation of the stones was disguised as bread.) And for our final speculative question: May we recognize a mysterious need of evil to imitate good, to follow, at whatever distance, or distortion, the "natural" human endowment to aspire *upward*?

Now to look at the question of compulsiveness from another point of view. According to Milton's concept, evil must also possess free will, but the freedom is characterized by the self-imposed restriction which Milton in the *Christian Doctrine* (I, xii) describes as "spiritual death." This death, figuratively considered, is the loss of "the life of the understanding"; it is also the loss of the "liberty to do good . . . which constitutes, as it were, the death of the will." The concept is a broad and penetrating one, able to account intelligibly for many different kinds of human experience.

Translated into dramatic inevitability, the concept lets us see that Satan is the victim of himself. Drama does not need to trace motivation back to a clearly defined, single, and ultimate spring. In drama the stream of motivation, once recognized above ground, following its natural course, allows us to believe in the existence of a real spring. We may speculate, legitimately and profitably, on what is below ground. If our desire for understanding is ambitious, we shall not want, or think we ought, to suppress our speculation. In the richness of its cognitive and mysterious ordering of experience great art invites our minds endlessly. But we may also, I should wish to add, content ourselves with the large satisfaction of experiencing as much as we can of the full order above ground.

To ask the question again: Why should Satan go back on his announced intention not to tempt appetite with what exceeds the natural and apparently lawful? What is the *one* source which underlies all the possible reasons thus far assembled? I do not like this question or quite believe in its validity, as I have made apparent. But the answer that I think will serve well enough is based on Satan's a priori loss of understanding and liberty to do good. Satan is demonstrably the victim of himself, and has ample opportunity to act out this role. What he says and does reflects an essential loss, which is the more marked because of his brilliant surface competence and awareness. As director of the stage he presents us with preparations and arrangements which mirror their author in ways he could not have anticipated. So, from the preceding scene, his scornful image of the beauty which exists only in the weak beholder's eye haunts the stage of the banquet scene. So do these lines:

> How many have with a smile made small account
> Of beauty and her lures, easily scorn'd
> All her assaults, on worthier things intent?

And we remember, with rich irony, Satan's accusing Belial of judging others by himself. Even a phrase, unremarkable in its context, will echo ironically: as Satan's obsessive reference to Belial's followers, "False titl'd Sons of God." The rejection of false transcendence by true transcendence has already been anticipated, we may remember, by the image of that confident queen of beauty *descending* from her throne to be discountenanced by "one look from his Majestick brow / Seated as on the top of Vertues hill."

Satan has to go on. He begins again, systematically, at a stage that does not really interest him. Mere material wealth, as the mere static possession of honor and political power, does not excite Satan's own intimate belief. This was apparent in the scornful reference to Solomon. It is true that Satan holds out wealth as means rather than end, but he gives wealth an independent emphasis and consequently the status of a formal temptation. If the intended victim accepts that price, then there will be no need to advance from means to end. If the offer fails, it has really been the introductory transition to the next offer; if the offer succeeds, it succeeds.

We may detect in the progress a kind of game of leapfrog played according to rules based on the Platonic concept of a tripartite soul. The appeal to appetite, as we have observed, was never pure and unambiguous; for the temptation of the bread involved a big transcendence, and the banquet invited a small, self-flattering transcendence from the appetitive to the passional. The links are interesting and significant. The banquet, with its illusion of transcendence, was presented as the height of carnal appetite and verged on the low appetite of the passional parts of the soul. What follows is the lower range of a higher transcendence.

If we look backward, we may infer that riches can also provide such banquets. If we look forward, we see that the less transcendent aspects of kingdom are being presented. Now we have the passional in terms of money feeding the appetite of the passional — a familiar, *low* basis of power looking up toward achievement rather than looking down from the *high* intoxication of that imagined achievement. The image of feeding is the hinge on which both temptations turn; for money is offered as the real bread of political power, to gain friends and followers, and to "feed" "at thy heels the dizzy Multitude." But the transcendent appetite has already had its authoritative expression in the soliloquy that precedes Christ's dream. It is a bold image that unites in perfect harmony the appetitive, the passional, and the rational in the soul of a religious hero:

> fed with better thoughts that feed
> Mee hungring more to do my Fathers will.

Christ's answer is "patiently" serious, except for the glancing reference to what he may accomplish in poverty and the fine, reverberating reference to the crown which "is but a wreath of thorns." Wealth without the virtues is "impotent." It cannot gain or keep power — witness history. The virtuous heroes of worldly kingdoms are cited, and this is important for the record. Most important of all, the problem of kingdom is now for the first time raised. The true honor of the worldly crown is based upon responsibility, but self-rule better deserves the name of king.

> But to guide Nations in the way of truth
> By saving Doctrine, and from errour lead
> To know, and knowing worship God aright,
> Is yet more Kingly, this attracts the soul,
> Governs the inner man, the noblest part,
> That other o're the body only reigns,
> And oft by force, which to a generous mind
> So reigning can be no sincere delight.

The answer suddenly transcends the limited argument of money as means, and transcends the next stage, when Satan will patiently offer the kingdoms of the world descending like queens of beauty from their thrones. Serious though the passage is, the stage director has been given an ironic cue to proceed to the kingdom of the mind, if anything. But if Satan has to be deaf, the drama profits. For brilliant though Christ's speech is, it is too concentrated and too final; it needs more room and action to play out the implications. Besides, there is no more reason for Satan to be convinced by this verbal demonstration than by the evidence of the baptism.

A DIGRESSION ON
POETRY AND POLITICS

IF WE step back entirely from this drama,
further back even than the moral traditions associated with the
symbols of "the world" and "the kingdoms of the world," we may
make a useful discrimination drawn from political theory. Erasmus, leaning on Plato and combining a moral simplicity of
orientation with some experiential sense of the complexity of
action, proclaims no one "fit to rule who has not assumed the rule
unwillingly and only after persuasion."[1] To desire power is to
disqualify oneself as foolish, ignorant, or wicked. The facts of
morality and the facts of political existence do not quite square
here, even for the Renaissance and less for us. (I may as well state,
in advance, that Milton's poem, as a poem should, stands primarily
on the moral facts.) But part of the moral basis, at least, rests on
a traditional attitude now standard, if variable, in modern political
"representation." Political rule denies personal gratification (to put
aside the old problem of realizing the perfect in the world of action) because the burdens and obligations of rule are public, not
private. Erasmus, reinforced by Christian ideals, echoes Aristotle's
familiar principle, that the standard of rule, the true form, is the
common, not the private, interest.[2]

This would mean that, even without a unique hero and a particular dramatic situation, it would be commonly recognizable that
Satan's political attitude is special, and obviously wrong. True,

the needs of the world, or parts of it, are adduced, and the advantages, at least to Israel and Rome, if Christ will assume rule; but Satan does not put much heart into this lure.

Another political attitude worth pausing on is the one reflected by the widespread admiration in the Renaissance for ancient Rome, which furnished countless moralizing examples of the political advantages of primitive virtue and simplicity. Montaigne went so far as to identify ancient Rome with Paradise (though for a special intellectual maneuver neither Milton nor his Satan could have liked, that of relating the decadence of Rome to the corrupting effect of knowledge).[3] Satan's Parthians are no doubt intended to suggest something of this attraction of primitive simplicity — the young nation on the rise, defying the power of the great old nation in decline, young and not yet corrupted.[4] But the trouble with Satan's presentation is that the primitive is not here endowed with any notable virtue to corrupt. The Parthians are mere fighters, though good ones, beautifully organized, and with a native strategy frustrating to the Roman concepts of war (though a military man might think that strategy better adapted to resisting the Romans than to conquering the world). They are presented in their primitive simplicity of power — a tool ready for use, admirable only for its limited utility and for its fierce animal efficiency. The best commentary on the Kingdom of Parthia is the political commonplace that the honor of rule is proportionate to the dignity of the subjects.[5] The commonplace also applies to the offer of Rome, and to part of the presented appeal of Israel. These kingdoms, whatever their attractions, represent the rule over inferior men. Christ does not use this argument, but instead a more profound one based on the concept of inner freedom and moral dignity; yet familiar political considerations make Satan's offer of the kingdoms as disproportionate and irrelevant as the offer of the luxurious banquet in the wilderness.

If we step a little closer to the established scene of the poem, we may observe that it is not only his hero that Milton has chosen well, but his *time,* when no noble and puissant nation is rousing herself after sleep. It is a time of political (and moral and philosophical)

64

low ebb. The choice offered is between a rude militaristic nation
and a decadent one with its best time behind it.

Let us turn to some of Milton's political and moral ideas. They
are clear enough as they are expressed by the action of the poem,
but it is useful to look at them separately, uncomplicated by the
special conditions of the poem, which are both narrower and more
comprehensive in scope than any of Milton's prose articulations. I
think a fundamental issue can be stated thus: Milton's political
theory is based on his moral theory, on the individual state of man.
The ideal state is a union of ideal individuals, and what is true for
the single state of man is true, by extension, for the multiple state
of the nation. The order of duty is, first, to God, then to self, then
to neighbor. The real political arena is the self, where duty must be
understood and managed. Self-mastery achieved by obedience to
truth is the best preparation for executing the commands of truth;
thus obeying and ruling are one (a Platonic unity which Aristotle
in his *Politics* goes out of his way to contradict). The greatest effort,
then, must be made in the self, where true liberty is to be gained
and held, a model for government under justice.

But who are one's neighbors? And what of the duties which do
not clearly originate from transcendent truth, or from the striving
of the self to know and hold that truth? Neighbors may be educated and persuaded; that is one kind of political answer. But what
of the new, unforeseeable duties which are generated by the
stresses of neighbors living together in one historical time and
place, stresses complicated enough within a nation, but added to
by the conflicting interests of neighboring nations? The moral answer may still be individual, and hold good for the individual; but
the political answer may not be able to wait for education; and it
must respond to the human sources of question, if less well than to
the divine sources, at least well enough. Divine patience is eternal,
and even its minor deflections work in long rhythms that human
patience can admire more easily than emulate.

As political *thinker* Milton seems to have added nothing new;
as moral thinker he did not need to; as moral poet, our chief
concern, he could touch nothing that did not become new. He is

baffled by the political problems, though he does not know this as clearly as we know it — from our vantage point of increased political knowledge, from the command, which we enjoy, of a richer choice in historical perspectives, and from our deep personal experience of immersion in perplexity.

It is not that Milton naively underestimates the practical difficulties of government. If he cannot successfully bridge the gap between theoretical and practical, he is not without distinguished company. Perhaps his most serious failing, given our privileged view of the historical time, is a lack of any substantial sense of the reality of social forces. But this failing, one must admit, only increases the gap which would still, Milton being Milton, remain. If we understand the man, his peculiar strengths and virtues were not imaginatively at home in politics. Nor should we expect anything like the immediate sense of political realities, and the shadows of their depths, that Shakespeare seems to draw in with his natural breath. Milton can breathe *some* of that air, quite enough for his poetry and its elected problems, but at his best he breathes a different air. It is not that he devoted a less-gifted part of himself to the public prose, but too much; he spread himself thin and forced into expression more than was capable of becoming his real self. In the poetry, where he exercises an absolute imaginative dominion, the power of rightness is unfailing as it breathes into the immediate problems that larger air which unites in poetic form the immediate with the final.

In addressing Oliver Cromwell Milton displays, rather impressively, his sense of the immediate problems of government. He knows the necessities of political intelligence: "to send out your anxious mind, your thoughts, to the remotest parts; to watch, to foresee." (VIII, 229.) But "means" for accomplishing important ends are *assumed* to be occupying Cromwell's attention and engrossing his soul, and they are assumed with little evidence of specific interest. Milton's most tangible suggestions are directed toward negative actions: toward separating the problems of the church from those of government, toward a moderate revising of the laws and education, toward not trying to perfect the state at once. He identifies the hero with the state, but in doing so he boldly asserts their inseparable need to resist encroachment on liberty ("he who forcibly seizes upon the liberty of others, is the first to lose his own"). (VIII, 227.) He emphasizes, tactfully yet frankly, the dangers inherent in power; and if the great office demands a leader instructed, almost, by divine colloquy, that is not a flattering reassurance to Cromwell but a reason for establishing an advisory council of trusted men; and the nominations are forthwith made under the rhetorical color of feeling himself compelled to commemorate the names of famous men.

The cautions, the sturdy grasp of the negative — these bespeak Milton's practical good sense, his feeling for the "contrarieties" of human existence. For all his zeal, when it comes to the point of establishing the City of God on earth, Milton shows an unzealous awareness of difficulties. This awareness perhaps ought to be associated with his stubborn unwillingness to despise the body, and with his belief (on both theoretical and empirical grounds) in the impracticability of passing laws for virtue, and even with his belief in the Second Coming (which in his creed does not solve or dismiss human complexities, but keeps them in a workable perspective). To illustrate this last I can think of nothing better than Milton's use of the Osiris myth in *Areopagitica*:

From that time ever since, the sad friends of Truth, such as durst appear, imitating the careful search that *Isis* made for the mangled body of *Osiris*, went up and down gathering up limb by limb still as they could find them. We have not yet found them all, Lords and Commons, nor ever shall do, till her Master's second coming; he shall bring together every joint and member, and shall mold them into an immortal feature of loveliness and perfection. Suffer not these licensing prohibitions to stand at every place of opportunity forbidding and disturbing them that continue seeking, that continue to do our obsequies to the torn body of our martyred Saint. (IV, 338.)

Milton's grasp of the negative is always impressive — whether as a poetic strategy for legitimatizing incredibly fine illegitimacies, like that fair field of Enna, in the best of all possible poetic worlds where every evil is made a necessary good; or whether as an intellectual-moral strategy for maintaining a concept of limits within which human experience can find its forms of meaning. The point deserves further treatment but would lead me too far astray. I had better offer it as suggestion and hope that it interests the reader, adding only one big thing more: Milton's grasp of the negative seems to me a fundamental source of the great poetic tension he achieves, and also the incidental source of many brilliant moments of tension which can apparently be explained in as many ways as there are critical minds.

The speech to Cromwell is noble and courageous in the political doors it refuses to leave shut. But in addressing the citizens Milton is freer to express more positively his chief political interests. A minor item in the praise-advice to Cromwell indicates that direction: the new leader must *persuade* the people to leave the old and corrupt institutions for a new and better discipline. Persuasion is of the mind, and the body politic is to be treated as capable of reason. At least that is what Milton needs to think, and tries hard to think. If he can feel and maintain less imaginative sympathy for the body politic than for the body human and individual, that is perhaps part of another story which, though interesting and important, need not affect the poetry in any immediate way. The formal grounds of the political concept are both Platonic and religious. The dispelling of "errors from the mind," as the imparting of "the heavenly light of truth," belongs to God alone; man has the right to use only reason, admonition, and prayer. If sword and scourge are used, it is as if these errors, which "are seated in the mind," were instead seated "in the body." (VIII, 179–81.)

But sometimes the body politic is thought of as mere body. This is likely to happen when the spiritual government of the church is under consideration, and is conveniently to be contrasted with the standard use of force by secular government; or when Milton's high concern with civil and religious liberty is not directly involved, which seems to withdraw the soul from his state. His curious proposal of a "grand Councel" as substitute for the imminent return of the king, reveals this bent. The council, somehow impossibly above politics, is to take care of the ordinary business of government: "being thus firmly constituted to perpetuity . . . there can be no cause alleged why peace, justice, plentiful trade and all prosperity should not thereupon ensue throughout the whole land." The ordinary business of government seems here to require no special inspiration, or perhaps cannot be quite believed in by 1660. In contrast, the advent of the Second Coming is emphasized with a fervor not usual in Milton. The council will do its limited, and of course un-regal, job

with as much assurance as can be of human things, that they shall so continue (if God favor us, and our wilful sins provoke him not) even to the coming of our true and rightful and only to be expected King, only worthy as he is our only Saviour, the Messiah, the Christ, the only heir of his eternal father, the only by him anointed and ordained since the work of our redemption finished, Universal Lord of all mankind. (VI, 133.)

The point to be made of this, I think, is less that Milton is now withdrawing from the world, a Christ in the desert, than that the true basis of his political interest is now being demonstrated — this time not by how he advances but by how he retreats. I do not mean that he is falling back all the way to hope in the Second Coming; the rhetorical occasion for long-range antiroyalism is exploited too opportunely for us to hold this simple interpretation of the above passage. When the practicability of his true political interest is baffled, he retreats, not to a personal belief in the Second Coming, though he is willing to use that idea rhetorically on his audience to cover the maneuver; but he retreats personally to the "practical" but morally unimportant scheme of the council. Finally he retreats, if out of politics, to the basis of his interest in politics, to the fundamental political unit, the soul of a hero.

But Milton's political history is more complicated than I have been making it, for I can afford to be concerned only with what concerns the poetry, or rather my limited understanding of the poetry, bound by my intelligence and my range of interest — to offer these as synecdoche for the whole state. I want to return now to what I consider Milton's chief political interests. When not in a tactical retreat, Milton tries to think of the body politic as having a rational soul able to respond to the persuasion of truth. In turning from Cromwell to the citizens, he emphasizes, as bridge to the truth, justice:

For, if, to be able to devise the subtlest expedients for filling the treasury; if, to furnish out sea and land forces, with the utmost expedition; if, to treat warily with the ambassadors of foreign states; to enter, with dexterity, into coalitions and treaties, be accounted by you more grand, more useful, more wise in a state, than to administer uncorrupted justice to the people; than to succour the oppressed, and those who are injuriously afflicted; than to give to every man his free, unshackled right — when you have suddenly found those grand things to be delusive, and the things which are now thought little and are neglected by you shall prove adverse and destructive; it will then be too late for you to discover how great has been your error. Again, the fidelity of the armies and adherents, in whom ye confide, is uncertain, unless it be maintained by the authority of justice alone: and wealth and honours, the objects of pursuit to most men, easily change masters. (VIII, 243.)

And justice, of course, is dependent on liberty, and liberty is dependent on the discipline of temperance.

Unless you banish avarice, ambition, luxury from your thoughts, and all excess even from your families, the tyrant, whom you imagined was to be sought abroad, and in the field, you will find at home, you will find within, and that a more inexorable one. (VIII, 241.)

Liberty gained in war but lost in the more glorious warfare of peace provides a "salutary lesson" — for posterity. But the idea of liberty remains constant and available, though not to those who have corruptly lost their chance. For true liberty is an inner order, an achieved balance, not mere abstinence; if it is broken from within, by voluntary choice, then it is lost, like a leg, or like fatally ruined health (these are my illustrative images, not Milton's). Such liberty so lost cannot be restored, whether by a Cromwell or a whole nation of Brutuses — and no real deliverer would if he could, or could if he would. Genuine liberty " a good man alone can properly attain." As for the many (if they are not true multiples — somehow — of "a good man"), they may try by arms again and again, but they will only change their slavery, not end it. For the practical demonstration of this concept of liberty based on the individual's possession of his soul, Milton appeals to history, to law, and to nature. The deranged man, incapable of ruling himself, becomes, like a nation, the ward of others. If you wish to continue free, he concludes, begin by being wise, or repent. "Learn to obey right reason, to be masters of yourselves." (VIII, 241–51.)

That is the heart of his doctrine, and it is difficult, and individual. When he caps what is individual with some general social advice intended to be practical, the applied science of moral liberty (which is clear, and familiar, and fully worked out by the moralists for the single "good man") becomes something less than practical, even for a community of saints — unless it be a small community, a kind of Little Gidding with restricted activity in the world, and not much molested by the world because not much in competition with the world, but possible to admire and even cherish, as the world cherishes the possibility of perfection in dreams, or cherishes the small, noncompetitive models of perfection in the parks and reservations of the world open for holiday visits. "Abstain from factions," he says, from "hatreds, superstitions, injuries, lusts, and plunders." This concluding political advice is more like beginning moral advice. The thinness of its applied moral imperative does not, I think, misrepresent the nature of Milton's own engagement. As I see the issue, his deepest intellectual, moral, and imaginative resources are either not available or not competent when applied to political problems.

But we have not yet isolated Milton's most important basis for political truth. Justice may be a bridge to that truth, and dependent upon the human foundation of liberty, which is dependent upon the discipline of temperance. But what of the other, the superhuman foundation for the bridge? The obedience to right reason is the exercise of justice and temperance in the virtue Milton calls piety, which is Platonic wisdom with Christian additions. Piety embraces that orientation toward the truth by which all the other virtues orient themselves. If the other virtues are true sources of political power, this is the source of sources. Piety is the first subject of his advice to the citizens. True liberty, he begins, cannot

71

be gained or lost by arms: it is born of piety, justice, temperance. Unless by real and sincere piety toward God and men, not an idle and wordy, but an efficacious, an operative piety, you drive from your minds superstition, which originates in an ignorance of true and substantial religion, you will not want those who will sit upon your backs and upon your necks, as if you were beasts of burden; who, though you are the victors in the war, will sell you, though by no military auction, as their plunder to the highest bidder; and will make an excellent market of your ignorance and superstition. (VIII, 241.)

The duty to God and neighbor, mediated by the duty to self, derives from God, from an anthropology that conceives of man as made in God's image, with man's faculty of reason the lens which, when corrected, most truly reflects that image. Man's bridge toward God is met by God's bridge toward man, which is love. Knowledge meets love in love. Knowledge not truly oriented diverts into superstition, which is idolatry, ignorance of the proper object to love. The moral-political issue is between knowledge as power and knowledge as love. First, let us look briefly at the political implications of knowledge as love.

In *The Reason of Church-government Urg'd against Prelaty* Milton cites the "wisest of the heathen," Plato, to the effect that "persuasion certainly is a more winning, and more manlike way to keep men in obedience than feare." Therefore, laws for civil society ought to be prefaced with a discourse:

showing how good, how gainful, how happy it must needs be to live according to honesty and justice, which . . . would so incite, and in a manner, charm the multitude into the love of that which is really good as to embrace it ever after, not of custom and awe, which most men do, but of choice and purpose, with true and constant delight. (III, 181.)

But the knowledge persuading men to love is not to be won from learning alone; something further is required:

We may see even in the guidance of a civil state to worldly happiness, it is not for every learned, or every wise man, though many of them consult in common, to invent or frame a discipline, but if it be at all the work of man, it must be of such a one as is a true

knower of himself, and himself in whom contemplation and practice, wit, prudence, fortitude, and eloquence must be rarely met,
both to comprehend the hidden causes of things, and span in his
thoughts all the various effects that passion or complexion can work
in man's nature; and hereto must his hand be at defiance with
gain, and his heart in all virtues heroic. . . . And therefore all the
ancient lawgivers were either truly inspired as *Moses*, or were such
men as with authority enough might give it out to be so, as *Minos*,
Lycurgus, Numa, because they wisely forethought that men would
never quietly submit to such a discipline as had not more of God's
hand in it than man's. (III, 186.)

But even the discipline descended from the authority of God's
hand must have something more. The inspired knowledge of himself and all men, possessed by the lawgiver, possessed and still
"operative," able to work in the world, must also be inspired
knowledge of God. The two ends of the bridge must meet in
love.

Moses therefore the only Lawgiver that we can believe to have
been visibly taught of God, knowing how vain it was to write laws
to men whose hearts were not first seasoned with the knowledge
of God and of his works, began from the book of Genesis, as a
prologue to his laws; which *Josephus* right well hath noted. That
the nation of the Jews, reading therein the universal goodness of
God to all creatures in the Creation, and his peculiar favor to them
in his election of *Abraham* their ancestor, from whom they could
derive so many blessings upon themselves, might be moved to obey
sincerely by knowing so good a reason of their obedience. (III,
182.)

In *Paradise Regained* Satan offers Christ the kingdoms of the
world. A main argument of the offer, though there are variations,
is that the Messiah cannot without *means* fulfill the prophecies
concerning him. The virtues, even under the authority of divine
prediction, require means, and the means offered are those of political power. Satan skillfully raises the questions of power, but
keeps away from the questions of inspired knowledge and love.
The poetic dilemma is a deliberately false one, for Christ's kingdom
is not of this world (at least not as Satan understands the world).
But the political dilemma is a real one. How is piety to make oper-

ative in this world its otherworldly idea? How is the self to unite duty to God and neighbor? Bacon's narrowing of the question, in his essay "Of Great Place," would have been acknowledged by Milton as a partial truth, but fatally dangerous as the whole truth. Bacon wrote: "But power to do good is the true and lawful end of aspiring. For good thoughts (though God accept them) yet towards men are little better than good dreams, except they be put in act; and that cannot be without power and place, as the vantage and commanding ground."

In the choice between a political wisdom based on *what men do* and a moral-poetic wisdom based on *what men ought to do,* Milton is fully committed to the latter, which he proclaims the real source of human power. And if the positive arguments do not promise any sure success in the political world's body, the violation of them constitutes a negative poetic argument that the world's heart responds to. After all, the compromising equilibrium of states dissolves, but the eternal moral verities go on unmoved, or at least move at a more nearly geological rate in the human heart. Their comment is always available at the failure of the compromises, and who can wisely say the comment is wrong? Besides, we know that moral or mythic logic is hard to set up as operative in successful competition with other kinds of logic; however true mythic logic may be to the depths of the human psyche, that truth emerges most successfully perhaps when violated, and then it makes operative an inexorable logic. The thin, clear, dry light of man's positive reason emerged in Greece. But this did not dispel man's other wisdom in the dark continuity of the soul. That wisdom does not seem able to produce clear, cooperative systems by refinement and extension and argument; but it is terrible and true and undeniable in the great argument of violation.

In *Paradise Regained* Milton is morally, poetically, dramatically right. Christ's kingdom is not of this world; his kingdom is the church, which governs the inner man; his role is that of symbolic illumination for the mind of man. The practical reason of prudence is united with the other virtues to serve a pure vision of wisdom which serves God. Knowledge of the fountain of knowledge is obedience, within and without, a "way of death" as positive moral example. Within the world of self this dying is true living. In the poem the symbolic role of illumination is radical and exacting, but it is also rich and dynamic. Milton intends no literal allegory which could be translated as meaning that every man should do precisely thus. The hero and the circumstances *are* unique, metaphorically relevant to every man, but who could presume a literal identification? This is part of the sustained tension of the poem, the dynamic degree of the reader's relationship to the hero's dramatic demonstration, intellectual, moral, and religious.

In prose, to make a limited point, a clear and final distinction between reader and hero is easily made. In *A Treatise of Civil Power in Ecclesiastical Causes,* Milton quotes John, 18, 36: "If my kingdom were of this world, then would my servants fight." Milton's comment is interesting, not only for the relative disparagement of civil power, but for the unequivocal separation between the divine metaphor and an immediately practical human concern:

This proves the kingdom of Christ not governed by outward force; as being none of this world, whose kingdoms are maintained all by force only; and yet disproves not that a Christian commonwealth may defend it self against outward force in the cause of religion as well as in any other; though Christ himself, coming purposely to die for us, would not be so defended. (VI, 22.)

The separation is reasonable, for a limited point in the more nearly literal world of prose argument; though in the poem so clear a division between the metaphor and the reader's literal concern would be ruinous.

In the poem the degree of relationship between reader and hero is dynamic, and will depend on every reader's experience as he reads, and as he takes personal inventory. The symbol, then, is radical and wonderfully sustained through a long action, but it is also flexible and individual in its applicability to the world of political action and the individual reader's understanding of that world. The symbol is no model for practical action, but that is not to deny the relevance of the symbol to the source of action. The life of the spirit may not translate well into the life of the body politic, and it may be more difficult to establish the fault than the consequences, but the two lives struggle on in a marriage harder to dissolve than to abuse. I quote for its relevance to our problem a brilliant analysis by Eric Voegelin, from *The New Science of Politics*:

The death of the spirit is the price of progress. Nietzche revealed this mystery of the Western apocalypse when he announced that God was dead and that He had been murdered. This Gnostic murder is constantly committed by the men who sacrifice God to civilization. The more fervently all human energies are thrown into the great enterprise of salvation through world-immanent action, the farther the human beings who engage in this enterprise move away from the life of the spirit. And since the life of the spirit is the source of order in man and society, the very success of a Gnostic civilization is the cause of its decline.[6]

We are dealing with a rich theme; so perhaps I may postpone my concluding remarks a little longer and add something from my personal experience. During the weeks that followed the end of World War II, I had the opportunity to talk with many hundreds of Germans. They were still suffering from shock, and relief. Much of what they said I thought influenced by their immediate state, and I felt my share of human sympathy for their conditon and its causes. But one attitude in particular astounded me, and I thought it transcended their immediate state and projected a cunningly distorted representation of "the life of the spirit." The usual catalogue of self-apologies, the usual distribution of blame — these were familiar to me, and I was not, I say, humanly unsympathetic. But politics were blamed for the German tragedy, politics as politics. And the solution proposed was that Germany should renounce politics. For what? Of course, for the life of the spirit. The most eloquent statement of this view I heard from a former mayor (Nazi) of Bayreuth. Germany, he said, must once again become a nation of poets, philosophers, and scientists. But no more politics. What Germany needed was an efficiency expert, someone like that extraordinary American businessman Henry Kaiser, the name an unimportant coincidence, who would put the country on a sound economic basis, run it efficiently, while the nation concentrated its most important energies on the more important business of poetry, philosophy, and science. I mention this to remind the reader that, though poetry and politics may not enjoy a completely successful marriage, there are worse states — like that of poetry and national efficiency living in sin. The reader may think Milton's proposal of a grand council a seventeenth-century version of the mayor of Bayreuth's proposal. I suppose it perhaps is, though Milton's intentions, and much of the circumstantial emphasis, were very different. But his poem, even when it deals directly with the temptations of politics, is not itself tempted into absurdity.

The moral dilemma of Milton's poem is imaginatively correct in its statement and in its solution. It perfectly fits the unique hero and his unique role. It is richly relevant (if less perfectly fitted) to the individual soul of the morally imaginative reader. The poetic dilemma is an ultimate moral one for which a political solution would be inadequate. The terms of the poem explore, but deliberately prevent, a political solution, and prevent that by a poetic solution that is imaginatively right. The radical commitment of Milton's basic political interest does not work in the political world, but it does work, triumphantly, in the poetic world he created. And this considerable achievement is not performed by sleight of hand, by tricky disappearing acts, but by a full imaginative confronting of a profound issue fully contained by the terms of the fiction, and true to the high order of the poetry and its exacting laws; and all this with no imaginative cheats! What I have just said, though great praise, also admits the limitations of the poem. Like other true poems, it is first and most concerned with being true to itself, and so fails to solve its elected problems except in terms of its own poetic fiction. But in remaining true to its own fiction it may perform services of no small importance to human beings. It may exercise and purge and strengthen the moral imagination of man, even political man.

THE KINGDOMS OF
THE WORLD

LET US begin by remembering a peculiar pattern of the temptations which precede the offer of the kingdoms of the world. The appeal to appetite was never pure and unambiguous; for the temptation of the bread involved a big transcendence; then there was a kind of retreat as the banquet invited a small, self-flattering transcendence from the appetitive to the passional — the banquet being both the height of the appeal to carnal appetite and the lowest level of appeal to the passional parts of the soul. The transitional offer of wealth appealed directly to the passional, but at the lower range of a potentially higher stage.

Something of the same pattern is repeated in the temptation of the kingdoms. First, as with the bread, the appeal of a big transcendence, glory, is tried, though it is not pressed in any concentrated, systematic way. Then there is a retreat followed by a systematic progression up the scale. (It is to be noted that when Satan jumps the proper stage of systematic temptation he does not make the kind of tangible, firm offer which would not allow him to drop his price as he retreats to begin again. The temptations of the bread and glory are quite different in this respect from those of the banquet and the kingdoms.) So now we begin at the top of the scale, with the appeal of glory; then we retreat, to begin again, with the offer of the small, specific Kingdom of Israel, and then continue up the scale to Parthia and Rome.

78

Satan opens the temptation of glory with direct flattery of Christ's person. Though flattery, it is accurate. He praises the perfect temper of the hero, whose mind, heart, and words are in perfect accord with each other and with the shape of goodness, wisdom, and justice. He would prove an infallible oracle to kings and nations; or if military deeds were required of him, he would prove an irresistible leader, the kind of inspired leader who could lead a few men to victory against the whole world. This is flattery; but if we understand Milton, and the Renaissance mind, and the portrait of the hero thus far presented to us, we are probably to understand this as true, or at least quite within the range of probability. The kingdoms of the world *are* Christ's, and his rejection is not asceticism but definition. In one sense, of course, if this potential power *is* possessed by the hero it will make unnecessary Satan's help to the rule over Israel or Parthia. And the flattery is directly repeated, but as program to specific political action, in the case of Rome. All Christ will need to do in order to unseat Tiberius is appear with his regal virtues and begin noble deeds. If this were a real offer, then, Satan would seem to be undercutting his own office as assistant. But it is less an offer than an exploratory general titillation. Self-aggrandizement is the theme, under the flimsy veil of concern for the world's deprivation. Glory is praised as the highest, the most strenuous pleasure of the most elevated spirits. (The image is that of ascending fire, as it was in the hero's autobiographical reflection on the "heroic acts.") And the pleasure is cunningly linked with an insistent weaving in and out of the worry of time: it is late but not too late.

The answer coolly shakes down the subject of glory. A familiar Renaissance definition is used, that human glory is the reflected judgment of one's inferiors and therefore susceptible to all the distortions of vulgar ignorance. This no doubt sounds more shocking to modern readers than it did to Milton's contemporaries, but even they must have noticed to what austere extent the Christ of intellect was being elevated over the Christ of feeling.[1] That is a fact of fictional presentation and not to be debated with, at least not before all the evidence is in. The harsh argument, and this one must observe, is a necessary part of the rejection of an independent human glory. But Christ softens the argument with some important qualifications. The judgment of the wise is not spurned, but the wise are few and the approval of the few does not constitute glory. Furthermore, a deliberate turn of language implies a kind of natural antipathy of the many toward the one "who dares be singularly good." Glory achieved through unflattering, "singular" goodness, and not established by the judgment of force, will need the sanction of some other judgment, presumably divine. True glory, then, is not the reflected judgment of inferiors, but the reflected judgment of God, which is true judgment. That glory may extend to earth (it begins by God's looking toward earth), and then presumably the minority of the wise may join their voice, but the more familiar home of glory is heaven, where the many are wise. Then Christ turns to the false transcendence of superhuman military conquerors, which receives an unsparing analysis, and reduction to the subhuman.

After this, with the direct claims of human glory quite demolished, Christ turns around to allow some room for indirect claims, under the hypothesis that there may be some "good" in the idea of glory. First, the *means* of attaining glory may be quite different from those which Satan suggests: namely, "By deeds of peace." The prime example, again, is Job, "Made famous in a Land and times obscure." The second example is Socrates: "who next more memorable?" So if there is any good in glory, and if it really exists on earth (without the promulgated record of a heavenly decision), then it must be sought thus, by not seeking it. The examples rather strongly suggest that there is human glory, even pagan glory; for the military deed of Scipio Africanus plainly is admirable and deserving of human fame, *if* it has not been corrupted by the improper motivation of desire for fame. As logical argument, as the defining statement of a man who knows in advance precisely what he means, the speech is far less impressive than it is if we read it as a process of thought defining itself in motion, under the pressure of concrete dramatic circumstances.

Let us follow this viewpoint a little further to see where it leads us. The argument first emerges as a direct answer to Satan's basic appeal, and so undermines the basis of glory as human. The piety of proper relationship is insisted on, the judgment of God and not the judgment of man. Most harshly treated is the idolatrous human transcendence which extorts from the human, by force, the judgment and devotion due only to God. But what is most interesting about the speech is that Christ does not stop there, as he very well might have done if he were intent only on expressing the pious difference between the human and the divine. Once the idolatry of direct claim to glory is disposed of, Christ shows himself willing to admit the possible validity of human fame, even where divine judgment is silent. The good deed, whether of peace or war, piously done for itself (and therefore in proper relationship with higher truth), and not done for self, may deserve glory whether God's judgment has been announced or not. Socrates and Scipio, though pagans, emerge as potentially genuine heroes. Christ's own orientation is exemplary, that of true being toward the *source* of being; of course he will not seek glory for himself:

> I seek not mine, but his
> Who sent me, and thereby witness whence I am.

(This reintroduces the drama of knowledge into the problem of glory, and Satan will not be comforted by this taunting invitation to discriminate between the metaphorical and the literal, and thus know the *who* by the *whence*.)

The speech has not closed a door it is quite possible to close between the human and the divine, between the divine and the human. Action in the world, the heroism of peace or war, is not despised — the effect is quite to the contrary. And one result of this for the drama is to leave still open the final definition of Christ's kingdom, and also the final understanding of that early aspiration for heroic acts. The hero is austere, intellectual, disciplined, pious; but he is still facing the problem of how to complete his mission *in* the world. The question of what to do in the world still stands between the depth of descent into the self and the transcendence of his "mission high." He does not rest on the absolute argument for rejecting the world and the possible "good" in glory. And one final note on a door left open at least a wide crack: the moral status of paganism is not being disparaged by a new morality; and that, whether as an indication of the continuing importance of the world, or whether as a mark to measure the progress of the hero, must interest us.

Satan's rebuttal, with a fine emphasis of personal accent, defends glory as a good sanctified by the example of God. God seeks glory, He created for glory, orders and governs for glory, requires glory in heaven and on earth and from good and bad without exemption, receives glory promiscuously, exacts glory. The rebuttal provokes feeling from the protagonist, who replies "fervently" now that the attack is directed not at him but at God. Glory is defended as part of the order and discipline of freedom under goodness. It is an external sign important chiefly as an internal opportunity for moral action. Gratitude (as the unmentionable Stoics also perceived) is the only full answer to obligation. The external sign tests the freedom of the inner response: if the response is directed toward goodness, gratitude is felt; if not, the moral order breaks. But even God's glory is in an essential way like man's, indirect, not sought. God did not create for glory "as prime end," but for goodness, and to make that goodness "freely" communicable. The bridge between human and divine is thus asserted in the continuity of the moral order, and a significant point of likeness emphasizes that continuity.

Then Christ reverses the method of definition he used in the earlier treatment of glory, when he began by excluding the possibility of human glory and then moved far toward admitting the hypothetical possibility. Now, having emphasized the similarity between human and divine, he emphasizes the necessary difference. The creature has nothing but what has been given him by the Creator; besides, as further disqualification, there is the matter of the first act of ingratitude, by which man fell. (Here we have, casually introduced, a crucial distinction drawn from the historical truth of Scriptures; before the Greek philosophers present their competitive way to truth we are made to see in operation a basic piece of knowledge that they lack.) But having asserted the difference between man and God, Christ can again make final room for human glory:

> Yet so much bounty is in God, such grace,
> That who advance his glory, not thir own,
> Them he himself to glory will advance.

This does not contradict the method, described earlier, by which Job's glory was established. But it is more general, and it is intended, I think, to accommodate the real existence of glory which has not received God's announced judgment. If the glory truly exists, then perhaps we may guess that it has fulfilled the conditions laid down in Christ's final statement. Since God is all truth and goodness, both Socrates and Scipio were advancing His glory, and may have received this sanction for their own.

The problem of glory has not been exhausted, but Satan's immediate interest has been, and any hope for a quick profit from the proposition that never got stated as firm offer. He drops the subject as he dropped the subject of bread, and as he will seem to, but not quite, drop the subject of the transitory kingdoms. The offer of the Kingdom of Israel begins, not as offer, but as advice and suggestion. The political problem is presented, and then the wrong, both civil and religious, to be righted. Zeal and duty are appealed to, and occasion, the matter of timing (which any student of David's career ought to know something about): "Raign then; what canst thou better do the while?" But this is general, and a sparring suggestion.

The answer is in terms of time. It is quiet and terribly final in its expressed resignation to God's "due time." It reaffirms the unity of obeying and ruling. It glances at the present function of insults, snares, violence, and proposes a formula of behavior ruinous to Satan's prospects: "Suffering, abstaining, quietly expecting / Without distrust or doubt." This quiet expression of patience provokes a "fervent" reply from Satan, "inly rackt." It is one of the most exciting moments in the drama; suddenly things appear to be opening up, as if a real break in the contest may come. The speech needs quoting; it is a masterly exhibition of dramatic art and language:

> Let that come when it comes; all hope is lost
> Of my reception into grace; what worse?
> For where no hope is left, is left no fear;
> If there be worse, the expectation more
> Of worse torments me then the feeling can.
> I would be at the worst; worst is my Port,
> My harbour and my ultimate repose,
> The end I would attain, my final good.
> My error was my error, and my crime
> My crime; whatever for it self condemn'd,
> And will alike be punish'd; whether thou
> Raign or raign not; though to that gentle brow
> Willingly I could flye, and hope thy raign,
> From that placid aspect and meek regard,
> Rather then aggravate my evil state,
> Would stand between me and thy Fathers ire,
> (Whose ire I dread more then the fire of Hell)
> A shelter and a kind of shading cool
> Interposition, as a summers cloud.
> If I then to the worst that can be hast,
> Why move thy feet so slow to what is best? . . .

I agree with Cleanth Brooks that "a real weariness breathes through the speech" and that Satan is "in deadly earnest" about attaining the end.[2] The language and rhythm are those of immediate complete feeling: which is not to say that the imaginative identification of poet and antagonist is more nearly complete than heretofore, but that the identification of the antagonist and his very self closes, or almost closes. We have heard the impressive human voice of evil before, the accents of personal emphasis, but always with subtle exaggerations, the overtones of the dramatic self. Now for an extraordinary moment the dramatic self sounds lost in, identified with, the real self, and even stripped of a dimension of self-consciousness we have been led to believe was not only in the role but in the self acting that role. We are startled by the "new" Satan who suddenly appears, and by the unexpected turn in a drama, all the lines of which have seemed firmly laid down and following out their appointed course. For a moment we feel we have misunderstood the old drama, or that it is turning into a new one for which we have no bearings at all and so may be lost by the very next move. It is a moment of extreme pressure on the audience. It is the kind of high dramatic tension we experience, I submit, only in great dramatic art.

But the big initial surprise, when we have looked at the speech more closely, also has a harvest of smaller surprises. The weariness at the beginning of the speech is a *reckless* weariness, in language, rhythm, and idea. Notice, for instance, how Satan clings to the theoretical, and verbal, formula: since he has lost hope he must have lost fear. He is like Macbeth at the end of the play, clinging hopelessly to his hope in the verbal charms, with something of the same recklessness, and with the verbal ruins of his moral conscious- ness marking the ruins of what was real and so still in existence and piping the tune he dances to. And for the fear verbally dis- missed there is the torture of expectation, an imaginative hell for the mind cut off from the truth of the imagination and forced, as Satan is, to experiment with inadequate translations of divine metaphor into the humanly literal. Besides, as the rhythm opens up from its tension of the anguished staccato and points toward a resolution in hope (and what would be for the drama a further tension, a recklessness beyond this recklessness), two further fears creep into expression: the fear of hell and the greater fear of God's wrath.

There is also a small, special harvest of ironies which have sud- denly come ripe. The two counter-rhythms of return briefly cross here. For the protagonist it is a return to the source of being, but by a way not yet clear to him, a way that he must discover and follow but wait for; and he must wait patiently and prepared, while preparing himself; and wait in expectation without torment, though he knows the path lies "Through many a hard assay even to the death." For the antagonist it is an impatient, willed return to the source of being he chose and ignorantly willed: the evil which is his good, the independent self cut off from true being, the hope of despair, the end which is not a new beginning but the end of choosing, willing, expecting, the hoped-for end of self, the port of worst. The protagonist waits, in perfect resignation to time and God's will, for the worst-best. The antagonist hurries, forcing his

resignation to time and God's will, for the best-worst. And yet
Satan's weariness, like the Satanic sincerity of self which rings
through the passage, is ready to turn weakness into strength, despair into hope; is ready, even, with incredible boldness, to force
time so radically that the "new" antagonist threatens to create the
new drama and the new protagonist who will be Saviour to Satan!

This is the biggest surprise; it is an excess that surpasses irony.
If Satan is willing to use his sincerity, as any other resource he
possesses, in the service of his will, though in order to will the end
of his will, nevertheless, we are dramatically convinced that he is
tempting himself as sincerely as he can. Were this not Satan, we
should have even less reservation. It is difficult to resist his rhythm
as he entertains the possibility, and the image bursts on us with an
utterly surprising opened horizon of drama. It may be an illusion
in the desert, like the pleasant valley in which Satan's banquet was
prepared, but the illusion invites Satan's mind, and even expresses
part of that mind — the hot desire for the respite of coolness, the
shade, though *transitory*, of a summer's cloud.

For a moment, too, they are brothers again,[3] or still; for relation
holds, and they are both sons of God. I feel this as myth though I do
not quite understand it. I think of biblical rivalries for the divine or
patriarchal blessing: Cain and Abel, Isaac and Ishmael, Jacob and
Esau, Joseph and his brothers. In Christ's original elevation as
favorite son, Satan fell. And now he knows he is doomed to fall
again at the next elevation. Lucifer is the "Autumnal Star" who
shall fall down, and Christ is "Our Morning Star then in his rise."
They are joined together in time, in destiny, not as enemies who
are strangers but as enemies who are brothers, one the beloved
champion of the Father, one disinherited and cursed. But they are
joined indissolubly together until the end of time, each to play out
his role in relation to the other. I think, without understanding
their myths, of other divine brothers or twins: the Dioscuri, the
Cabiri, the Açvins. I think of the long, inexhaustible tradition of
the psychomachia. For a moment one brother seems to be appealing to another, and we skirt close to a whole new imaginative range
of drama, into which floods, for a breathless moment, not only the

destined role of the Saviour, but thoughts of the prodigal son and the rejoicing in heaven over a sinner saved, and thoughts of the boldest of all solutions, that of the problem of evil. It is a bold moment, after which the two brothers resume their classic pose of opposition and the drama proceeds according to plan.

The spell is broken and the tempter goes back to his job. There is no offer made and no pause to permit a counter-offer. The temptation is produced by Satan for himself. But it is not quite acknowledged, and so not quite offered or rejected. The performance, as far as we can see, has been gratuitous, and this time less a brilliant display of footwork than a kind of compulsive dance.

One thing further needs noting, and it is easier to see this after we have got out of the dramatic dazzle of the moment. Satan has not yet understood the hero's course of action. Nor for that matter has the hero. Both know the available evidence, and they know that the arena is the world, the kingdom of men; both are agreed that personal endeavor and means will be required. But their understanding is different, as their approach to prophetic metaphor is different. Satan's mind has revealed itself as constricted, the complete and worldly master of the material concerns of mind, but imprisoned in that mastery, and unable to understand anything beyond this fixed range. The torment of expectation is not only the torment of his guilt and of his eternal restlessness; it is the torment of *not knowing*, of feeling himself incapable of knowing, of experiencing the failure of his literal mind to understand the baffling metaphors in their own terms or to translate them successfully into his terms. Satan has fixed on one of Christ's three functions, his role as king. But the metaphor has not been understood, or translated. And while he is fixed on this role he is really exercising and developing Christ's role as prophet, which is to provide illumination for the understanding of man. The point I have been heading toward is this: in the genuine agony of the moment Satan's imagination bursts through the apparently fixed limits of his mind. He drops his "rational" obsession over the problem of Christ's kingdom, and imagines, or intuits, that third function of the Messiah, so far unimagined and about to disappear again from the scene of consciousness — the sacrificial role of priest. So if the sincerity is not perfect, the agony at any rate is real. And this *is* for the moment a new Satan, one whose mind can in a burst of free anguish rise to the imaginative truth beyond the immediate appearances that blind him.

Satan returns to his own mind and his rational experiments at understanding. He begins, remarkably, in a way that demonstrates how much he knows, how nearly right he is, and therefore how essential is what he does not, cannot know. Brilliance of mind he has. But something is always fatally missing, some faculty of "life" which has died in the understanding; and though the loss may be *felt*, it cannot be *known*, and could be known only through the faculty itself. Perhaps Christ is lingering, he suggests, detained "in deep thoughts" "Of the enterprize so hazardous and high." And so he perceives that valid relationship between the depth of descent into the self and the height of transcendence. But his experimental solution is in terms of his shrewd knowledge of human experience, and his own intimate experience — in terms of fear, now the timidity of inexperience. He speaks from superior knowledge, he thinks, like an *alazon* in a Socratic dialogue; he is the man of the world and cities patronizing the country boy who has only thought about these things (perhaps read). Still, Satan does recognize — it is part of his perplexity — the evidences of human perfection; but the idea of perfection without experience is a problem too baffling for Satan to stay with. He tries to limit the problem to the one aspect of timidity, and in doing so he will receive, though indirectly, a full answer concerning Christ's experience. (Finally, Satan will receive the direct answer on fear.)

The vision of Parthian might follows, a brilliant description for a poet who has disclaimed competence at that kind of heroic writing. With his familiar mastery of the small denominations of time, Satan sets the scene: "And just in time thou com'st to have a view . . . for now. . . ." Then, opportunely, the vision acts itself out for the beholder's eyes. Or almost does; for some details are imaginatively expanded beyond the physical possibility of the moment, and a great historical excursion into the rich romance of battle occurs under the mere sanction of a poetic negative. Milton has tampered with the perspective here, I think, in a way that calls attention to itself. A narrative voice seems to have intruded without warrant into a spectacle set up by Satan and then viewed directly by Christ. Milton very much wants that addition of romantic chivalry, to adorn the plain beauty of this naked military power and lend it a kind of cosmetic charm cunningly, but visibly, superimposed.[4] Satan, too, wants that addition, and since he swells with pleasure and confidence, I suppose he must take responsibility for the false effect. The hocus-pocus, like the whole show, is part of the extravagance of trying to make attractive for this second Adam a rather plain second Eve.

Satan's argument begins in terms of fear. The Parthian might, so impressively displayed, will provide security for the hero. Then Satan touches on the need for personal endeavor, and continues to the main argument, the practical necessity of human means even in the fulfilling of divine prediction. According to the facts of human politics, the throne of Israel cannot be secure between two powerful and contending states unless allied with one of them. Finally, he sweetens the appeal to reasonable fear with the bait of political and religious charity, the hope of freeing the ten lost tribes.

It is toward this last that the bulk, though the less immediately relevant part, of Christ's answer is directed. His denial of obligation to the lost children of Israel must be seen as more than a local discrimination. The point will soon be made more strongly, perhaps with a developed personal clarity, in reference to the politically lost Romans. (We may remember Milton's warning to Englishmen, that if through their own self-corruption they lost the chance for liberty which they had earned, they could not then be freed by the external agency of any leader.) We know the grounds for the denial of responsibility — that true liberty is internal, not external, and that only a regenerating call from God could renew the moral basis for liberty. But the point, surely, is more than general, as it is more than local. The process of self-definition has been going on. The youthful aspiration for heroic acts is now being further refined toward the real program of salvation, and it would seem that the youthful concept of "persuasion" has also been clarifying itself. I suggest that the articulated acceptance of the need for personal endeavor, turned back to Satan as a taunt, is relevant to the condition of the lost brethren. Being lost, they are incapable of endeavoring unless they are inspired by some wondrous call from God which will persuade them to repentance and the endeavor for sincerity. And I suggest that persuasion is being understood by Christ, or is beginning to be understood, as the endeavor of being ready for inspiration: to speak the wondrous word of God.[5]

The first part of Christ's answer is brief but more immediately relevant. It cuts through the "wisdom" of human politics and experience to moral principle: the luggage of war and the politic maxims are an argument of human weakness rather than of strength. It is a moral insight that reflects devastatingly on all the appeals of false transcendence; they are all distorted and distorting answers to the fact of human limitations and dependence; all are self-deceiving evasions that unrealistically turn weakness into frightened strength; but the way to true strength is another way, and that is what Christ is teaching by example.

The vision of Rome is then prepared, without verbal transition by Satan but with some prefatory images of compulsiveness which speak for him. Most notable is that of the swarm of flies in vintage time, "About the wine-press where sweet moust is powr'd" — a striking anticipatory symbol of the sacerdotal role not yet entered in, though the flies are there already. This vision, more concentrated and intricate than the one of Parthia, Satan takes full creative responsibility for; and how he contrives it "were curious to enquire." (It is no doubt an ironic version of the archetypal vision of the heavenly city, a new Jerusalem prepared as a bride adorned for her husband.) As rhetorical description of place it is designed to lure the eye; the interpretation that then follows makes its appeal to the mind. This kingdom — and not Israel, which does not really interest Satan, for it is small and both politically and strategically unimportant — comes closest to the kingdom of the mind represented by Athens. Rome is the height of worldly power, but that power is not the primitive nakedness of the Parthians. Rome expresses the material grandeur which represents the transcendence of the political mind. The representation is not only that of wealth, "wide domain," and "long Renown," but it is also that of culture: "Civility of Manners, Arts, and Arms."

The bait of charity is again drawn across the path, now as pure political charity. (To look back briefly: the stones turned to bread would provide food for self and the "wretched"; the acceptance of the banquet would relieve nature and her "gentle Ministers" of their troubled shame over the hunger of the lord of nature; the affectation of "private life" was depriving "All Earth her wonder at thy acts"; the acceptance of zeal and duty would free "Thy Country from her Heathen servitude"; the acceptance of Parthia would deliver the ten tribes, as their fathers were delivered from the land of Egypt.) These last two advance the political under the lure of the religious. But now we have the purely political, the suggestion that Christ enter his role of redeemer-king by saving political sinners, "A victor people free from servile yoke." The suggestion is linked with the moral and political horror of Tiberius' person and rule, and with the ever-present, reassuring argument of the ease with which Christ may accomplish this end, the ease being a natural product of the corrupt situation and the noble endowments of the hero. Finally, the argument returns to its basis in *Realpolitik*:

> Aim therefore at no less then all the world,
> Aim at the highest, without the highest attain'd
> Will be for thee no sitting, or not long
> On *David's* Throne, be propheci'd what will.

That Satan's reasoning is "plausible" to the world, Everyman had better admit, and draw his inference. For this display of the endeavoring wisdom of strength also defines an innate weakness — the dynamic nature of power which is founded, not on consent, nor even on an equilibrium of power, but on the stability of a peak that will not stay still, "the highest," "all the world."

The answer is a complete translation of the political terms into

moral terms, this time with no peremptory cutting through to principle. Christ begins wittily by filling out the picture of luxury-mag-
nificence with details which Satan might have produced as for
another banquet: "(For I have also heard, perhaps have read)."
This provocative parenthesis, which anticipates the beginning of
Christ's answer to the temptation of Athens, answers indirectly
what has not been answered until now, Satan's patronizing concern for the timid inexperience of a rustic hero. The knowledge is
there and comprehends experience. Satan's empire of petty time
is invaded by the mocking account of what goes on in embassies —
the "tedious wast of time" hearing the honor of lies and "outlandish
flatteries"! Then Christ replies directly to the political temptation.
He has not been sent for Tiberius, "nor yet to free" the once virtuous Romans, on whom he passes judgment fully and clearly. Since
it is a moral judgment it has the sharpness and finality which we,
as readers, recognize as a true voice of history. And then Christ
presents his own version of how he will come into his kingdom. He
borrows two prophetic symbols from the Book of Daniel, the over-
shadowing tree and the great, smashing stone. They are symbols
of power not humanly predictable, and beyond Satan's rational or
imaginative range. They refer again to God's time, and bafflingly
unite the promise of endeavoring with the promise of means:

> Means there shall be to this, but what the means,
> Is not for thee to know, nor me to tell.

Finally, as the last episode in the temptation of the kingdoms,
Satan announces the price. These valuable gifts have not been free
but require the famous gesture of worship. If we have been following the poem correctly, this can mean only one thing. It is a temptation, of course, but hardly a temptation to accept the price. A
bargainer like Satan does not expect a customer uninterested in the
merchandise to become interested upon hearing the full price, or
the details of financing. Besides, in this kind of bargaining the
price is not likely to be unknown, though unmentioned. Satan's
breach of the code for the proper conduct of the craft of tempting
has been to dare "to utter" the impious price. Plainly what Satan
is playing for is his opponent's response. The old technique of

beginning a temptation out of order by the classic scale, and higher, is now being reversed by a surprising jump downward and backward, as if this phase were just beginning instead of ending. What can Satan expect but the satisfaction of his limited tactical objective? If this *is* the Son of God, and is successfully provoked, then Satan may learn, however sadly, the fact. The protagonist has been conducting himself as a man, though perfect, and has shown himself capable of feeling, most notably in the defense of God's glory. If he is provoked to anger he may act, and so reveal what Satan wants to know. Any action at all would be a relief to the baffled Satan. One does not know how far Satan's knowledge of the issue goes, but if it goes far enough he may realize that, if the hero can be got to act anything on his own, Satan will have won.

THE KINGDOM
OF THE MIND

SATAN is "with fear abasht," but not too abashed, at the failure of his overt impiousness. He has merely been practicing the business of personal justice, and concerning himself with his most proper concern: which has been to test by rational experiment, to try to understand, and finally to challenge that symbolic "title" Son of God. He is almost graceful, and he is impressively patient in his admissions of defeated concern, and in the nonchalant way he drops the ruined subject:

> Therefore let pass, as they are transitory,
> The Kingdoms of this world; I shall no more
> Advise thee, gain them as thou canst, or not.

But he simply turns with no serious effort to conceal what he is doing, to another trial in terms of his lordship over the world. True, he makes a kind of imaginative attempt to identify himself with the hero. The tone is a strange depature for Satan, not ironic but perhaps patronizing in the strain of imaginative effort: "the childhood shews the man / As morning shews the day." And Satan applies his trained way of thinking to the problems facing a hero whose kingdom, by process of elimination, must be a kingdom of the mind to be gained by persuasion and for the governing of the inner man. The tone is quiet and reasonable.

> All knowledge is not couch't in *Moses* Law,
> The Pentateuch or what the Prophets wrote,

94

> The Gentiles also know, and write, and teach
> To admiration, led by Natures light;
> And with the Gentiles much thou must converse,
> Ruling them by perswasion as thou mean'st,
> Without thir learning how wilt thou with them,
> Or they with thee hold conversation meet?
> How wilt thou reason with them, how refute
> Thir Idolisms, Traditions, Paradoxes?
> Error by his own arms is best evinc't.

But still the basis remains unchanged, and Satan makes no effort, perhaps he cannot, to conceal his concept of mind as power. He does not hesitate to attribute spatial existence to the mind, and activity like the activity of one kind of matter dominating another:

> Be famous then
> By wisdom; as thy Empire must extend,
> So let extend thy mind o're all the world,
> In knowledge, all things in it comprehend.

The vision of Athens is first presented as pure description, the beautiful object not speaking for itself to the beholder's eyes, but fully interpreted by the guide to the vision — with some details added which are beyond the scope of sight:

> Look once more e're we leave this specular Mount
> Westward, much nearer by Southwest, behold
> Where on the *Aegean* shore a City stands
> Built nobly, pure the air, and light the soil,
> *Athens* the eye of *Greece*, Mother of Arts
> And Eloquence, native to famous wits
> Or hospitable, in her sweet recess,
> City or Suburban, studious walks and shades;
> See there the Olive Grove of *Academe*,
> *Plato*'s retirement, where the *Attic* Bird
> Trills her thick-warbl'd notes the summer long,
> There flowrie hill *Hymettus* with the sound
> Of Bees industrious murmur oft invites
> To studious musing; there *Ilissus* rouls
> His whispering stream.

This holds an imaginative surprise for us, because it is a vision of pure beauty. Satan, the despiser of beauty — which stands "In the admiration only of weak minds / Led captive" — is here making his bow, though brief, to an incomprehensible weakness.[1]

But the purity of the beauty does not last long, for it is digni-fied with an access of power:

> within the walls then view
> The schools of antient Sages; his who bred
> Great *Alexander* to subdue the world,
> *Lyceum* there, and painted *Stoa* next:
> There thou shalt hear and learn the secret power
> Of harmony in tones and numbers hit
> By voice or hand, and various measur'd verse.

Even when the concept of mind as power goes unexpressed, it is never far below the surface of Satan's argument. The most success-ful concealment is in the praise of Socrates, from whose "low-rooft house" empire seems impossibly remote. But Socrates "water'd all the schools" of philosophy, and what do the schools offer?

> These here revolve, or, as thou lik'st, at home,
> Till time mature thee to a Kingdom's waight;
> These rules will render thee a King compleat
> Within thy self, much more with Empire joyn'd.

Christ's reply is exceeded in length only by his autobiographical soliloquy. The famous "rejection" of Athens has been much com-mented on, and I want to add my interpretation to the many on record. It is a crux of the poem, Satan's chief temptation and Christ's chief answer. I shall continue as much as possible on lines I have been following — but with one important difference. Satan's motivations, the drama of his mind, will no longer provide us with significant cues to the action. But this, though I have not pointed it out as such to the reader, has been a changing shift in balance for some time. Christ's mind completely dominates the action now, while Satan must maneuver within the diminished range of unat-tempted possibilities.

Since a great deal is at stake here, it may be best to begin by con-sidering the speech against some of the background of conven-tional expectation, and out of dramatic context. Whatever we observe this way cannot be final, as the obvious wrongness of mind-as-power cannot answer all the dramatic questions; but we ought not omit anything useful to explain a speech that has troubled so many readers.

That the main lines of the speech do not contradict the long record of Milton's thinking on the subject of wisdom has been soundly and perceptively demonstrated by Irene Samuel.[2] I find my reading of the record in substantial agreement with hers. Learning has no independent value by itself, but like other valuable human things must be brought into the order of a higher harmony if it is to be wisdom. Wisdom in the individual is achieved by the proper order of learning and by its organic absorption into the unity of the good life. Temperance in learning is like the temperance we have studied elsewhere, not mere abstention, but the strenuous discipline of subordination and superordination uniting in the individual the faculties and virtues under reason; but reason in the individual is not a self-contained end to itself: it points to action in the world, the duty toward neighbors, and it fulfills the larger harmony by pointing toward the source of reason in God.

Let us look at this from another nondramatic point of view. The basic text for the rejection of Greek philosophy is the second chapter of the Epistle to the Colossians. In Christ "are hid all the treasures of wisdom and knowledge. And this I say, lest any man should beguile you with enticing words. . . . Beware lest any man spoil you through philosophy and vain deceit, after the tradition of men, after the rudiments of the world, and not after Christ." It is a text on which the primitive church can found its argument for the superiority of the single truth of Christianity to the multiple, competitive opinions of the philosophers. And, for quite different reasons, it is a text which underlies Montaigne's skeptical attack on reason, and underlies the less skeptical Bacon's ground-clearing concept of the Idols of the Theatre. Milton, no despiser of philosophy, though of the "cheats" of learning and "scholastical trash," never considered philosophy the high point of learning. God has "never sent us for ministers to the schools of philosophy, but rather bids us beware of such 'vain deceit.' "[3]

I want to mention one further piece of background, the conventional argument for the superiority of Scriptures as a literature of knowledge and power. Christ says many of the familiar, time-worn things in rebuking the high claims of Greek literature, and quite properly, since they are going to be said for centuries. (There are some small differences, however, which loom large in the context, as we shall notice presently.) Perhaps there is no one basic text to be cited, but this, from the Second Corinthians (4, 7) may serve as a relevant example: "But we have this treasure in earthen vessels, that the excellency of the power may be of God, and not of us." Origen, in commenting on this, makes the point that in the style of Scriptures no human eloquence is mingled with the truth of the doctrines, which are not dependent on the rhetorical arts of words or the human wisdom of philosophers, but on "the manifestation of the spirit and of power." The apostles converted hearers without the arts of Greek dialectics or rhetoric. "Had the doctrine and the preaching consisted in the persuasive utterance and arrangement of words, then faith also, like that of the philosophers of the world in their opinions, would have been through the wisdom of men and not through the power of God." The defense of the style is that it speaks the language of the heart, to which both unlearned and learned best respond, and that it speaks from inspiration. For even truth does not reach the heart unless God's power is granted to the speaker, so that "a grace appear upon his words." [4]

Now let us return to the passage and the dramatic context. Christ's answer opens with the gnomic taunt:

> Think not but that I know these things, or think
> I know them not; not therefore am I short
> Of knowing what I aught.

The answer is to be, among other things, an extraordinary demonstration of knowledge. But still, this ought to remind us, we are witnessing no philosophical debate with all the premises and definitions on the table. It is a contest with evil, for the highest stakes; and though the hero's mind is clear and definite, it is actively in motion, and not obliged to be straightforward or confidential with a cunning deceiver. Besides, though the moral center

of the stage is clear and illuminated, in the shadows, lending their
dim outlines to the drama, are the primitive and mythic predecessors of this contest, whispering the importance of the concealment
and discovery of identity.

The next statement is the famous declaration:

> he who receives
> Light from above, from the fountain of light,
> No other doctrine needs, though granted true.

The first impression of this, I think, is that a striking assertion has
been made, perhaps a claim for gnosis. The contrasting fact of the
demonstrated hungering to do God's will, until now heroically sustained, is the background against which this impression is made.
The emphasis may even seem, by contrast, to be fierce, a kind of
Dionysiac sprint in what has been an Apollonian marathon. Christ
has been so completely oriented toward the *other*, toward the
source in God; the patience of his un-knowing [5] has been so pious
and athletic, that the present declaration bursts on us with a shock,
and we take it to be an emphasis on self. The impression, it turns
out, is not quite accurate, but the imaginative surprise is right; and
something of this latter will continue, legitimately, through the
scene and on to the end of the poem. An important turn of the
drama is now occurring and we do well to be shocked into attention, for there are other surprises in store. At such moments the
mind may run well behind the feelings.

We could stop to look more closely at that light from above, but
we had better go on, for the speech is an evolving one that will
return to this declaration at a point where we can understand it
more fully. Christ continues with a review of the schools of philosophy. The doctrine of the schools is not true, but false, or little
better than dreams, conjectures, fancies, "built on nothing firm."
Socrates, "the first and wisest of them," professed to know only
that he knew nothing. (This is a quiet, and fundamental, correction
of Satan's version of the Socratic wisdom.) Then the various schools
are dismissed briefly, except for the Stoics, who receive the full
treatment due them as the type of "Philosophic pride." Some of the

concluding remarks make serious distinctions that are probably meant to apply to all the schools:

> Alas what can they teach, and not mislead;
> Ignorant of themselves, of God much more.

The specific bill of their ignorance includes these essential items: the creation and the fall. Without knowledge of these events, and what they mean for man, philosophy lacks a "firm" basis. The treatment is brief and states understood distinctions without argument. The ethical ignorance of self, we may assume, will be basic if the philosopher does not know that man was created by God in His image, and that man fell by a simple but comprehensive act, "Degraded by himself, on grace depending." The ignorant arrogation of glory to self is the result of not recognizing oneself as creature, not knowing about the first act of ingratitude. (Christ has already used that argument in defining glory.) Finally, there is the dangerously misleading concept of God "as one regardless quite / Of mortal things." Without the essential knowledge, writ large in Scriptures, of God's love for the world and man, there is no real basis (we may interpret) for Eros, no bridge between the human and the divine. Interpreting further, we may add that the great principle of persuasion, by which man rationally governs himself and society, will lack the voice of divine inspiration; man's heart will not be "seasoned" in advance to accept and love the good, persuaded by the knowledge that what is good is God's will expressed through His love. If these understood arguments are accepted (as we know they may be), then perhaps it was not too harsh to call philosophy dreams and conjectures. Besides, the real issue, as we return to it, is not learning but true wisdom:

> Who therefore seeks in these
> True wisdom, finds her not, or by delusion
> Far worse, her false resemblance only meets.

At this point the general claims of learning are associated with the claims of philosophy, and the further relevance of the light from above may be seen:

> However many books
> Wise men have said are wearisom; who reads

Incessantly, and to his reading brings not
A spirit and judgment equal or superior,
(And what he brings, what needs he elsewhere seek)
Uncertain and unsettl'd still remains,
Deep verst in books and shallow in himself,
Crude or intoxicate, collecting toys,
And trifles for choice matters, worth a spunge;
As Children gathering pibles on the shore.

The distinction between learning and wisdom is ancient and standard, though every age must make it for itself, and every individual
in that age must make it for himself. The distinction is prefatory,
whether articulated or not, to every new idea. It is now being
articulated because it has to be, because Christ is now not only
demonstrating wisdom, as he has been doing all along, but he is
declaring his own wisdom.

The architectonic knowledge of self and the "spirit and judgment equal or superior" I take to be expressions of the light from
above. Let us look more narrowly at what is involved. The reference to judgment is, I assume, a version of the Platonic theory of
knowledge, which considers the internal endowment of judgment
the basis of knowing, not the external information that comes in
through the senses. The concept may be aristocratic in practice,
for every man's judgment will not prove itself adequate to the
truth. But the point, and it is a real point here, is that the light
of truth is common to all and single, and available to the endowment of judgment. Even that apparently lofty parenthesis, "And
what he brings, what needs he elsewhere seek," is neither a flat
rejection of books, as it may seem, nor an exclusive, unique claim
to knowledge by the speaker for himself or for any man.

The speaker, we must not forget, is talking about wisdom and
not about learning. His point is, I think, practical and defensible:
that we do not learn wisdom from books unless we bring to the
books a judgment and spirit capable of receiving wisdom; and if
they are capable of receiving wisdom, then they already possess
within themselves the chief endowment for wisdom. And if wisdom
is common and available, then the inner potential may be realized
by other means: by study of the self, by inspiration; by study of

101

other books, especially the book of books, which speaks directly to the spirit and may make it equal. Christ is not proposing an educational program. Nor is he describing his own curriculum — this is a point I shall want to return to. He is defining wisdom and declaring his own.

Self-knowledge, in the familiar extensions of Platonism, was the recovery of being never absent, the knowledge of the logos in the soul, the light within received from the "fountain of light," and uniting the self deeply and truly understood with the source of self in the highest truth. And if truth is one and the same thing, then it must be available, theoretically at least, by the same means to every man.

At this point it is relevant to quote some of Milton's comments on the reading of Scriptures. In *Of Reformation* he defends the "easiness" of Scriptures against the "importunate clients of Antiquity." The difficult passage expounds itself so: it tells us "how little it imports our *saving knowledge*." For whatever "is most necessary to be known is most easy." It asperses the mercy, truth, and wisdom of God to say He requires obedience but makes the commands ambiguous and obscure; that is the devil's suggestion.

The very essence of Truth is plainness, and brightness; the darkness and crookedness is our own. The *wisdom* of *God* created *understanding*, fit and proportionable to Truth the object, and end of it, as the eye to the thing visible. If our *understanding* have a film of *ignorance* over it, or be blear with gazing on other false glisterings, what is that to Truth? If we will but purge with sovereign eyesalve that intellectual ray which God hath planted in us, then we would believe the Scriptures protesting their own plainness, and perspicuity, calling to them to be instructed, not only the *wise*, and *learned*, but the *simple*, the *poor*, the *babes*, foretelling an extraordinary effusion of *God's* spirit upon every age, and sex, attributing to all men, and requiring from them, the ability of searching, trying, examining, and by the Spirit discerning that which is good; and as the Scriptures themselves pronounce their own plainness, so do the Fathers testify of them. (III, 33.)

The simplicity of truth is here asserted, but we had better not overlook that Miltonic emphasis on the attributing to all men the ability of searching, etc., *and* the requiring of the same from them.

Milton, though an athlete at learning himself, does not, as moralist or as man, deny the claim of the simple good man to goodness. Such a man, like the Christ of the speech on wisdom, may without any particular learning not be short of knowing what he ought. Unlike the learned fool or the learned hypocrite, "a plain unlearned man that lives well by that light which he has, is better, and wiser, and edifies others more towards a godly and happy life." (III, 163.) We are glad to have Milton say and feel this, and not exempt the possibility from Christ's speech. We note with interest that Milton thought the early Fathers found the Bible easy, and were able to avoid sophisticated errors even though only "two or three" of them knew Hebrew and few knew Greek. But still we ought to recognize that the "plain unlearned man" is not the chief object of Miltonic instruction, or interest. He is not to be thought of as deprived of the truth of wisdom, and he may get it his own way. But there are other ways to the same truth; and since these more engage Milton's interest, and belief, we must no doubt think of them as better ways to the same end.

If the early Fathers, without the equipment of much learning, could find the Bible easy, and that with "scarce half the light that we enjoy . . . why should we doubt, that have all the helps of Learning and faithful industry that man in this life can look for, and the assistance of *God* as near now to us as ever?" (III, 33–34.) What God attributes He requires, and learning is a good if well directed. Nor is Milton's God uninterested in learning: He will not "suffer true learning to be wanting, where true grace, and our obedience to him abounds: for if he give us to know him aright, and to practice this our knowledge in right established discipline, how much more will he replenish us with all abilities in tongues and arts, that may conduce to his glory, and our good?" (III, 163–64.)

The pursuit of learning is a strenuous activity. Is wisdom easy? May we infer that the "plain unlearned man" lives well by naturally following the natural light he has? Hardly. (Though "but one thing is needful," for Milton it is not "implicit faith.") Men are never too busy or too humbly unlearned to study the Bible in their mother tongue, and to attain "full persuasion of heart" by their own individual effort. In explaining the composition of his own *Christian Doctrine* Milton wrote what we recognize to be central in his intellectual belief: "It was also evident to me that, in religion as in other things, the offers of God were all directed, not to an indolent credulity, but to constant diligence, and to an unwearied search after truth." [6] And wisdom, like knowledge, is a "burden," for God "requires the improvement" of entrusted gifts. The possessor must, as part of the burden of improvement, determine "how and in what manner he shall dispose and employ those sums of knowledge and illumination which God hath sent him into this world to trade with." [7]

Where does this long excursion bring us? I trust, back to the hero's own dramatic demonstration of the endeavoring after wisdom. Our early insight into Christ's intellectual endeavor is now being fully, and surprisingly, acted out. I had better begin by summarizing my analysis of the consciousness revealed in Christ's autobiographical soliloquy, the personal revelation that precedes the first encounter with Satan and serves as evolving commentary on all the temptations. The child's first response was intuitive, the desire to learn, know, and do. This, we may now say, was the first recognition of the light from above. That recognition was accompanied by the inseparable intuition that the light must be better understood, by endeavor, and that the understanding must express itself in action. (This last has been an issue all through the drama, and is not yet dramatically settled.) The second stage of consciousness evolved from the first; this we may describe as discursive and disciplined, the study of the law, in which the intuitive was verified and strengthened.

The third stage, the aspiration for heroic acts, I have described as a kind of human intuition, an earthly interpretation of the divinely inspired need of the understanding to express itself in action. The fundamental desire of knowing-doing sought specific ends based on a human, a social orientation, and requiring the completely human discipline of force. The child, though innocent of any evil in his heroic ideal, nevertheless recognized for himself the basic gap between the human and the divine represented by the use of force. (It has been Satan's task to make possible the full demonstration of how political power is attached to the human, and how the means become end.) The fourth stage redefined what might be public good in terms of knowledge. Persuasion was the key, the humanly-heavenly proper means which reasserted the right bridge between the intuitive and the discursive, between the truth of righteous things and real public good. Persuasion was the proper means for the understanding to express itself in action. The fourth stage, then, represents the return to original intuition, but with the support of a fuller human discipline of reason and intellectual experience, including the rejected course of action.[8]

This fourth stage has been continuing throughout the poem, with the hero improving his gifts, becoming what he is, and still wrestling with the problem of employing his "knowledge and illumination." Much of the development and definition of this fourth stage has been part of our dramatic experience. But not all of it. We saw that, after the mother's contribution of special knowledge, the son returned to his inspired study of the law and prophets, and from this study he drew some further inferences, though mounting to no higher stage of knowledge. We have been told that all his activity at home has been contemplative, and we have been witnessing in these dialogues that the judgment is equal or superior to the books studied; and, further, that this wisdom gained through study is capable of judging authoritatively whatever is presented before it, even when presented in cunning disguise. And most important of all for the present purposes, we were not told in the soliloquy, and Satan's intelligence did not get all the facts or else made some lazy assumptions — at any rate, both antagonist and audience share the dramatic surprise of learning only now the extent of the protagonist's reading and thinking in private.

Perhaps we ought not be so surprised, for we have seen in steady installments a remarkable command of whatever intellectual experience or knowledge was sufficient to the problem at hand. From this point of view, we are seeing no more than what is sufficient now, though fuller, and more detailed, and basic. But we are surprised, and with good reason. This is no mere "rejection" of Athens. Christ knows what the Greeks know, and besides he knows what they do not know. And the latter is more important. He has almost completely, by direct demonstration, undercut Satan's argument of persuading the heathen by means of their own knowledge. Christ has that knowledge and finds it inadequate for wisdom, as the concept of persuasion dependent on that knowledge is for him inadequate. Part of our surprise comes from learning the extent of the hero's preparation. What he said, casually, about expecting to endeavor and about there being means, now echoes in our consciousness with substantial force.

I said earlier that a striking assertion seems to be made in the claim of light from above, and that Christ is now declaring his own wisdom. Since then I have been at some pains to show that the claim is general, common to true wisdom and the way it must be acquired. The speech, I am now ready to say, is both general, relevant to Everyman, and particular, the dramatic acting out of illumination by the prophet whose role it is to provide illumination for the human understanding. He is not only saying it in speech, he is doing it in a drama of knowledge. The expression is action, it is happening now. Christ has needed these efforts and helps in order to know that he does not need them, and the rejecting of the kingdom of mind is only the dramatic occasion, though an important occasion, for what is really occurring. The image of God, which resides chiefly in the mind of man, and was inspired by as much of the divine breath as man could avail himself of to achieve by his own efforts the perfection of his image — that image is now in the act of emerging. And in the emergence the inessential is being stripped off.[9] By the next stage, after this drama, when Christ re-enters the world and history, he will have stripped off the "learning" now displayed; or, rather, that is what Milton's hero is doing now. The desert of the mind is littered, rather impressively by now, with what is no longer needed (though if we are to believe the fiction, it *was* needed) — and not only because this is an absolute moral drama, but because, as Milton says nicely in another connection, "No marble statue can be politely carved."[10] The kingdom of the mind really is Christ's, but on his terms, not Satan's. The kingdoms of the world really are Christ's, as he sternly reminded Satan, and rejected the offer of them. So is the kingdom of nature his, though the rule is not to be expressed by banquets. But the kingdoms are authoritatively rejected by their real possessor, though not for the sake of rejection, but for the purpose of defining the self and the terms of possession.

One thing more on this subject. I said that the declaration concerning the light from above seemed surprisingly to be an emphasis of self. It is not insofar as it is general. But still, something of the personal remains even beyond the dramatic definition of mind now occurring, something we may still feel as Dionysiac in an Apollonian drama. For the efficacy of the light from above depends on sameness, the similarity of the object of truth to the subject. This is rehearsal, or first inkling, of what is to happen on the tower.

If the reader is persuaded by the interpretation thus far, what follows will present little difficulty. The defense of Hebrew literature is based upon the same discriminations as the defense of true wisdom. That literature is a true reflection in words of the light from above. The inadequacies of Greek literature are ultimately the same as those of Greek philosophy: they are those of ignorance in basic matters, of false or diluted inspiration derived more from man than God.

Modern readers, more literary than religious, and used to respecting the idea of the classics, though perhaps not reading them, but used to feeling a degree of devout respect which Milton never quite achieved in a lifetime of devoted reading — such modern readers, and I am one of them, cannot avoid some sense of shock at the hard judgment now pronounced. Besides, the modern concept of poetry has not quite freed itself from the over-big defense of Matthew Arnold, that poetry was to take the place of religion; or from the over-little defense of I. A. Richards, that poetry was to promote equilibrium in our still-unpurified intellectual economy by the salubrious indulgence of pseudo-statements. Poetry as the modern handmaiden of psychology has perhaps regained some lost ground, as the handmaiden of economic theory perhaps lost some, of cultural history gained some. But the social status of a handmaiden, much in demand, and loved from time to time but amid much quarreling over the purpose of her charms, is likely to suffer from excessive attentions and insufficient respect. In Milton's time the function of poetry could be less talked about and more accepted. *Paradise Regained* is a poem.

The modern reader, as the historian can tell him, ought to be shocked, not at the judgment pronounced, but at the judge's moderation and learned competence, for he has plainly read and considered all the evidence in the case. The historian can cite hundreds, perhaps thousands, of similar judgments passed on the case by deputies of deputies of the present judge. As an amateur historian who knows only a few of the more celebrated cases, I am impressed by the moderation of this judgment. We had no right to expect it, given the tradition of passing and repassing this judgment, given the antagonist, given the protagonist and the special conditions created by the drama, conditions that the drama must remain true to, given our standard expectations of how any new idea will treat an established idea that stands in the way. Christ uses, as he must, the conventional arguments that his deputies will use in history, yet with some small (necessarily small) and significant differences. The priority in time of Hebrew poetry, that overworked point, is mentioned only in passing; the chief superiority is that of art inspired by truth.

What is most important is that Christ does not absolutely dismiss Greek poetry. For poetry was not presented as having absolute claim to true wisdom, but as having claim to the "secret power" of harmony, as being able to claim the sponsorship of Apollo, as claiming best to describe important human conditions, as claiming to teach "moral prudence" best and most delightfully. Poetry, as music, is for Christ a "solace" with which he may, if he wishes, "delight my private hours." Solace in the human affairs of even a perfect man is, we may assume, necessary, dignified, and valuable. It does not pretend to true wisdom in any direct or absolute way, but neither can it be cut off from wisdom and still be valuable. At its best it may even come very close, though without making any high claims. But all human claims to wisdom, as we have been required to notice, are fraught with dangerous disabilities.[11] (Poetry, which "nothing affirms" and nothing claims, may have some extraordinary advantages; but I add this, as a modern reader, to modern readers.)

We may remember that Christ was content to deny the direct human claims to glory, but he did not stop there, as he might have done. He went on to re-establish the proper possibility for human glory; and if there was anything to share, pagan heroes would share it too. Greek poetry is not so liberally admired as pagan heroism. For that matter, the Socrates who suffered death for truth seems more admired than the philosopher who sought truth in life. (This is not quite fair perhaps, for different kinds of judgment, on different grounds, are evoked, and in different contexts.) But the province of Greek poetry is less roughly handled than the military and political kingdoms of the world. And poetry, as we have noted, does not have to be denied philosophy's claim to wisdom. There is harshness, no doubt, in Christ's reference to the cosmetic epithets, but one could hardly expect him to take a liberal view of Greek mythology. What is left, after the epithets have been removed, is inferior to the songs of Zion, and "Thin sown with aught of profit or delight"; but still "thin sown," which would surprise many Christians to hear. And an important second thought makes the thin somewhat less thin:

> Unless where moral vertue is express't
> By light of Nature not in all quite lost.

The claim of the orators, being more limited, is still less challenged. They are allowed something, but less than the prophets.

The defense of Hebrew poetry and prophecy is the defense of inspiration, defense of the verbal record in art and instruction of light from above, defense of the identity of beauty and truth. In the poetry "God is prais'd aright, and Godlike men." And this is "from God inspir'd." The prophets teach "As men divinely taught," and they teach the real rules that govern the happiness or fate of kingdoms. Measured by the wisdom or art expressed by inspiration from the fountain of light, works that are inspired by man, or love of country, or the light of nature, are found inferior. They are not rejected. They are not needed by any man desiring wisdom, and for solace and instruction he can do better elsewhere. They are certainly not needed by Christ, and never less needed than now. But still, the light of Greek culture, though thin and diluted, is not like the false glitter of Satan's "radiant" courts.

If we regard this as an autobiographical poem (which would be a serious charge) then we must be disturbed by the emphasis and by the peremptory treatment of things Greek. But we may be comforted by the thought that Milton is writing a poem, and though it may be a poem truly inspired, still it is a poem and not a retraction. It may be more truly inspired than Greek poetry, but it hardly claims the authority attributed to Hebrew poetry. It has particular dramatic commitments to fulfill and must be true to them. As a dramatic speech, taken in its context, what Christ says ought not disturb us — at least not if we like poetry well and intelligently enough to want to defend the Greeks. Nor ought we expect that the context must translate perfectly and without loss or change to other contexts. Truth may do that, but not dramatic or poetic truth. As drama the scene speaks for itself, and magnificently. It is a big scene for the drama of knowledge. Nothing remains except the proof that wisdom believes itself.

Let us conclude by stepping back from the scene again, to look at it from two further, and different, perspectives. We knew to begin with that the offer of mind-as-power was morally wrong, but that perspective was not a very useful guide to the dramatic meaning of the scene. Now that we have examined the scene we may consider, as a kind of postscript-footnote, a similiar perspective. The vision of Athens is the only vision not strictly contemporaneous. Why? May we say that there is not much to offer that is strictly contemporaneous? It is a kingdom of the mind historically played out in the time-present of the drama. Having shown itself incapable of mastering time, it is hardly to be offered a second chance by a hero with another vision destined to sweep the world. Even within the strict limitations of power Satan's offer is a little peculiar — one hesitates to say soft. (This is postscript and perhaps all wrong.) It is as if — to illustrate only the point of timing and power — Lenin, riding in his sealed train back to Russia and revolution, could have been tempted by the offer of a perfect old utopia, or of the command of Stoic kingliness, or of complete Christian humility.

And one final point. I want to raise this question: How much of Christ's speech could have been said by Christ, or Christianity, or a seventeenth-century Christian poet; how much could have been known, or known, could have been said in words and images without the aid of the classics and classical philosophy? This is relevant to us as human beings, as inheritors and transmitters of culture; it was certainly relevant to Milton as man and poet. But it is not in the same way relevant to us as readers of the poem — any more, say, than Christ's talking English, and blank verse, both of which are the long results of cooperative development and tradition, now being individually used in a unique way. It is all absurd, if we carry on a running debate with the imaginative details. But the essential argument is not absurd, and we have to accept the imaginative conditions of artistic expression, here as anywhere.

THE WAY OF DEATH

THE exploratory argument of my concluding essay on *Paradise Regained* is this: Milton revives the old ascetic notion of dying to the world, and transforms it to express his concept of Christ's drama by going back of the ascetic idea (as a good Renaissance humanist, as a seventeenth-century Protestant, as John Milton), and back to the sources in the philosophical, the religious, the mythic "way of death"; and revives and transforms the oldest version of this cathartic human wisdom into a path of action leading, not to the denial or rejection of the world, but to the acknowledgment of the world as the proper theater of man's endeavor, though that acknowledgment is governed by the terms of a purifying definition. Perhaps I now had better add this: the definition is not a philosophical or political one laying out a complete course of action to be proved true or false empirically; it is a poetic definition, and so must gain its assent by the agreement of heart and mind, not oblivious of the claims of stomach, back, hearth, bed, bourse, throne, or heart or mind separated from each other, but not required to satisfy those claims in their terms; the poetic definition is required only in its own terms to wring assent, however secret or silent, from these claimants, and this is assured if heart and mind are in agreement.

Let us begin by looking, though not very methodically, at some aspects of the religious, the mythic, the philosophical "way of death." I want to make a few useful points and distinctions before turning back to the end of the poem and then finally turning to some concluding remarks.

Perhaps the best religious text is I John, 2, 15–16: "Love not the world, neither the things that are in the world. If any man love the world, the love of the Father is not in him. For all that is in the world, the lust of the flesh, and the lust of the eyes, and the pride of life, is not of the Father, but is of the world." The versions, the variations of this are innumerable, and the *contemptus mundi* is only one popular form. Milton's Christ must not, perforce, "love" the world that Satan offers him. So the debate, the whole pattern of rebuttals, may seem to be leading to the inevitable end of dying to the world. But before we leap to the conclusion that the poem is a *contemptus mundi* of unparalleled endurance, we had better note some remarkable absences. Chiefly, we ought to wonder why the great theme of death, loved but not exhausted by the poets, should be so patently ignored. If Christ is dying to the world he is doing so without the benefit of the slow, rich brooding over death which might have been expected if the author had been Shakespeare, or Drummond, or Browne, or Taylor; nor is the theme evoked with any of the peremptory imaginative splendor of a Shakespeare, a Donne, a Raleigh. If the theme is there it is there as cold idea and not as warm fact.

We are all acquainted with the familiar uses for moral lessons of the Idea of Death, and how inspiringly it may lend itself even to usually undistinguished eloquence. But Milton's use is not the familiar one of tempering lust or pride or desire for the mortal by vividly producing the common, reluctant end, and applying to it the alternating ardor of rhetorical amplification and the chill of rhetorical reduction. Milton's Idea of Death is in the mind, not the body; the end is a purified beginning, a dying to the false as an achieved or re-achieved basis for true living, a return to Paradise not through innocence but through experience, not in dream but awake and with the eyes fully opened. All the emphasis of the moral lesson is on living well.

Let us next turn briefly to the mythic "way of death." I shall lean on a single quotation from Mircea Eliade's *The Myth of the Eternal Return*, where I find the issue admirably stated:

Can we see, in this tendency toward purification, a nostalgia for the lost paradise of animality? [This is a reference to Hegel's remark that only the animal is truly innocent.] Or, in the primitive's desire to have no "memory," not to record time, and to content himself with tolerating it simply as a dimension of his existence, but without "interiorizing" it, without transforming it into consciousness, should we rather see his thirst for the "ontic," his will to be, to *be* after the fashion of the archetypal beings whose gestures he constantly repeats? . . . it is more probable that the desire felt by the man of traditional societies to refuse history, and to confine himself to an indefinite repetition of archetypes, testifies to his thirst for the real and his terror of "losing" himself by letting himself be overwhelmed by the meaninglessness of profane existence. . . . It is the profound meaning of primitive behavior that is revelatory; this behavior is governed by belief in an absolute reality opposed to the profane world of "unrealities"; in the last analysis, the latter does not constitute a "world," properly speaking; it is the "unreal" *par excellence*, the uncreated, the nonexistent: the void.[1]

There are other ways of looking at mythic experience, of course; and I plainly do not mean to suggest, by quoting this impressive interpretation, that Milton's poem is "primitive" all the way and represents the profane world as unreal and uncreated. Milton will not yield up the world to the devil, or even the things created in the world, like arts and sciences and government, though there was plenty of precedent for the opinion attributing these to the devil. What Satan has got control of he has got by usurpation, and that puts an entirely different light on the matter. Milton holds to his belief in an undamaged correspondence available between this world and reality. But the ancient gestures of the soul retain their cathartic wisdom for the poet, a wisdom he wishes to save and direct. As poet Milton is also modern and sophisticated; the "dying" of his poem does not correspond exactly to the mythic way, any more than to the ascetic religious way. All I wish to do now is point out the available analogues in psychic experience, for they are analogues which serve the experience created by this poem.

Even when they are modified and redirected into the new myth, they carry with them, below the level of thought, the old feelings of rightness in the familiar gestures, in the rhythm of the path now being followed, in the remembered footing of the well-worn places. I shall return to this difficult subject in interpreting the last temptation, though I shall not promise to make the presence of mythic gestures clear and convincing.

The third "way of death" I wish to introduce for its probable relevance is the philosophical. These categories, it should be understood, are more convenient than absolute. I accept what seems to be the plausible modern opinion, that the ancient philosophers did some basic borrowing or inheriting from ancient religion: which opinion, if it does not prove that the truth is therefore the truth, may only push some basic problems further back into the dark. But to the point. The philosopher's life as a rehearsal for death may be considered as a ritualistic purification. By the ritual of reason the soul may ascend in concentrated thought to gain knowledge from the other world of gods and spirits. Or true virtue may be considered, as in the *Phaedo* (37–38), an initiatory purification, after which the soul that departs this life perfectly pure, the soul that is a true lover of wisdom, will dwell among the gods. Plato, having accepted the Heraclitean "intuition that nothing in the sensible world is exempt from change, but every form of matter is perpetually dying and being reborn in a different form, could only declare that the permanent reality was immaterial and accessible only to pure thought." [2] The "way of death" then is founded on the belief that the world of reality is elsewhere. Plato tries to bridge the unbridgeable Parmenidean gulf in many ways: through anamnesis, inspiration, love, the vision of the Good, dialectical knowledge of pure forms. And in the philosopher-king he tries to make reality work in this world, and in the concept of imitation, the best possible world of the Demiurge. But the doctrine, as history shows, remains a doctrine that encourages the desire for pure withdrawal, for complete rejection of the world. And the doctrine carries its chill message even in the flush of practical experience and total immersion in the activities of the world, whenever we are forced to recognize (like Shakespeare's Brutus or Cordelia) how the idea is modified by action. (Plotinus ascribes to magic that seductive misdirection of thought: "Magic exercises its influence on every action, and on every active life." IV, iv, 43.) And yet, there is no reason for acceding passively to the historical demonstration. The philosophical "way of death" did not absolutely need to follow through the logic of withdrawal. Plato must have been of more than one mind on the subject, and the Pythagoreans, who formulated the doctrine, were apparently important in fifth-century politics .

Let these remarks, then, serve as introduction to our major concern, that of interpreting the end of the poem. Christ's "way of death" will be seen as related to the background just sketched, but still distinctive. From our final vantage point we should be able to look back at the interpretive path we have inched along, and see at least some of the pattern and some of the implications all at once.

When the kingdom of the mind is refused and transcended by the definition-declaration of wisdom, Satan is left "Quite at a loss." All of his ammunition is gone, we are told; and when he returns after the night of terrors, it is "with no new device." The terrors and the test on the tower, then, are not new temptations, and certainly not the high points in the drama of temptation. The ascent has already been won, the high point crossed, and we are moving on the summit, about to enter on the downward slope, or already upon it, we cannot be sure. Milton is making extraordinary dramatic use of the summit (as he will in *Samson Agonistes*), for the summit is that long moment in dramatic time when the tide has inexorably changed, but not all at once, not clearly and with mechanical neatness, not canceling out all the signs of the old rhythm with silent indifference, as if they were merely errors, or had not even existed.

As audience we may expect to breathe hard, and sweat, and shake a little, and in the alleviation of pull not be sure whether we still feel the old pull, or no pull, or a new pull. If we are learned, and philosophical, and quick, we may clearly grasp the argument and realize that Satan is finished and has played out his whole string. Perhaps we do know this in our quiet armchairs. But the rhythms of intellect and feeling are at one with each other only for brief moments during a drama, if at all; only at the end, and in the afterglow that follows the end, do the two grope their way toward each other, or brilliantly coincide. We may know that Satan is finished, and Satan may know it, but he has not acted it. The momentum of the drama continues without pause. There are changes, there are admissions that all is over, but the audience is not ready to leave yet. The momentum continues unabated, new things crowd in. If it is really over, why does one not feel as if it were over? One waits for the feeling. If Satan is only venting desperate rage, that will be an interesting cold fact to record later in an intellectual or dramatic paradigm; it is no cold fact now, and though a choral voice says it, the commentary is running counter to the dramatic action and so producing the very tension that helps prove the play not finished.

And the last two episodes, in spite of what the choral commentary seems in part to say, are treated as temptations, though not quite new ones. Satan may have nothing new to offer, but the drama has. The external logic of the theme, the formal, if uncodified, procedures governing contests between good and evil, may have been carried through and so satisfied, or exhausted. But the internal logic, if I may speak so, all the possibilities of which are not realized by the traditional formulas of moral science or moral art, but lie deeply latent and can be released only by the unique artist (and only after they have been released can they be recognized as having been there at all)—that internal logic has not been satisfied, or exhausted. This drama, in spite of its rigidly prescribed conditions, has not been lacking in the right kind of dramatic surprise. The small examples are many, very many, and constitute an important part of the poem's imaginative quality, of which they are an external sign. If I confine myself to major examples I think of these: the first encounter with Satan, the suddenness and the special turns; the second conference of the devils, and the banquet which adds surprise to surprise; the episode of the "port of worst";

the declaration of wisdom. With all these experiences behind us, and while we are moving in a dramatic momentum that has not yet slackened, with the major issue over and yet not over, with last things not yet defined — at such a time we should at least expect that the surprises are not yet over. In the hands of a great artist the last turn of a theme is not likely to be the least. And so these last two episodes, though not new temptations, are not casual after-thoughts, of the artist anyway.

Satan at a loss, with nothing further to offer, begins to lose his extraordinary patience and to offer insults; not the sly, provocative insults of the fancy footwork, but insults that seem more to serve the needs of self-expression. (We are moving, we shall discover, toward a final range of comedy.) "What dost thou in this World?" he asks with exasperation, and gives the scornful answer that is a joke but baffled: "the Wilderness / For thee is fittest place." He lectures and predicts regret for the fastidiousness which has refused the help of Satan's mastery of timing. He reads the stars and sees the literal phase of the sacerdotal career to come. But still in the stars there is that kingdom, and Satan cannot quite discharge his bafflement by ironically twisting the definition of eternity:

> A Kingdom they portend thee, but what Kingdom,
> Real or Allegoric I discern not,
> Nor when, eternal sure, as without end,
> Without beginning; for no date prefixt
> Directs me in the Starry Rubric set.

Then we have the first of our two episodes, the night of terrors. As formal temptation, it is anticlimactic, whether considered ethically as a test of fortitude, or theologically as an effort to bring about distrust in God and the anxious clinging to "the pride of life." The temptation offers nothing; at best it can be transitional to an offer that can be accepted, as flattery or suggestion has performed the office of transition in the past. But this transition is the strongest and most sustained thus far, granting, as it does to Satan, the long-delayed relief of apparent action. In retrospect, perhaps even now, this will seem a fitting expression of desperate rage. The potential anxieties of the hero are now being worked over at the crudest level, for we have retreated to anxieties without names or even distinct forms. Satan has retreated into a dark sabbath of relief from the work of persuasion, and is attempting to make fear do that work. He has tried this before, but always with names for the anxieties and in the name of persuasion, according to the standard rules for significant moral corruption. In a way, this is the banquet reversed: not a solicitous nature offering its beautiful all to its lord (and vanishing abruptly with the brief horror of the sound of harpies' wings and talons), but an angry nature threatening with an excess of horror for the sake of excess. And the scene is, also like the banquet, an ironic image of Satan expressing himself; for horror, one would like to say, even more than beauty stands "In the admiration only of weak minds." [3]

But there is another way to look at the scene. Throughout the whole drama Satan has been performing an office he does not, cannot, comprehend. It is an office that lies, not only outside his understanding, but outside his will. We have recognized before that there is a kind of compulsiveness in evil; but we have thought that this had better be considered a mystery, an inner logic working its own dark course, and to be directly explained only at the risk of explaining it away. Yet no formal turn of the drama has depended alone on the office outside Satan's understanding and will. He has always had, quite properly, his *own* motivations, and his own controlled, if incomplete, understanding of his motivations. And the night of terror is, one may say, sufficiently motivated by Satan's need for the relief of "positive" action after the grueling exercise of patience, and after the last and greatest defeat has been registered in the formal course. And he knows, we are told, that his power is not yet expired. So what happens is hardly a violation of Satan's character, but is a plausible expression of that character at this stage and in these circumstances.

Yet there is that necessary office casting its shadow on everything Satan does. And as the drama nears its close, and as Satan approaches the end with all his formal, regular gestures used up in failure, and all his most hopeful, or illusory, motivations frayed thin by defeat and so diminished perhaps in conscious control — as these happen, the shadow of Satan's office more nearly assumes, or becomes, his dramatic role. Once, when Satan articulated his "port of worst," the dramatic self seemed for a moment to become identified with, lost in, a real self that threatened to emerge and undo the appointed course of the drama and transform it into a new drama. Now we are at the other extreme. The dramatic self is becoming identified with, lost in, the shadow of the office. Personality, the dramatic role — these are still active, still capable of providing brilliant comedy and the kind of impressive action that can dominate a scene for an extraordinary moment. But when they collapse they reveal, not the ruin of formidable strength, but the thin substance of illusion, the final shadow of unwilled existence, the allegorical extension of a dramatic role already acted out and consciously lost, now finally possessed by the driving momentum it seemed to be driving, the after-throes of that comprehensive spiritual death Satan has been acting out, the death of the understanding and the will. This is real death, the progressive privation of light ignorantly achieved by the prince of darkness. In counterdirection, Christ's "way of death" is the way of life.

Satan's office, not toward himself but outward toward Christ, serves the drama of knowledge. The temptation of the kingdom of the mind evoked, as formal answer to the highest formal temptation, the impressive definition of wisdom. That was the highest point of Christ's illumination. And since this is drama, the expression of the highest point was the acting out, the achieving of the experience on the stage before us, now finally arrived at by due dramatic process, achieved by the protagonist and shared by the audience. The antagonist served the result, and the highest point of his hope became the lowest point of his despair. He now has no higher point left untried, unless we allow him a verbal paradox of a higher transcendence of despair. But the protagonist has, beyond the illumination achieved, a still higher point to achieve. And Satan still serves.

As temptations, the last two episodes, we have noted, are not really new. And, formally considered, they are anticlimactic. But they are also wonderfully dense, and hard to label satisfactorily,

120

for they weave tightly together in a subtle recapitulation much of the moral drama already experienced. When we come to the tower I shall try a little sorting and labeling, in order to describe the artistic intention.

But there is, as I started to say, another way to look at the scene of night terrors. What I have in mind is not the formal temptation but a special service now being performed by Satan for the drama of knowledge. Let us consider the highest point of Christ's illumination as analogous to, not identical with, the first true ecstasy of mystic illumination, the sense of brilliant identification with the source of light. I do not want to be misunderstood, I am not saying that Christ's experience *is* that of the mystic at this stage. What I mean is this: Milton is fulfilling the old gestures in order to create his new myth. A new myth which did not repeat the old gestures would be a hopeful monster indeed. If Christ's symbolic role is to provide illumination for the understanding, and by more than a dialectical example furnishing effective notebook arguments with which to confute evil, then his experience ought to encompass the "deep" patterns and movements by which men have realized the heights of understanding. I am not interested in arguing that the mystic experience is *the* archetype of intellectual illumination. I offer only this, I think modest, argument: the substantial pattern of the mystic experience, like the patterns of the philosophical, religious, and mythic "way of death," retains a kind of authoritative wisdom, and something in the pattern, the gesture, the movement below the level of thought, is repeated in the movement toward wisdom of this drama of knowledge.

Let us continue. The dark night would then follow the high point of intuition and would precede a still higher point. That night is what Satan provides, but with a difference. The darkness and the terrors before the consummation are all external, trumped up by Satan to provide the right trappings for the experience, though that is not his intention. And the new hero who is undergoing the old experience, which is now being rationalized and transformed into a new myth but without missing any of the old steps — the new hero is revealed as completely superior to the old experience, continuing in his quiet progress, fulfilling all the old rhythms, passing easily through the old trials, but in his own way, which renews and transforms.

For a single illustration I quote from Plutarch's famous account of the divine marriage of the mystery cults:

At first wanderings and wearisome hurryings to and fro, and unfinished journeys half-seen as through a darkness; then before the consummation itself all the terrors, shuddering and trembling, sweat and wonder; after which they are confronted by a wonderful light, or received into pure regions and meadows, with singing and dancing and sanctities of holy voices and sacred revelations, wherein, made perfect at last, free and absolved, the initiate worships with crowned head in the company of those pure and undefiled, looking down on the impure, uninitiated multitude of the living as they trample one another under foot and are herded together in thick mire and dust.[4]

To describe the ascent of Eros, Plato borrows from the marriage and revelation of the Eleusinian mysteries. I mention this as a reminder of the occasional closeness of the philosophical "way" to the religious and mythic. Plutarch's account, I am assuming, maintains in general, if not in exact detail, elements of the experience which are common and fundamental, whether as part of the mythic inheritance of recorded religion, or whether as part of the solitary mystic's individual experience as he has tried to express it.

For the hero of a new revelation, there are differences. There are no sweat and wonder, no trembling, and the terrors do not terrify. But the terrors are there, and an unfinished journey, and a master of the mysteries to disturb with "ugly dreams," and to set a stage other masters might well envy:

> and either Tropic now
> 'Gan thunder, and both ends of Heav'n, the Clouds
> From many a horrid rift abortive pour'd
> Fierce rain with lightning mixt, water with fire
> In ruine reconcil'd: nor slept the winds . . .

In addition, Satan can call on expert assistance:

> Infernal Ghosts, and Hellish Furies, round
> Environ'd thee, some howl'd, some yell'd, some shriek'd,

Some bent at thee thir fiery darts, while thou
Sat'st unappall'd in calm and sinless peace.

It is the last line which controls the whole experience, and absorbs it into the new revelation. The terrors are followed by a wonderful light, and pure meadows, and singing, but not those of the old revelation. I quote the whole passage, for it is a remarkable one:

Thus pass'd the night so foul till morning fair
Came forth with Pilgrim steps in amice gray;
Who with her radiant finger still'd the roar
Of thunder, chas'd the clouds, and laid the winds,
And grisly Spectres, which the Fiend had rais'd
To tempt the Son of God with terrors dire.
And now the Sun with more effectual beams
Had chear'd the face of Earth, and dry'd the wet
From drooping plant, or dropping tree; the birds
Who all things now behold more fresh and green,
After a night of storm so ruinous,
Clear'd up their choicest notes in bush and spray
To gratulate the sweet return of morn.

The dark night is over but the new revelation has not come. It is a beautiful morning, and welcome; it is *the* morning, and does not go uncelebrated. The hero says nothing, and we are left to our own feelings, and those expressed by the poem, at the joyful return of hopeful nature. His act is natural; he is found on the sunny hill, "Back'd on the North and West by a thick wood"; but he says nothing. There has been no "looking down on the impure" yet, no revelation. But the master of the mysteries returns "in wonted shape" to push matters to a conclusion.

The next scene is dominantly comic and harvests ironies not quite ripe until now. Satan is remarkably cheerful, "in a careless mood," as if refreshed by the relief of a night's work that at least made things happen. He delivers a brisk and cheery lecture on the significance of the portents. It is the old subject: the night was an omen that the perfect season was being missed by faulty timing. However, the lecture falters for a moment as he is caught in his old obsession:

> no man knows when,
> For both the when and how is no where told,
> Thou shalt be what thou art ordain'd, no doubt;
> For Angels have proclaim'd it, but concealing
> The time and means.

But the formal phase of argument and reply is over. Christ continues walking and answers "in brief," over his shoulder at it were. The Satan of the crude anxieties, attempting to persuade by fear, and with no unrefuted arguments to offer, cannot begin the debate again.

Then the false morning mask of Satan disappears, with all his flimsy cheerfulness of recent acquisition, and all that long-suffering patience carefully matched against the protagonist's patience. "Swoln with rage," he answers in a rage that releases all his comic perplexity:

> Then hear, O Son of *David*, Virgin-born;
> For Son of God to me is yet in doubt,
> Of the Messiah I have heard foretold
> By all the Prophets; of thy birth at length
> Announc't by *Gabriel* with the first I knew,
> And of the Angelic Song in *Bethlehem* field,
> On thy birth-night, that sung thee Saviour born.
> From that time seldom have I ceas'd to eye
> Thy infancy, thy childhood, and thy youth,
> Thy manhood last, though yet in private bred;
> Till at the Ford of *Jordan* whither all
> Flock'd to the Baptist, I among the rest,
> Though not to be Baptiz'd, by voice from Heav'n
> Heard thee pronounc'd the Son of God belov'd.
> Thenceforth I thought thee worth my nearer view
> And narrower Scrutiny, that I might learn
> In what degree or meaning thou art call'd
> The Son of God, which bears no single sence;
> The Son of God I also am, or was,
> And if I was, I am; relation stands;
> All men are Sons of God; yet thee I thought
> In some respect far higher so declar'd . . .

We are getting a recapitulation of Satan's first approach to his problem. This is where he came in, and after all that has happened he is still there, retelling it all in a kind of comic-opera song, but with the addition of the charming dramatic candor about the baptism, and with an authoritatively final comic statement on the subject of the literal-metaphorical title Son of God. The verbal comedy of this last is now fulfilled, though the idea has a little further service to perform.

The speech continues in angry sincerity which aims only at the relief of expressing itself, and is, if here only, not baited. Christ *is* to be the fatal enemy, at least that is what "all best conjectures" indicate. And so Satan has attempted, with "good reason," to understand his adversary, and "To win him, or win from him what I can." And he confesses that he has found him.

> Proof against all temptation as a rock
> Of Adamant, and as a Center, firm
> To the utmost of meer man both wise and good,
> Not more; for Honours, Riches, Kingdoms, Glory
> Have been before contemn'd, and may agen.

Satan serves the drama of knowledge here, too, against his will. For he is affirming, on proved authority, that all men *are* the sons of God, and that the hero, however impressive his behavior, has done nothing that man cannot do, has not done, may not do again. It is an important affirmation and comes at an important moment, just before Satan is to exceed the bounds of human possibility. The comic has not lifted the tension, though it has been working richly against it.

The last temptation is brief and sudden, like the first, which it resembles interestingly. It also comes without real preparation, for the terrors of the night, whatever they intended, have accomplished nothing; but all the other temptations were carefully graduated, and when the offer of glory deviated from the order it only emphasized the order, which was promptly resumed. But the temptation of the stones, the request for a major transcendence through miracle, though under the humble colors of hunger and charity, came without warning, and did not maneuver for a position perhaps to be used later, but aimed at finality. And Satan on the tower has all at once arranged an issue that must be answered finally, one way or the other. The physical excitement of the first encounter in the drama is answered fully, as the form completes itself, by the abruptness, the fierce violence, and the sudden release of surprising action, an action held back through an entire drama, openly but fearfully longed for by Satan and secretly longed for by the audience.

The nature of the temptation and the nature of the answer must occupy us for a while. The problem is partly the problem of the terrors. According to the formal plan the temptation may be considered, ethically, the test of fortitude; theologically, the general test of trust in God specialized as "presumption." These may do as labels, but the final action of a complex drama is not happily described by labels. And this final action brings together thematically much that has already happened. The test is, formally, on a lower level and anticlimactic, but not in a simple way, without countermotions. The test proves, as a kind of review examination, the demonstrated mastery of all the lessons. The test requires the proof, as I said in the preceding essay, that wisdom believes itself. I had better quote the passage, so we may have it before us.

> Till underneath them fair *Jerusalem*,
> The holy City lifted high her Towers,
> And higher yet the glorious Temple rear'd
> Her pile, far off appearing like a Mount
> Of Alabaster, top't with golden Spires:
> There on the highest Pinacle he set
> The Son of God; and added thus in scorn:
>   There stand, if thou wilt stand; to stand upright
> Will ask thee skill; I to thy Fathers house
> Have brought thee, and highest plac't, highest is best,
> Now shew thy Progeny; if not to stand,
> Cast thy self down; safely if Son of God:
> For it is written, He will give command
> Concerning thee to his Angels, in thir hands
> They shall up lift thee, lest at any time
> Thou chance to dash thy foot against a stone.

This last vision from a great height recalls the other visions of the kingdoms. The motion of return to the source of being Satan sarcastically translates with his effort at metaphor, "thy Fathers house." And the old argument of power receives its last variation, "highest is best." The choice that Satan has prepared is between Christ's asserting himself in miracle (I assume from the "Spires" and from Satan's tone that standing is not humanly possible),[5] and this would be like turning the stones to bread; or between Christ's accepting the probability of miracle if, not standing, he falls-or-casts-himself down, and this would be like accepting the miracle of the banquet.

For an anticlimactic temptation on a lower level it is a cunning one, and ought both to surprise and impress the reader. The trap, Satan thinks, will evoke the assertion or intervention of miracle, or else an assertion of self by the hero, an effort to do the humanly impossible and stand. When the effort of the perfect man fails, he will have been put in the ambiguous position of acting out what Satan said. When he falls he will indeed require a perfect will and consciousness to be sure that he has not jumped. The hero has refused all suggestions, rejected the false dilemmas, heroically not acted, but discriminated, clarified, declared, while patiently not acting but preparing to act. Now Satan thinks that he must act, one way or another, and from Satan's will; that he must accept from Satan, as from his God, if not dominion, then the terms and the *time* of his revelation, or else death, no "way of death" but death.

The reader is likely at the moment to be impressed more by the apparent absoluteness of the trap than by its representing a sharp decline in the moral drama. This is as it should be, for even a moral drama should be drama. Stripped of all his false claims, the antagonist, having pursued the logic of his "way of death" to its conclusion, is now declaring his essential wisdom. At the point of exhaustion, what emerges, dangerous and fascinating, is that final shadow of unwilled existence, the brute, mechanical end of his momentum.[6] Satan's literal, material mind has finally come to the device of persuasion that is most expressive, most sure to give him his answer. If we look at things more coolly than the situation itself permits, we can see that Satan, in abrogating his permitted dramatic role, has broken the rules of his proper office as tempter, and so invoked forces that have hitherto maintained their neutrality.

(Milton never meant that free will denied all possibility of divine intervention; where there is God's grace there must be God's wrath too: witness the war in heaven.) In his moral exhaustion Satan has exceeded his office; he is not trying to persuade, to corrupt; he is threatening bodily death; he has put everything in one maniacal attempt literally to *know*.[7]

The answer is not literal, but Satan's response to it is literal, and material: he falls. Still, he is caught up for one last time in the comedy of the stage he has ordered, and the reader sees that Satan has not been let down simply. Here, at Satan's highest-lowest point, which exceeds the moral drama by receding out of it, the whole perspective of transcendence is reversed, and unwittingly revealed. Christ, raised aloft in the middle region of air, "looking down on the impure," though not himself in the company of the "pure and undefiled," is invited to the final revelation of transcendence. And the pull is, as it has been all along, *downward*, spiritually, intellectually, physically. This is the literal direction now revealed, the Satanic apocalypse, the power and glory and kingdom of mere death.

But there is another revelation, brought on by Satan, the fruit of his efforts, though not of his consciousness; and even the control of the timing is, by a delicate adjustment, raised beyond his power to predict or imagine. The answer comes:

> To whom thus Jesus: also it is written,
> Tempt not the Lord thy God, he said and stood.
> But Satan smitten with amazement fell.

What has happened? Surely not that Christ is directly replying to Satan's challenge by finally declaring himself, by saying: thou shalt not tempt *me*, the Lord thy God![8] That would be to violate the whole discipline, so perfectly sustained, of Christ's moral and intellectual example: the witness of whence he is by the seeking of glory not for himself but for Him who sent him, the hungering to do the Father's will, the full confirmation of intuitive knowledge by rational discipline, the acting and not-acting as perfect man, but man. What has happened is more surprising, and true to the drama.

The flesh becomes word. Christ says it, and then becomes it. The full revelation occurs, the miracle of epiphany, theophany, but not as an act of will, not from the self.[9] The rational discipline holding to the light from above now becomes part of that light. The intuitive is confirmed in thought, word, and deed. Inspiration, the inspired word of God, the power of the wondrous call of God, true glory — the final statement occurs here, now, in action. And this is the final comment on the theme of persuasion.

What has the office of evil performed? The first thing to note is that man has won all the significant, inner victory by himself, aided only by the due endowments of man. That was the real contest and victory, but evil could not stop itself with the mere knowledge of defeat and without the experience. When evil exceeded the due limits of power from below, the unlimited power from above manifested itself, and the manifestation served as complete act. The hero has been descended into the depths of himself during a long initiatory withdrawal. He has been tracing the labyrinthine mazes of self, preparing *to act transcendence in the world,* but withdrawn into profundities which lie deeper than the level of direct concern with the world as world or the self as self. The tempter has tested the center of knowing between the height of transcendence and the depth of descent. The depth has not been described, and perhaps not directly expressed. Perhaps Milton thought the subject inexpressible; or needing, in a poem that is a drama and not a meditation, only to be expressed in action, as the external result of an internal experience. But it is clear that Milton wanted his hero to go through the significant motions of searching the depths, wanted him to repeat the old gestures — whether as an ancient, necessary act of the soul in search of its truth, or whether as the fulfillment by a new myth of the tried and true gestures of the old myths. The hero, we have been reminded, has descended into himself, tracing the desert wild, wandering the woody maze. And Milton has wanted to express a relationship between the depth of descent and transcendence, the "mission high," the end of being on earth. Satan has provided the means of expressing, of dramatically realizing, that relationship. He has formulated, as only the master of the world's wisdom could, the options to be stripped off. His high offers of the world, his highest-best, have demonstrated themselves as the lowest-worst.

As man, though perfect, Christ's first intuition was of goodness. One may think that he did not need to know good through evil; but his mission requires acting in the world, and evil has helped, or else the drama means nothing. Evil has provided the opportunity, and the apparatus, for the soul descended into self to define that self in terms of the world; to recover the common likeness of the soul to the God transcending and uniting all souls, and to do so not in solitary meditation or rapture, but in the thought of action. In refusing to imitate God directly, and so wrongly, by transcendence, Christ maintains the difference, the distance between God and man; but he does so while demonstrating the similarity between man and God, by acting out the perfection of the image of God in man. This, one may now see, is what in another way he did in defining glory and wisdom: he asserted the difference in order to make possible the similarity. Even the light from above was received, and acknowledged, and from above. Now he comes into the true patrimony of likeness, and the Apollonian gesture of recognizing God as the measure becomes, in very motion, the Dionysiac gesture of identification, as grace is shed on the word and it becomes act.[10]

In my concluding pages I want to return to my announced theme from the vantage point I think we have reached. We have come to the end of the poem after a long and detailed process. I must now try to say, from the advantage of our present perspective, and so with some difference, what I said at the beginning: that this poem is about life, and about proper endeavoring in the world.

First, let me quote a contrary opinion, so that I may quarrel with it:

Contemptus mundi was never carried further by medieval pope or doctor of the Church than it was by Milton in this poem. Disillusion like his may have been possible only in the twilight of the Renaissance; and perhaps the denunciation of ancient culture that consummates Christ's refusal of even the noblest earthly glory could have come only from a spirit to whom classical literature had

130

promised the vision of ancient civic liberty that is painted in *Areopagitica.*[11]

The *contemptus*, religious decorum tells us, could be carried further by no one than by the protagonist of this poem. But Milton did not interpret the decorum so, and the poem he wrote is consciously organized in another direction. Milton is not trying to declare the business of the world bankrupt. By inveigling, Satan has got control of some of the world's enterprises, but his power is "usurped," and not complete; nor is the world incorrigibly rotten. Christ is not the first to refuse the false allurements of Satan, as the devil himself protests. Old heroes, and old human possibilities, are respected by the hero of this poem as he prepares to contest for the dominion — of the world. It is not the world of Satan's understanding, to be sure, but a world purged of the idolatrous preferring of man, or Satan, to God.

To see Christ's answers, not as a positive process of self-definition, but as a retreating series of refusals, is to assume the dramatic perspective of Satan. It is true that Satan is the initiating agent who makes the proposals, but Christ's mind does not so much react as act. His positive vision penetrates the shallow patterns of empirical knowledge offered him by Satan. And yet, to the credit of the poem, Milton does not supply Satan with fatuous propositions. What Satan says makes very good sense, as we only too well know. It is the business of the poem to convince us that in this drama the sense is an absolutely wrong sense. As for the translation of the symbol, to what extent this demonstration is literally true and practicable for Everyman — I shall try to say something further on that soon. But this much at least ought to be obvious: the demonstrated wrong sense of Satan cannot seem irrelevant to the imaginative experience of the imperfect men who participate in this drama as audience. It is the business of the poem to convince us, but as a poem. We shall have to look, not to the medieval doctors but to the poets, for an arraignment of the world based upon an intimate, solid, imaginatively realized knowledge of the forces of the world. For Milton the choice between knowledge-as-power or knowledge-as-love has to be a dramatically proved choice, the simplicity of truth tested by the complexity of error. There is no willful, peremptory turning of the back on the world, or Satan; but the knowing of good through evil, before and without evil, but through and beyond evil. (The filial virtue is, in this poem, exposed, though "untried," and in order to "exercise" itself and to "earn" salvation.) Already, with the seventeenth century turning toward its last quarter, the old truths had become harder to realize, without pious surgery. But Milton's answer is no simple imagining of a world before Bacon, or Machiavelli.

As a poetic argument we are given a wonderfully contrived and sustained illusion. By the brilliance and length and dramatic interest of Milton's treatment, the whole scope of the temptations deceives, and deliberately. But that impressive deception runs its course and is revealed in its true dimension. Satan has nothing to offer but man's power over man or nature, for the sake of power. As a victim of self pursuing an inevitable course, Satan illustrates, or rather, surveys and establishes the *limits* of evil, so that captive minds may cease to admire.

A smaller, more local, poetic argument worth noticing is one provided by the style. There is a remarkable shift in tempo and manner after the episode of Athens. Actually it begins a little earlier, with small signs, and with the shifting of Satan's consciousness away from the dramatic center of immediacy, to return only for the final comic harvest. (Here are, briefly, some of the small signs: the expression of the need for endeavoring and means, the purified expectation of time, the moral optimism that ends Book III and begins Book IV, the defense of inspiration.) But after Satan's last legitimate move has been countered, the whole swing is, rapid and optimistic, toward a confident end. The last night rises unsubstantially, the mere privation of light. The storm is briefly and fully resisted; morning in the desert comes like dawn in Paradise; the poise of the brisk and "careless" Satan quickly explodes in a comic recapitulation of his dilemma; and he is treated as one who has lost the status of tempter.

But the great poetic argument is of course the hero. Milton gives us the rarest and most hopeful of images, wisdom without bodily decrepitude, early, with the hero young, at the flower, unbruised. Wisdom enters into its earned and granted kingdom before entering the world, but not without having experienced the world. Christ holds heroically to his wisdom, and advances from intuition to confirmation, passing through the dangerous trial of translating intuition into what will be the greatest public good, and doing so without any merely human substitutions or additions, whether the prompting comes from his own early hopes for heroic acts, or whether from the external suggestions of Satan.[12]

The high point of the experience, for the hero and the audience, is the miracle on the tower. But after that the poem moves into the new beginning which is the end of the poem. Milton is under no obligation to continue with a new drama, but the sequel is too well-known not to be implied in what has already been acted out. In his early autobiographical soliloquy Christ decided "to try" persuasion rather than "heroic acts." Though not further discussed, that decision has been a major subject of the poem. The contest with Satan has been a contest that has also defined persuasion. Satan has moved from argument, though argument which liberally used fear and force in various representations, to the naked fear and force that represent the essential weakness of his strength. Christ's concept of persuasion has deepened, or so we may assume in drama, where the meaning is what happens. He has been teaching himself as preparation for his end of teaching the world, but all of the impressive intellectual faculties and accomplishments displayed have been moving with increased emphasis toward the final form: inspiration. He is to teach without temporal office, and not the law but the inspired word, the wondrous call; and that great persuasion is to be confirmed by the persuasion of his exemplary act.

The hero's example to the living is to identify man's end with reality, and so to return the end to the beginning, to raise Eden again, though in the waste wilderness. The first great step in the hero's economy of salvation (and Everyman is to attend this closely) is to put his own house in order. For destiny is individual — this is not an easy lesson and does not grow easier with time. Now

Everyman is not the Messiah — this is as obvious as the fact that a moral example ought not be "average" moral behavior. Our hero is "private," individual, but unique; he wins all of the important internal victory as a man, up to the miracle of revelation; his drama is familiar, repeated, representative, but also unique. Milton nowhere insists on the literal identification of the reader with the hero; the tension of that relationship is maintained throughout the poem; it is for every man's conscience to assess the symbolism. For the hero (for Everyman?) putting his house in order proves to be identical with the return to the source of being. But that return is not a withdrawal from the world in rapturous contemplation. Truth originates from God, not the world, and is answerable to God — but in the world. The return is a return to God's will, and that means God's will for man and the world, and that means God's love; and that means all the preparation was preparation to act in the world, to act God's will and love in the world. All of the hero's descent into the self and all of the antagonist's offers of transcendence have clearly recognized, and reiterated, this end of being on earth: action. And the final acclaim of victory is the acclaim of one soul perfectly in order, and so ready to act perfectly the greatest task of God's love: "Now enter, and begin to save mankind." Now . . . enter . . . and . . . begin.[13]

SAMSON
AGONISTES

THE FIRST DARK STEPS

IT IS easier to believe that the arts share common forms than to talk sensibly on the subject. The idiom of each art, and each artist, is too intimately individual to translate without gross distortion. But the critical imagination, I believe, may be educated without the distortion of inadequate words. My understanding of my own experience, for example, is that, though I am barely literate in music, I have come to see many potentialities of poetic form by first having experienced them in music. Both arts, it is obvious, require the dimension of time for their development; they move by sound; thematic materials are repeated, varied, explored, evolved, returned to an original or an intermediate stage for the comparison which may both confirm the distance traveled and constitute a new turn of development; silence (the plastic space of sound) is formed and forms, surrounding as it does each sound and the successions of sound; rhythms make their angles and curves that play against each other in independent shapes becoming a final shape; textures (the qualities in combination of sounds, or rhythms, or thematic materials in process) perform in mysterious ways, dominating moments with an imaginative authority that may linger unsubsided even in the final resolution of what one would like to think is *the* form, but cannot therefore quite be sure; dissonance and harmony endow each other with significant existence.

137

I believe all this, but I have enough sense, I think, not to try to make these matters too clear. (Apparently I also should have acknowledged my debt to the visual arts, to which my remarks on poetry and music owe something.) The occasion for my raising the subject is the poem I am about to interpret. *Samson Agonistes,* more than any other long poem I know, with the possible exception of Eliot's *Quartets,* does not only share common elements of form with music, but seems to insist on the musical nature of its form. That is not the right way of putting it perhaps, and I do not intend to try to demonstrate a pure "musical form" in the poem. I shall try to be content with my, admittedly, crude emphasis, and point out the analogies to musical form only when they are important enough, and of themselves clear enough, so that even inexact pointing may serve critical description. For the most part I shall interpret the work in my usual way, as a poetic drama, a companion piece to the dramatic poem *Paradise Regained.*

The opening of the play, while doing its proper task of introducing the action and getting it started, advances rich thematic materials which are to be developed. There would be nothing remarkable in this, for it is a familiar method of narrative and dramatic art, if it were not for the degree, which is remarkable. Almost nothing serves this first stage alone. Large theme and small, directly stated, or innocently appearing as an adorning or illustrative image — they occur with a density too concentrated for us to apprehend on a first reading. Yet they do, I am convinced, communicate the fact of the density by the manner of communicating. Something I cannot name in the imaginative quality of the details and in the tone (as recognizable anywhere, in isolation, as, let us say, the texture of sound achieved by Beethoven in parts of the last quartets) — something commands our expectation that these things mean beyond the moment. We are not to be deceived but amazed. At the end of the play we shall find some of the same density, as themes crowd in for their final appearances and remind us of their individual and significant histories.

I want to look at Samson's first speech, his only monologue, and note some of its thematic anticipations as well as the larger pattern of movement it makes in the dramatic progression here begun. The opening lines, describing mere physical situation, also suggest the internal drama to come:

> A little onward lend thy guiding hand
> To these dark steps, a little further on;
> For yonder bank hath choice of Sun or shade.

(I take the titles for my first four essays in this section from phrases in the first two lines.) Here he feels "amends,"

> The breath of Heav'n fresh-blowing, pure and sweet,
> With day-spring born.

This physical consolation, while it establishes at once Samson's capacity for feeling, and what that means, and his capacity for responding to the hopeful movement of nature, can hardly be limited in this drama to the immediacy of the physical and the natural. Next, the feast of the Philistines now does in a small way what it will do in a final way: their *superstition unwillingly yields him rest*. And so,

> Retiring from the popular noise, I seek
> This unfrequented place to find some ease.

But at the end of the play it is in the frequented place amid the popular noise that he seeks and finds ease, to body and mind.

The opening may be considered an introduction containing major thematic anticipations. Then, with the mention of the tormenting thoughts the style shifts, and the themes are presented with powerful immediacy as they refer from past to present. The main theme is the promise of Samson's destiny: the great exploits, the benefit to Abraham's race (the important relationship with the community here for the first time introduced), the specially prescribed breeding, "As of a person separate to God." This last introduces a subject of sustained importance: the mark of difference on Samson, the heroic morality, the tragic guilt. The main theme of the promise ruined, which has been stated and partly developed, then proceeds in two further developments marked by two significant interruptions.

First there are the facts of his present condition:

> Betray'd, Captiv'd, and both my Eyes put out,
> Made of my Enemies the scorn and gaze;
> To grind in Brazen Fetters under task
> With this Heav'n-gifted strength.

The facts of blindness and imprisonment are fiercer than in their
first expression; they will undergo several further modifications,
thrilling ones. Now the facts come with an immediate power of
terrible scorn and detachment. The tension between the feeling of
extreme self-hate and the cold intellectual thrust of distance from
the identity of self produces a feeling that seems beyond feeling.

> Ask for this great Deliverer now, and find him
> Eyeless in *Gaza* at the mill with slaves.

The friction of self-hate and detachment gives a special tone to
Samson's words, and we respond to their immediate power. But if
we borrow from our later perspective, as we may legitimately do, so
long as we see only what *is* here now — for most of us in fact are unable to respond with anything like full consciousness to the immediacy of a thick dramatic texture — if we assume the right
perspective, we shall see that the personal in the psychological
equation is present, and strong, and most susceptible of interesting
development. For instance, the description of himself as betrayed
implies in Samson's mind some inclination to look at his calamity
in the special terms of the grieved self looking outward toward
the external causes of the grief. I do not mean that we should expect
now any full recognition of the nature and the clear causes of the
grief; for the emphasis points, as it properly should, to the freshness of the grief and the state of mind of a tragic hero newly facing
that grief.

Something in Samson, a vital endowment, recognizes the bent
of the personal and stops to make the right moral gesture:

> Yet stay, let me not rashly call in doubt
> Divine Prediction; what if all foretold
> Had been fulfilld but through mine own default,
> Whom have I to complain of but my self?

This, the first expression of justice and individual responsibility,
interrupts the main theme of the promise ruined, and gives tempo-

rary pause to the expression of the personal. But not for long, since the feeling has too much force to remain still. The acknowledgment of responsibility, the first sure step of moral reintegration (if we may judge by the case of Adam), marks the moral stage at which this drama begins; but for the moment Samson uses the acknowledgment as a means of continuing past it, with his personal and less detached expression of anger at himself, and with a contempt for his "impotence of mind" that carries over to the triviality of his gift of strength. Then a second, and stronger, interruption is invoked:

> But peace, I must not quarrel with the will
> Of highest dispensation, which herein
> Happ'ly had ends above my reach to know.

A sincere reference to God's will provides no easy rhetorical transition, and Samson means what he says. He simply turns from the sincere reference to a sincere personal restatement, not building on the pious gesture, but making it in order to define and admit the personal. (It is enough for him to know that strength is his ruin and the source of all his miseries.) The piety also marks a formal stage at which the drama begins, but resignation in God's will is at the end of a longer path than even the full acceptance of individual responsibility. Samson makes the essential gesture, not as transition to the personal but as acknowledgment. He is about to speak the pure personal, the self grieving for the self with no tension of irony, and without the leisure or luxury of anger and scorn. He pours out feeling as feeling, out of lyric necessity. The gesture is the formal sign, which the pious will not mistake, that he is not questioning God's will but *must* give expression to his pain. Milton is presenting this with a clear discrimination in mind; for instance, in contrasting stoic apathy with true patience, he describes the standard biblical view: "for sensibility to pain, and even lamentations, are not inconsistent with true patience; as may be seen in Job and the other saints, when under the pressure of affliction." (*Christian Doctrine*, I, 10.) (This is a point we shall have to return to in treating Manoa.)

The lament for the loss of sight is the final and authoritative expression toward which Samson has been moving. It is an intimate identification of the self with its grief. After the dark weariness of the opening, with its inner movement of small but hopeful responsiveness to feeling; and after (1) the initial statement of the promise ruined, and the first development; after (2) the grim tension within the self, the angry feeling and the terrible separation; after the first interrupting gesture, and (3) the anger that continues but with less detachment — now, finally, after the gesture that clarifies and releases, the pure singleness of feeling speaks the concentrated and sustained anguish of its inner necessity. The development moves out from what began as a major theme, the promise ruined, but then evolved in terms of personal responses to that theme, and at last has abandoned the theme to give independent expression to what has been a dependent response.

If I have been accurate in my analysis, the new theme repeats the form we have so far traced: it has an introduction and a triple development.[1] First, there is the prefatory statement of personal grief, "Blind among enemies." Then the theme of light is invoked as "the prime work of God," but the extension is from the felt perspective of self, the humble imagination that grief might have been eased by sight of nature's "various objects." Then the personal grief is developed as physical condition, the unsheltered stage of being dark in light, as the former champion writhes with indignity over his foolish helplessness:

> I dark in light expos'd
> To daily fraud, contempt, abuse and wrong,
> Within doors, or without, still as a fool,
> In power of others, never in my own;
> Scarce half I seem to live, dead more then half.

The last line introduces the second development, the treatment of darkness as death in life. First, there is the hopelessness of the "dark, dark, dark." Then the "great Word," the "prime decree" of light, is again invoked in lament for the loss. This is developed in a larger imaginative dimension than the grief of the physical condition, which was related to public attitudes, was indignant, and capable of a local, physical imagining. But the light not seen is felt as silence and lonely space. The physical fact of light is then developed as an idea that turns through the extreme of an excruciating physical imagination that intimately fondles the heart of the grief:

> Why was the sight
> To such a tender ball as th' eye confin'd?
> So obvious and so easie to be quench't,
> And not as feeling through all parts diffus'd,
> That she might look at will through every pore?

Then, third, the movement turns back to the personal grief, uniting the themes of light and dark, life and death:

> As in the land of darkness yet in light,
> To live a life half dead, a living death.

He is "Buried, yet not exempt" from "all the miseries of life." At the sound of approaching steps the thought of the indignity of staring returns, and the affliction of "insult."

With the coming of the Chorus we have an external measure for the internal revelation of the monologue, and the first external help arrives for the internal deliverance. Most striking is their description of him. We accept, as we must, the first physical account and the brilliantly contrasting history of what he was. But in between they infer his internal state from the external appearance:

> As one past hope, abandon'd,
> And by himself given over.

This, from the available evidence, we must question. The moral gestures toward responsibility and Providence indicated a stage well this side of despair.[2] Tragic heroes who speak in beautiful verse of great vitality may perhaps not be judged by normal standards of prose control and rhetorical order. But the quality of the grief, its height of expression, and the terms — all bespeak a tormented hero who feels his torments as things alive in an unabandoned self. He is no more abandoned than he is resigned. His grief is fresh enough to hurt. The anger and self-contempt are too powerfully felt and expressed to represent despair; so is the exacerbated sensitivity to insult, and to the staring, and to the thought of himself "still as a fool." The Chorus will soon make the occasion for the correcting of its error.

After a formal transition by Samson, the style an impersonal, cultivated voice of high tragedy (like the one Samson used when he first heard the intruding sound of steps), he recognizes friends and speaks in still another voice, not the private one we heard, but a public one. It is hard to describe a voice, but let us say that it has the control of dignity, a sense of the difference and the distance between external and internal ears. Is it that sense, controlling more than voice, which makes him say of his blindness, "Yet that which was the worst now least afflicts me"? Our immediate response is to the pathos of the deceit, and we have no way of being immediately sure of anything but deception. As time goes, it has been too soon for such an important change to have occurred. But dramatic time can make its own laws, and if a hero says an incredible thing that later becomes credible, or utterly convincing, when did it first begin to be true? We need not try to answer the question so, but we are being encouraged by the drama to look beyond the obviousness of deception. First, we should make some allowance for the effect of this audience, which symbolizes the community. As not-self [3] they may inspire the dignity of deception. But they may also bring a help to Samson which gives the first words — premature or not, we cannot tell — to an internal change that will occur, that may now be occurring, or can do so only after the words are spoken. At the very least, we are being reminded, again, that the internal Samson is not static, and that the signs of movement are many and subtle.

The presence of others returns the hero to the larger aspect of his failure, not merely to the promise ruined, but beyond that to the trust betrayed. This, even as he says it, counters the illusion that sight could have eased his grief:

> for had I sight, confus'd with shame,
> How could I once look up, or heave the head,
> Who like a foolish Pilot have shipwrack't,
> My Vessel trusted to me from above,
> Gloriously rigg'd; and for a word, a tear,
> Fool, have divulg'd the secret gift of God.

The small illusion may be countered, but not the pressure of the intimate anguish. He makes the frank display; it is a public lament before the community, the rhythms beating like a fist upon the chest; it is frank, but not terrible like the private lament. Still, the shame now can imagine a kind of shelter in blindness, but not the sense of folly, which strains to see how it is regarded by others: "Am I not sung and proverbed for a Fool / In every street?" His explanation is the one that we heard before, that the gifts of strength and wisdom were disproportionate. The tone is now less angry, and the detachment is deliberately casual, presented like a public fact.

The Chorus responds properly, the way Samson himself responded in his monologue, for they share the same piety: "Tax not divine disposal." But they see the fault in a more human way, in terms of man's weakness with woman. They offer the voice of human comfort, the sympathy which would limit the fault, or at least limit the sorrow. They will, as they properly should, go further in that direction than Samson; but there is a gap, we may already begin to see, between their morality and his.[4] The human emphasis continues, and the Chorus, expressing the communal curiosity under its dramatic license, asks about the strange marriages.

The implications of the reply tell us more than the reply itself. The first marriage was a means of beginning Israel's deliverance. The legal defense of this comes later, in answer to Dalila; now it is defended, as it was to his parents, as an inspiration coming from God:

> they knew not
> That what I motion'd was of God; I knew
> From intimate impulse.

The inspiration of God is a familiar and hard fact, in no way altered by what has befallen the hero; what he knew he knows. But that certainty is followed by a less inscrutable uncertainty as he comes to his error, the second marriage:

> Was in the Vale of *Sorec, Dalila,*
> That specious Monster, my accomplisht snare.
> I thought it lawful from my former act,
> And the same end.

The first feeling for Dalila — we may guess, in spite of himself — is to be heard in the softened beauty of the line that announces her. This may be, in poetry as in music, a true signature of feeling. And in the opposite expression, the harshness of his backing away, we may hear another version of that first feeling. But there is a deeper revelation in his rationalizing of the act. He has done an extraordinary thing: he has interpreted intuition by analogy! [5] (We may be reminded of that third stage of consciousness described and rejected by Christ, the answering of divine intuition in terms of the human intuition of heroic acts.) There is more than a suspicion that the trust of God was here, perhaps for the first time, symbolically violated, and the precious, individual favor of the "intimate impulse" rationalized in a logical analogy to indulge a "motion" from self. Samson does not go into the fine points of it, but he knows what he needs to know now, the real source of error and responsibility: "She was not the prime cause, but I my self."

The Chorus, moved by its own strange human reasons, expresses an ambivalance we shall need to comment on later. Samson's efforts are praised; "Yet *Israel* still serves with all his Sons." The answer to this hostility reveals *how* wrong they were in thinking him self-abandoned. Neither private nor public lament has turned him into a sewer to receive all faults. If he is to be a sacrifice it will be as heroic example, not scapegoat. The defense is positive and strong in a way we have not seen before. Certain individual qualities of the hero appear for the first time and mark an important advance in our dramatic knowledge. This last, we have no other choice but to assume now, is the same as the hero's dramatic progress. It is the leaders of Israel who must accept this blame, since, blind and deaf to the manifest signs of God's inspiration, they did not acknowledge "those great acts which God had done / Singly by me." Samson then proceeds to the specific history and tells it with clean detachment (different from his earlier detachment), and with a quiet, powerful dignity that reminds one of the early Othello. He ends with a ringing judgment we cannot believe comes from a man buried in his own disaster.

The strength of the self, evident in the anguish, is no less evident here. But now, under an unjust accusation, that strength shows itself possessed also of an amazing intellectual and moral clarity. Samson refuses to accept, though in the rubbish of his major ruin, the small addition of personal injustice. This gesture from the un-wrecked stubborn self is no less important than the object offered, which is the release of self in an acknowledgment of total responsi-bility for the public as well as the private failure. He refuses, now for the first time, now in terms of total defeat and despair, the temptation to *withdraw*. Instead, he accepts the challenge of a difficult theme, in difficult circumstances, and conducts himself with sure dignity; for he speaks justice, of the nation, and even of himself. But first he speaks justice of God, Who did the deeds. And after the Chorus has taken advantage of its lyrical license to make a graceful digression, Samson repeats his piety of justice; for in his energy of enunciation he did not forget either the humble fact of his fault or the glorious origin of his accomplishments:

> Of such examples adde mee to the roul,
> Mee easily indeed mine may neglect,
> But Gods propos'd deliverance not so.

For the moment at least, he has emerged from the "living death" with an uncommon vigor of mind and spirit. The path before him is long and still arduous, but he is well started. As we look back we can see that the signs have multiplied since the entrance of the Chorus. The special quality of his grief and the irritated sense of his own folly have developed in the public situation to a point where he can speak justly of himself, an accomplishment difficult even for unfallen heroes. Justice toward the self is more strenuous than the acceptance of individual responsibility. It is to be one of the hero's chief trials, and will require a measure of intellectual strength he has denied having.

A LITTLE ONWARD

MANOA introduces the most human voice
into the drama, the one with the widest range, and a full dramatic
and natural privilege to express that range. The voice is both
public, saying what ordinary men might feel, and individual to his
character and to his position as father. Finally, as spokesman for
ordinary humanity and as participant in the drama, he will be
privileged to express a purified human response to the tragic experience.

The first effect is different and shocking, partly because of the
quality of the new voice, which is recklessly willing to articulate
attitudes not yet articulated; but partly also because that new
voice repeats what has already been said, but turns it peremptorily
into the special expression of a new and forceful dramatic position. The Chorus, in its first recognition of Samson, spoke with awe
and pity (and with some remarkable poetic rhythms):

> This, this is he; softly a while,
> Let us not break in upon him;
> O change beyond report, thought, or belief.

Manoa roughly and abruptly condenses: "O miserable change! is
this the man . . ." He continues, as the Chorus did, to mark the
difference by recalling what Samson was, and in a similar rhythm:
"That invincible *Samson*." But he does not celebrate Samson's
previous glory so much as use it for a rhetorical contrast which is

148

unsparing. The Chorus drew its moral, that of medieval tragedy but, I think, not Milton's [1]: "O mirror of our fickle state." Manoa draws a similar kind of moral, as platitudinous, perhaps as misplaced, but certainly overpersonalized:

> O ever failing trust
> In mortal strength! and oh what not in man
> Deceivable and vain! Nay what thing good
> Pray'd for, but often proves our woe, our bane?
> I pray'd for Children.

The Chorus, whatever its ambivalance toward Samson, did not see him as ridiculous, though its presence reminded Samson of the fact. But Manoa insists relentlessly on the external view that mirrors what we know to be an internal torment:

> Select, and Sacred, Glorious for a while,
> The miracle of men: then in an hour
> Ensnar'd, assaulted, overcome, led bound,
> Thy Foes derision, Captive, Poor, and Blind
> Into a Dungeon thrust, to work with Slaves.

Those are hard words. They sing and proverb the great folly, and answer by specific demonstration the question the Chorus left politely unanswered. Manoa says nothing that the hero does not know, but (is it irrelevant to surmise?) Samson may need somebody to say this. Perhaps it is not too farfetched to think the same of Manoa's calling God's justice into question. So far we have had only one side of that matter, and this is a drama. Manoa's point of view is frankly personal: these were his prayers, his gifts, granted with pomp and solemnity, "desirable, to tempt." The loss, and even the ridicule, somehow seem chiefly his. And when he moves from the obviously personal complaint to the larger questioning of God's judgment, it still is plainly the special pleading, or complaint, of a passionate participant in a particular case.

It is easy to misjudge Manoa, especially if one is unacquainted with the Haggadah, or has never heard, on a grandfather's knee, the Old Testament God spoken of with respectful but authoritative familiarity. Manoa represents a people with an old, direct, and, as it were, family relationship to God; with no real history, even in error, not responding to or against that relationship. The certainty of the relationship makes possible unofficial latitude unthinkable or blasphemous in religions of more recent establishment. Milton's Manoa is complaining against God, and he can hardly be unaware, any more than Samson and the Chorus, of what he is doing. "For this did the Angel twice descend?" But lamentations are not inconsistent with true patience or true piety. He is transgressing and, I conjecture, he knows that God knows it, and that this is the grief of the father Manoa speaking, and not the piety of the son Manoa. Let me illustrate this from a brilliant fiction. In Mann's *Young Joseph* Jacob, grieving for his lost boy, has gone too far in expostulating with God. Eliezer calls him to task and Jacob replies:

Ah, thou God's-defender . . . Thou hypocrite . . . For what thou sayest I too could say, and thou knowest I am not duller of sense than thou. But I speak to Him otherwise, and even so am nearer to Him than thou! For one must defend God against His defenders, and protect Him against those who would protect Him. Thinkest thou He is a man, even of overwhelming power, and it is His side thou must espouse against me, a worm? When thou callest Him eternally great, thou utterest merely wind, if thou knowest not that God is still above God, still everlastingly above Himself, and will punish from above, where He is my healing and my reliance and where thou art not, if thou regardest thyself as between Him and me! [2]

Manoa, to Milton's credit, is complex, and I cannot present the whole case for my conjecture now.

Samson of course invokes the familiar and appropriate piety, even as a father to a son, or as the well to the feverish: "Appoint not heavenly disposition, Father." He defends heavenly justice by taking full responsibility for all the evils that have befallen him. The announcement is not new but the quality of the statement is. Previously the acknowledgment of guilt has been accompanied by private or public self-anger. But he defended himself against false guilt, as we noticed, with calm, dignified clarity, with justice toward himself. Now, defending, not himself but God against a false charge, the acknowledgment of responsibility rises to the level of presenting the whole case against himself, and passing judgment, with justice. It is an extraordinary performance, for he tells everything, all the intimate details of the bedroom folly, and he does this frankly and cleanly, to an embarrassing father, without suppression or excess. (If there were a trace of unheroic morbidity, I assume that we, as veteran human beings, could not possibly miss it.) The justice toward self and the suffering of tragic pressure are rewarded, if I may speak so, wtih a moral insight worthy of a great tragic hero:

> The base degree to which I now am fall'n,
> These rags, this grinding, is not yet so base
> As was my former servitude, ignoble,
> Unmanly, ignominious, infamous,
> True slavery, and that blindness worse then this,
> That saw not how degeneratly I serv'd.

We cannot pause to measure the progress of the hero, for much has been happening fast; and though this last step was a mighty one, the path, we know, still is long. We can, however, carry in our minds one unmistakable dramatic impression. It is this: Samson has reached the present high point of his forward motion by an intimately related series of small motions; the monologue gave us the most important inner potentialities, but they are being realized by the help — if misguided, or unintentional, or even hostile — of external challenge.

Manoa replies in a shocking descent from the objective "I" of the tragic hero to the subjective "I" of the comic parent repeating an ancient domestic pattern:

> I cannot praise thy Marriage choises, Son,
> Rather approv'd them not; but thou didst plead
> Divine impulsion prompting how thou might'st
> Find some occasion to infest our Foes.
> I state not that; this I am sure . . .

He acknowledges the suffering of Samson; it is enough and more than enough for the fault. But he is brief, and at the present stage, unemotional in his expression of the fact. He has a further suffering to reveal, the implications of which he is about to spell out. If he is not actually savoring the pleasure of pain, he has nevertheless made no effort to blunt the effect of his rhetorical presentation and the skillful approach to it. "A worse thing yet remains": the popular feast in praise of Dagon for the victory over Samson. Dagon will be *magnified* and God,

> Besides whom is no God, compar'd with Idols,
> Disglorifi'd, blasphem'd, and had in scorn
> By th' Idolatrous rout amidst thir wine;
> Which to have come to pass by means of thee,
> *Samson*, of all thy sufferings think the heaviest,
> Of all reproach the most with shame that ever
> Could have befall'n thee and thy Fathers house.

And that is the truth, even if the human voice that pronounces it is thin and weak; even if the rhythms are distressingly overpersonal,[3] and point and nag, like an inescapable voice out of a true bad dream of paternal pedagogy; even if the rhetorical clincher of the "father's house" is hoarded to the precious end.

Samson responds to the truth by acknowledging and dignifying it, and by something more. Manoa has revived the subject of the trust betrayed, and it has to be faced directly now; and not in terms of the relative proportions of strength and wisdom, nor even in terms of the promise ruined, the great exploits and the benefits to Abraham's race, nor in a metaphor of the foolish pilot shipwrecking. Samson goes beyond his personal failure, and beyond the failure of a national mission, to his failure as a representative, a champion, of God. He repeats, in humble confession, the truth of his father's judgment: he is responsible for the honor brought to Dagon and the dishonor brought to God. He adds, from his intimate knowledge as a former champion, specific details of the failure: he has encouraged "Idolists and Atheists" to open their mouths, has brought

> diffidence of God, and doubt
> In feeble hearts, propense anough before
> To waver, or fall off and joyn with Idols.

This failure toward his nation, this guilt, he accepts, and his own conscience produces the charge. This is the "chief affliction," the "anguish" of the soul which permits no sleep to the eye or rest to the thoughts. We have had to wait until now for this major expression of guilt, which has been brought out by the drama, by Manoa's unpleasantly personal but just charge, and by Samson's full acknowledgment, with voluntary additions .

He is not stimulated, or buoyed up, by this virtuoso justice toward the self. And no wonder. He has just achieved the psychological low point so far. Yet this performance, though perhaps less immediately impressive than the two previous demonstrations of justice toward the self, must be accounted a moral advance, and the high point so far. He has moved from defending himself against injustice to defending God against injustice, this latter by explaining his personal crime and accepting full responsibility for the personal punishment. Now he has moved to a full facing of his crime and its consequences, which exceed the personal and so, it may seem, the personal power to expiate by punishment, or to have any human relation to, except that of a despairing recognition. The high point of moral advance, then, is the low point of psychological retreat. It is not the time for full dramatic expression yet — that will come soon — but here we have the place marked, the point where the two lines cross.[4] What shall we call these lines, or is there a name? A Heraclitean way up and way down, where high point and low point are really the same if one has the wit to discover the unexpected by looking for it? Or should we say that the stubborn life of the self, upon which the life of the spirit has been steadily advancing, refusing despair and pronouncing justice, now has achieved the revelation of the spirit, the view that transcends self: which view is the enlarged despair the stubborn self was too witless, at first, or too wise to decipher? I like these questions but leave them.

Samson's answer to his revelation, not the full answer yet, is *withdrawal*. The temptation he refused from the Chorus, and that, in another form, he is about to refuse from his father, he now embraces for the moment and calls it hope:

> This only hope relieves me, that the strife
> With me hath end; all the contest is now

> 'Twixt God and *Dagon*; *Dagon* hath presum'd,
> Me overthrown, to enter lists with God,
> His Deity comparing and preferring
> Before the God of *Abraham*.

His piety is irreproachable; he is confident that God will soon "arise and his great name assert." It is irreproachable but not in character, and this play requires that one distinguish between common and heroic piety. And the hope that leans on God, as it should, cannot comfortably be linked with the champion's own hope for retirement. But his feeling, so natural and sharable, has not had any specific names put upon it. That is Manoa's office, to name the names, and to let Samson face his feeling as a proposal from without. Even a champion needs help from himself.[5]

Manoa seizes briskly on Samson's piety and interprets it as prophecy. Of course, God will not long "defer" His vindication, or allow the doubt "whether God be Lord." God will take care of God, nothing surer. But what of Samson? Manoa has plans for ransom. The Philistines may by now have satisfied their revenge; and besides, Samson being already in a state of broken retirement, "now no more canst do them harm." So there may be hope in Samson's hope.

Samson responds by clasping his guilt a little closer to him, in protection, as it were. It is not the whole guilt, for even a hero can hardly be capable of that feat as a continuous exercise. It is the crime of his "garrulity" that he offers, universally recognized as deserving contempt and scorn, the "mark of fool," exclusion as a "blab." And he has not kept "Gods counsel," a "holy secret." He deserves and prefers to "pay on" his punishment, to "expiate, if possible."

Manoa rises to the task of persuasion. It is the eloquent voice of ordinary morality, heightened by the special urgency of the father trying to confirm his son in the embrace of ordinary "hope":

> Be penitent and for thy fault contrite,
> But act not in thy own affliction, Son,
> Repent the sin, but if the punishment
> Thou canst avoid, self-preservation bids;
> Or th' execution leave to high disposal,

And let another hand, not thine, exact
Thy penal forfeit from thy self; perhaps
God will relent, and quit thee all his debt;
Who evermore approves and more accepts
(Best pleas'd with humble and filial submission)
Him who imploring mercy sues for life,
Then who self-rigorous chooses death as due;
Which argues over-just, and self-displeas'd
For self-offence, more then for God offended.

Who knows, the argument ends on a note of Belial-like hope, perhaps God already intends, not only to release you from "the strife," but to return you "Home to thy countrey and his sacred house," where you may expiate with offerings, prayers, and "vows renew'd," but at home.

The argument is a brilliant tissue of half-right and half-wrong. It would not be dramatically interesting, which it certainly is, if these were not truths misplaced. The main error, I think, is that the argument is founded on a special position of *self* (theological "presumption" masked as trust in God), and reasons from that base. With shrewd psychological casuistry it accuses Samson of being more concerned with the crime against self than the crime against God. Manoa, in addition to his authorized privilege as parent to stretch things for the seeming good of his son, is not without some justification. This is the way, inevitably, that heroic guilt looks to ordinary morality. Besides, Samson has just answered in terms of only part of his guilt, the garrulity; and Manoa, it has been plain, has missed the real point of Samson's "hope," as he has misjudged, or ignored, the moral stature of Samson's conduct. The audience has its privileged position too, and cannot mistake the true nature of Samson's guilt: it is for the crime against God. This is not to minimize from the very beginning the force and the necessity of the personal grief in Samson, but that has been serving — however grim that high point of moral revelation — neither self-preservation nor self-displeasure, but the dark and groping ways of the human discovery of God's justice. And the whole dramatic use of Manoa's argument is to exhibit for the audience the heroic nature of Samson's tragic guilt, which cannot possibly compound its crime against God by means of such self-comforting reasons. At the same time, the argument exhibits to Samson, and his audience, one set of positive consequences to the "hope" for withdrawal. Samson may not know what he wants to do, but he knows, with a knowledge deeper than thought or word, that he would rather sit still, as he is, than let his "hope" to be out of it lead him forward into new error, into a glib resumption of the life that would be moral death for him.

Samson makes no effort to meet his father's arguments in their own terms, which is just as well, and respectful of him. One may conjecture that Samson is, in a special way, exhausted or still shocked by the experience of the full moral vision. The answer on garrulity, while a good enough answer, was of a smaller dimension than we might have expected, a temporary recess in the forward movement. So what we get now is the first installment of a serious answer that has to get stated somewhere, and can serve best at this juncture to clarify a visible part of the moral issue raised by that expression of "hope."

First, inevitably from Samson, the affirmation of piety: he does implore God's pardon. But why should he seek life, to what "end"? (As a chosen athlete of God he had an end, now irretrievably lost. As a man, with a mere human character Miltonically conceived, he must have an end of being on earth, a burden of gifts to use and improve and make an accounting of. We remember the first intuition, the desire to know and *do*, of the protagonist in *Paradise Regained.*) What end can a self-ruined hero, fully facing his ruin, conceive of? The ruin must be faced before the question can be asked significantly, and the question must be asked, though in a blank personal darkness that seems the very landscape of despair, before any answer can become possible, before the personal darkness of death in life can be reversed.

Why should Samson seek life? He returns from the vision of the larger failure to the personal failure. He goes back to the stubborn self, back to the root, to draw moral strength from his weakness. It is a necessary gesture, now, before he can go on. He adds his version of what he was to those presented by the Chorus and Manoa.

156

In that happy springtime, when "great in hopes," and with "magnanimous thoughts," and "Full of divine instinct," and with "some
proof" already of his great promise, what end of life did he seek?
He swelled with pride "like a petty God," and fell into the trap of
"venereal trains" to soften in voluptuousness:

> At length to lay my head and hallow'd pledge
> Of all my strength in the lascivious lap
> Of a deceitful Concubine who shore me
> Like a tame Weather, all my precious fleece,
> Then turn'd me out ridiculous, despoil'd,
> Shav'n, and disarm'd among my enemies.

The self-contempt and the detachment of ridicule have not slackened, and he has not gone beyond them yet, as he must; but some
of the earlier intensity of feeling is not here. This is cold or cool;
there is no hating of self for the sake of self; the harsh comedy is
deliberate, and usefully serves his answer: having failed with all
these advantages, why should he try now? To what end? As an
argument against renewed life it is not very convincing, but it is
less an answer than a narrowing of the question. This, I think we
may say, has been made necessary by the high point of his moral
revelation and its aftereffect, the despairing "hope" to withdraw,
and by Manoa's turning of the negative motion within the self into
an attractive promise of an easy way out.

The Chorus, long silent, exercises its license to digress, and delivers a kind of musical-comedy aria on the theme of Samson's
alcoholic abstinence. It is one of the weaker moments of the drama,
serving chiefly to put a little time between the two parts of Samson's answer. But it is not quite irrelevant; besides anticipating
a turn at the end of the play, it does raise the larger question of
wholeness, the temperance which must be complete, and the
wholeness which includes the "end" of life and the being useful.

Why should he seek life? The personal failure, when everything
was most propitious, now is rounded out by a fuller vision of that
failure and the exhausted possibility of usefulness:

> Now blind, dishearten'd, sham'd, dishonour'd, quell'd,
> To what can I be useful, wherein serve

> My Nation, and the work from Heav'n impos'd,
> But to sit idle on the household hearth,
> A burdenous drone.

Withdrawal to the household hearth cannot attract him. Facing of
the full guilt revealed no means of full expiation, and here he is, an
unemployable hero, disheartened and useless. (It will take the
changing of only one term in that grim judgment to change everything.) The comic version of his past, that return to the root as a
moral reminder of the present, is now matched by an unsparing,
"comic" version of his future if he goes forward by withdrawing as
Manoa counsels:

> to visitants a gaze
> Or pitied object, these redundant locks
> Robustious to no purpose clustring down,
> Vain monument of strength; till length of years
> And sedentary numness craze my limbs
> To a contemptible old age obscure.

The sense of self in darkness exposed to light still is there, and
so is the sense of the ridiculousness and the indignity. But the
prophetic vision is less harsh, dealing, as it does, with natural facts,
and needing only to imagine the facts to reveal them as impossible.
Once it is said, it is clear that Samson will not embrace in domestic
familiarity these articulated terms of existence. If his life has no
apparent "end," neither can this be the "end" of death he seeks.
The desire for withdrawal, and "end" for him of the "strife," was a
legitimate human and personal error. But the visions of past and
future, both prophetic (in the old sense that prophecy reveals by
imagination the truth in either past or future), have helped define
what is not possible, and have helped define the heroic morality.
He is left still in his dark landscape, but he has not moved into
further error. He can see nothing beyond the blank facelessness of
undefined death, here in slavery where he earns his bread (a remarkably stubborn small fact of existence and a sign of his character). That death, still undefined, is "oft-invocated," still his only
"hope," and "the welcom end of all my pains." That death would

seem to represent complete withdrawal of the human spirit and mind. But Samson being Samson, this cannot be so.

> A little onward lend thy guiding hand
> To these dark steps, a little further on.

Manoa replies, but he has already done his best. Samson on a moral plateau still is distinguished, but his father tires fast, and the moral thinness and commonness at the heart of his best speech now lies on the surface. It is better, he says, to stay at home unemployed, and "bed-rid," and old, than serve the Philistines. He refuses to give up hope, though it is a glib and facile hope (and he indicates later some self-consciousness, which complicates both his role and our understanding of his character). It is as easy for God to restore sight as to produce a fountain; and Manoa persuades himself that the miracle will happen, for why else should the strength still remain in Samson's hair?

> His might continues in thee not for naught,
> Nor shall his wondrous gifts be frustrate thus.

It is a facile hopefulness, all right for a father but impossible for a tragic hero, and it emphasizes again the gap between their moral natures. That is part of the drama and we are supposed to see it. But we should also see that Manoa is voicing, for the first time in the drama, the present fact of remaining strength as a fact that belongs to the future as well as the past. For all his prophetic clarity and superior moral vision, Samson cannot see this. Nor should he yet, for Manoa's hope would be corrupting to him. But it is not corrupting to Manoa, or to the complicated rhythm of dramatic movement unfolding.

The gap between common and heroic morality looks both ways. This observation, and the question to follow, would be irrelevant to *Paradise Regained*, where the gap exists chiefly for the hero. But that is a different drama. In this drama may we not relevantly ask whether the two kinds of morality are not intimately dependent on each other? The question is not one of superiority but of relationship, necessary, reciprocal relationship. It is not a question usually asked of Milton's work, and so even a minor relevance gains added importance from that historical fact.

Samson has two reactions to his father's jarring hopefulness, which "seems a tune" indeed, as the Chorus will say in its lyric study of patience, "Harsh, and of dissonant mood from his complaint." The first reaction is a direct, and limited, expression of the feeling released at the moral high point of recognizing the full guilt. This high point, which I am calling the low point of psychological retreat, returns to the dark weariness at the very opening of the play; but with a more articulate self-consciousness, and with a rhythm hardly less burnt-out, expressing an exhaustion more than physical, and *now* without any discernible inner movement of hopeful responsiveness to feeling. Samson does not expect restored light, but "double darkness"; the presage is not even recorded as a hope, but as a mere fact of feeling. The "genial spirits droop," nature seems "weary of herself":

> My race of glory run, and race of shame,
> And I shall shortly be with them that rest.

Manoa responds with a cheerful and confident lecture on psychology, and analyzes away the gloomy "suggestions." His tone so jars against the authoritative tone of the hero that it is hard not to be angry with him, or to laugh. One indulges both, I suppose, and the drama certainly profits by this minor and superficial diversion from the unrelenting heroism of Samson's profound seriousness. Manoa has his light too, and we must respect it, however unwillingly. He is no hero, and he has a full human share of pride and resentment. There is a touch also of something like envy for his great son, perhaps nothing that requires invoking the name of Freud, but something common and domestic. Besides, it is the son and not the father who received God's blessing, and the father's loss therefore has this further complication. (One thinks of the iconographic tradition of painting Joseph a little off to the side, the eyes thoughtful and sad as he looks at or away from his son.) He has his moral obligation too: he

> Must not omit a Fathers timely care
> To prosecute the means of thy deliverance
> By ransom or how else.

These considerations (and some interesting developments later)
justify in a modest human way his limited vision, and exempt it
from severe, unqualified criticism. He is not heroic or tragic, but
he is not corrupt. He serves the drama of Samson better than he
knows; and he is elevated at the end *by* Samson, who draws up
the other vision toward his. Manoa serves, and he has to be there,
as he is, in order to be drawn up.

With the departure of Manoa what he has begun can move to
an important stage of fulfillment. In his second reaction to Manoa's
hopefulness, Samson bursts into a lyric lament which recalls, as it
is meant to, the lament for the loss of sight. The similarities and
the differences are instructive. There is no strenuous concern, as
there was before, over the personal indignity, the contempt and
folly. A minor factual statement at the end is overshadowed by the
major statement, the sense of desertion by God. The hopelessness
continues unmitigated, but not in terms of darkness as death. It is
the hopelessness of the desertion, and this thought goes beyond
the thoughts of living death and fixes on plain, undefined death
as the only imaginable remedy. We have nothing now quite like the
abstract imagining of the light not seen as silence. Instead, Milton
combines that terrible order of imagination with the kind of excru-
ciatingly physical imagination that considered sight in terms of
the "tender ball . . . So obvious and so easie to be quench't." For
the subject during most of the first two sections of the lyric is the
torment of mind, the physical hurt of thought, the idea of pain as
pain. I quote the first two sections:

> O that torment should not be confin'd
> To the bodies wounds and sores
> With maladies innumerable
> In heart, head, brest, and reins;
> But must secret passage find
> To th' inmost mind,
> There exercise all his fierce accidents,
> And on her purest spirits prey,

> As on entrails, joints, and limbs,
> With answerable pains, but more intense,
> Though void of corporal sense.
>   My griefs not only pain me
> As a lingring disease,
> But finding no redress, ferment and rage,
> Nor less then wounds immedicable
> Ranckle, and fester, and gangrene,
> To black mortification.
> Thoughts my Tormenters arm'd with deadly stings
> Mangle my apprehensive tenderest parts,
> Exasperate, exulcerate, and raise
> Dire inflammation which no cooling herb
> Or medcinal liquor can asswage,
> Nor breath of Vernal Air from snowy *Alp*.
> Sleep hath forsook and giv'n me o're
> To deaths benumming Opium as my only cure.
> Thence faintings, swounings of despair,
> And sense of Heav'ns desertion.

We must add the quality of this detachment to the other kinds of detachment we have noted in Samson. (To review briefly: the cold distance in tension with self-hatred, the cool detachment without hatred, the public objectivity of justice toward the self.) This is lyric and not concerned with justice, and not concerned with others. The detachment is not the other side of self-hatred, for there is nothing here that we should call hate; and yet there is an intensity of feeling raised to the highest pitch, as far beyond hate as it is beyond the personal. We need perhaps only to mark its height, and to recognize that the great height of this "impersonal" feeling matches the revelation of guilt which exceeded personal power to respond to, except by thoughts of despair and death.

But Samson is *trying* to respond, and the agony of mind that so struggles to express itself is not lost in despair. It is willing to go back, it must, to try again, whether to find some possibility missed, for it would suffer everything possible; or whether to suffer through to something beyond the impersonal, something that can be responded to or will grant response. Samson's capacity to feel, that sign of the essential self, is a thread of strength without which the whole moral fabric would be impossible. And a kind of resolution, or the beginning of a resolution, is suffered through to, is reached. It is a human hope, a human feeling that descends from the awful agony of mind. The hope is not available, but it is expressed and returned to, if only as desire, a human longing for that "breath of Vernal Air from snowy *Alp*." [6] The familiar though distant reaches of human feeling are returned to, after the terrible grandeur of suffering which strains at the limits of the human, the thoughts that "Mangle my apprehensive tenderest parts." In the return there is a kind of calm, as after an exhausting imaginative effort that rose to a limit and touched it. The source of his agony is the thought of God's trust betrayed. He has named that, and now he has named the end, which lies beyond the suffering of consciousness, beyond human capacity to feel except as non-feeling: the "faintings," the "swounings of despair," the "sense of Heav'ns desertion."

There is no place further to go. Having reached the end, and named it, he is thrown back on the beginning, on God. This has been the end of all the great personal effort, to recognize completely his human helplessness. The struggle of the self toward human justice has arrived at the overwhelming sense of divine justice. Zenith and nadir confront each other. If divine justice indifferently exists in an order completely separate from the human, then we have had the tragic experience. For Samson can go no further in the direction he has gone. Further personal effort will still be required, but on a different level, penetrating no further, but proving the clear possession of the limit reached. The forward motion attains one end here, with the full facing of the guilt. But that end is more than a limit to be held; it is also a new beginning that turns to and is met by the final end. For though Samson can advance no further toward divine justice, divine justice can advance toward him.

The human and personal become possible again. Samson goes back once more, but on a different, a quieter, level. He reviews his history still another time, but there are no further clues, nothing still beyond the one "hope" left, the "one prayer" for death. The detachment is without passion, without irony; there is a kind of calm, perhaps a kind of resignation, in the recounting. The justice toward self, here again briefly demonstrated, now approaches quite directly the subject of divine justice. It is the hero's one contribution to the other side of the dramatic theme, the case against God. But it is presented as a fact of the history, a fact that must be articulated, though not as complaint, in order that the dramatic expression of justice may be complete:

> But now hath cast me off as never known,
> And to those cruel enemies,
> Whom I by his appointment had provok't
> Left me all helpless with th' irreparable loss
> Of sight.

It is a fact, here modestly but impressively stated; it stands between Manoa's version and the great choral extension which is to follow.

The turning of the play has been occurring here. It has been occurring for a long exploratory time, ever since the hero faced up to the full revelation of his guilt. And now, finally, we are to come out of the deepest darkness. But even now there is one further exploration of the darkness to be made. The Chorus begins by considering patience, "the truest fortitude." The conclusion has a bearing on Samson's experience as we have been following it. Patience, though learnedly and persuasively praised by the wise, "Little prevails" with the afflicted,

> Unless he feel within
> Some sourse of consolation from above;
> Secret refreshings, that repair his strength,
> And fainting spirits uphold.

Samson has been brave in his patience, and just, but he has reached this impasse. All his progress brought him to this place and the knowledge of it. The Chorus, offering its comment from outside, can speak less hopefully than Manoa but less hopelessly than Samson. There is no bright promise of light in the "Unless," but there is a little glimmer. And in the prolonged darkness of the present landscape that glimmer marks the way up out of darkness.

But first the Chorus matches, in its elevated intensity of detachment, the lyric on the torment of mind. This is the play's great statement against divine justice, the full, short human view of the human condition. And though God is not tied "to his own prescript," yet if His ways *are* "justifiable to Men," *if* divine justice is not indifferent to human justice, then the great statement can be made, in a play, only if it is answerable. And it would not be worth making at all if it did not offer the challenge of a great statement.

> God of our Fathers, what is man!
> That thou towards him with hand so various,
> Or might I say contrarious,
> Temperst thy providence through his short course,
> Not evenly, as thou rul'st
> The Angelic orders and inferiour creatures mute,
> Irrational and brute.
> Nor do I name of men the common rout,
> That wandring loose about
> Grow up and perish, as the summer flie,
> Heads without name no more rememberd,
> But such as thou hast solemnly elected,
> With gifts and graces eminently adorn'd
> To some great work, thy glory,
> And peoples safety, which in part they effect:
> Yet toward these thus dignifi'd, thou oft
> Amidst thir highth of noon,
> Changest thy countenance, and thy hand with no regard
> Of highest favours past
> From thee on them, or them to thee of service.
> Nor only dost degrade them, or remit
> To life obscur'd, which were a fair dismission,
> But throw'st them lower then thou didst exalt them high,
> Unseemly falls in human eie,
> Too grievous for the trespass or omission,
> Oft leav'st them to the hostile sword
> Of Heathen and prophane, thir carkasses
> To dogs and fowls a prey, or else captiv'd:
> Or to the unjust tribunals, under change of times,
> And condemnation of the ingrateful multitude.
> If these they scape, perhaps in poverty
> With sickness and disease thou bow'st them down,

> Painful diseases and deform'd,
> In crude old age;
> Though not disordinate, yet causless suffring
> The punishment of dissolute days, in fine,
> Just or unjust, alike seem miserable,
> For oft alike, both come to evil end.

This also reviews history, a history in which Samson appears as one in a community of heroes, a community sharing the same evils with the less privileged. Having said the worst, the Chorus, like Samson, suffers through to a kind of resolution. As in Samson's lyric, the hope lies in the return to human feeling after the grandeur of suffering which strains the limits of the human and reaches beyond the human capacity for any response but despair. The theme of human hope half expressed by Samson, and then as a negative thing not available, turns at this most surprising moment into the direct lyric statement:

> So deal not with this once thy glorious Champion,
> The Image of thy strength, and mighty minister.
> What do I beg? how hast thou dealt already?
> Behold him in this state calamitous, and turn
> His labours, for thou canst, to peaceful end.

This tender human voice gently enters the play as something new. We have not heard it, we cannot mistake it, we shall certainly not doubt or resist it. The hope, the prayer expressed, is the right one, making its way without argument between the two extremes of hope expressed by Manoa and Samson. It is fully human in feeling but approaches the divine with purer vision than Samson, and with an undisturbed sense of the relation between human and divine justice. It prays only for "peaceful end," without names or conditions. It points the way up. I cannot forbear adding that the unheroic Chorus, like Manoa, is capable of seeing and feeling what still lies beyond the hero's vision.

A LITTLE FURTHER ON

DALILA appears on the dramatic horizon, gloriously rigged, "With all her bravery on, and tackle trim." A new range of the drama is now to be entered, and the tone veers like a wind in a new direction. We have had some small signs of warning, but now we are in full motion again. The comic, which was present without laughter in some of Samson's lofty, solitary eying of himself (the comic strained to an extreme, perhaps uncharted, range), and was present with uneasy but familiar laughter in the paternal display of unheroic, domestic differences, now enters with a new and fuller role to contribute. The gorgeous Dalila sweeps forward, and is hailed by the Chorus with all the fine sensuous excesses men respond to in, or attribute to, a beautiful ship. The comic has entered as part of the new expression of human feeling in the play. The Chorus, which gave the first full voice to that feeling, both introduces Dalila and makes the last comments. The choral view is human and unheroic. That view, which in the last scene pointed the way for Samson and expressed what was beyond his heroic vision, will now prove, as the rhythm of dramatic unfolding alters, to see less than Samson and to see more slowly.

The ship is transformed into something even fairer, and the Chorus responds as if enchanted:

> Yet on she moves, now stands & eies thee fixt,
> About t' have spoke, but now, with head declin'd

167

> Like a fair flower surcharg'd with dew, she weeps
> And words addrest seem into tears dissolv'd,
> Wetting the borders of her silk'n veil.

Nor is the magic charm of the beautiful woman coming submissive
interrupted by Dalila's words, which only confirm what the Chorus
described. The words and the movement of the words offer sympathy, more intimate, private, individual, than the best effort by
the Chorus. The voice is the voice longed for by the heart of grief,
perhaps the remembered voice of the mother, perhaps the deli-
cious voice imagined in a dream of the self consoling the self. It
is also the female voice Juvenal naughtily described as having
fingers.

The charm is raucously broken by Samson: "Out, out, *Hyaena*;
these are thy wonted arts." He gives her no benefit of doubt, and
brusquely pushes aside the principle of generous forgiveness. The
talent for ridicule, which has had no object thus far but himself,
enjoys the exercise of a different kind of detachment as he presents
the domestic comedy of the false wife repenting between decep-
tions.

To this harsh unreasonableness Dalila replies in the voice and
style of calm reason, soft and humble. But the style subtly changes
when she gets past her preamble of admissions. "To what I did thou
shewdst me first the way." She is brazenly right, as right as Eve
was when she too used the argument she had lost the moral right
to use. It is a maneuver to undermine justice in a relativism of injustice, and the claims of weakness to human generosity are ad-
vanced less as an argument than as a lesson in humiliation:

> E're I to thee, thou to thy self wast cruel.
> Let weakness then with weakness come to parl
> So near related, or the same of kind.

She warms to her subject and moves to a better argument — for
showing her talents. What if love caused what she did? History,
masculine chivalry, the bewildered efforts of well-meaning love, a
pitiful self-dramatization of Dalila "Wailing thy absence in my
widow'd bed" — all are woven into a brilliant demonstration that
is less argument than insult. She intended Samson to be, like a hero

of a popular song, "Mine and Loves prisoner, not the *Philistines*."
The relativism comes in again, like an underlying theme:

> These reasons in Loves law have past for good,
> Though fond and reasonless to some perhaps;
> And Love hath oft, well meaning, wrought much wo,
> Yet always pity or pardon hath obtain'd.

Samson is more impressed by her art than by the insults pretending to be arguments. He infers that she has come, not in "feign'd
remorse," as he at first charged, but in "malice." His answer is the
answer of justice toward the self, the answer which brought him
to the great impasse but is now suddenly useful again:

> I gave, thou say'st, th' example,
> I led the way; bitter reproach, but true,
> I to my self was false e're thou to me,
> Such pardon therefore as I give my folly,
> Take to thy wicked deed.

And Samson's own judgment of himself he describes, not inaptly,
as "Impartial, self-severe, inexorable." The relativistic plea of
weakness, available as excuse for even the worst crimes, receives
this harsh judgment: "All wickedness is weakness." (Samson's own
crime, he has said, was if not impious at least weak.) So Samson
answers with justice toward the self, with a hard moral judgment,
with the meeting of insult by insult, and with one thing more. The
argument of love, though a hoax, he cannot let pass, whether because of the dignity of the subject, or because of his own personal
involvement. He answers in a different way, with the simple reasoning of the heart: "Love seeks to have Love."

The second argument of Dalila *is* an argument, with no discernible surface insult, but with a drift more dangerous than insult.
What she did she did out of concern for the community, besieged
as she was by magistrates, princes, and priests,

> Sollicited, commanded, threatn'd, urg'd,
> Adjur'd by all the bonds of civil Duty
> And of Religion, press'd how just it was,
> How honourable, how glorious to entrap
> A common enemy, who had destroy'd
> Such numbers of our Nation: and the Priest

Was not behind, but ever at my ear,
Preaching how meritorious with the gods
It would be to ensnare an irreligious
Dishonourer of *Dagon.*

Only her love silently held out, until she yielded herself to a higher love of truth and duty, which "Took full possession" of her. The bawdy image is more revealing than honest; for this is a monstrous public seduction by the "grave authority" of common, public morality, which commands hard cash and a cold passion. It has many faces; Manoa sketched the suggestions of a few; this one is called, "to the public good / Private respects must yield."

This is a hard pill for Samson to swallow. He has mastered the most humiliating ridicule of self, Dalila's external view insidiously associating itself with, the nails intimately caressing, his internal view. He has mastered that by accepting the truth of it. The fact of his guilt is the acknowledged *weakness* that is a demonstrated source of moral *strength.* He has accepted the truth in terms of justice toward self: which dissociates her from that truth, since it is not justice she wants. But now she has returned with a more insidious intimacy, her own version of justice toward self. It is a version that illuminates, with a marvelous intricacy of reflection and shadow, Samson's image of self-justice.

Dalila's gift of beauty was not "proportiond ill" with wisdom; it was not "Proudly secure," but did "subserve where wisdom bears command." She did not go her independent way, trusting the "intimate impulse" of inspiration. She did not stand aloof, or walk like a petty goddess, "admir'd of all and dreaded." When her mute deeds offered deliverance to the community, and Philistia, unlike Israel, acknowledged those deeds and thought them "worth notice," Dalila associated herself with the good of the community, which was identical with the good of Dagon. Her love, that personal, individual, heroic force, did not divert her finally from the impersonal duty, civil and religious. For justice, honor, and glory, for Dagon and "the public good," she has become, if not a champion of her god, at the very least a holy harlot, the truest servant of her god and people.

170

It is a hard pill for Samson. It is not only self-justice that is being challenged by this parody, but the justice of Samson's God and community, which are being defeated and swallowed by a cynical relativism. Samson's God has chosen to work through the individual and through individual inspiration: which may be earned and deserved by the individual, but cannot be taken for granted without peril, cannot be generalized by a convenience of analogy, cannot be institutionalized in a permanent formula of "public good," for inspiration *is* individual. The truth is common to all, if they are able to see it and act it. Ordinary, unheroic morality, like that of Manoa or the Chorus, may, at some levels or stages, even see further than heroic morality, and may help. The truth which is common must be commonly available, otherwise ordinary morality could not be elevated by the tragic experience. Still, in Milton's view the wisdom of the people is a dubious and shifty one. As public wisdom it is external, a hodgepodge of proved inner truth and the various degrees of accommodation made to external pressures. But the wisdom of the heart is not dubious, and its knowledge is clear to both orders of morality. But the wisdom of the heart is public only insofar as the public is composed of individuals able to respond *individually* to the common truth.

Philistia is institutionalized morality. The princes and magistrates represent, not surprisingly, the convenient good, which also represents them. The priests, like their god, represent public good. There is no gap between the two orders of morality, they are identical, and there is no consciousness of anything missed. Philistia has usurped the essential right of the individual to his truth. Philistia says *it* is truth, and that truth is public good, a mystery not to be examined. Dalila has been debauched by that "grave authority" — or this would be so if we could believe her. But it is time that I stopped interpreting for Samson and Milton. Samson has a direct reply to the challenge.

He has no intention of accepting this humiliation. He has anticipated that "feign'd Religion" would be where her "circling wiles" would end. (He is not entirely right; her circle has not closed yet.) The hypocritical claims of false religion he answers by the reason-

171

ing of the heart. If her love had been sincere, it would have "taught"
her "Far other reasonings, brought forth other deeds." He chose
her from among his enemies,

> lov'd thee, as too well thou knew'st,
> Too well, unbosom'd all my secrets to thee,
> Not out of levity, but over-powr'd
> By thy request, who could deny thee nothing.

We have had several versions and partial versions before, but none
quite like this. It is possible, I suppose, to say that Samson is making an argumentative point and is not literally accountable here.
But the point is too important for Samson to cheat now; he has
earned, by strenuous demonstrations, the right to be believed.
This must be the point implied, but passed over for whatever reason, in his explanation of the second marriage. He told the Chorus,
"I thought it lawful from my former act." But why Samson should
have confused intuition with analogy he did not say. We sus-
pected, from that extraordinary act and from something in his
tone as he spoke of Dalila, that he had rationalized a "motion" from
self, and that he had here symbolically violated the trust of God.
Now I think we can be sure. What is more important is that this
hero of self-justice has found one further thing to reveal and face.
It adds little to the guilt, though something to the clarity. And from
his human weakness of love, though it led, in a motion counter to
hers, to the highest betrayal, he can quote as argument the common wisdom of the heart.

A wife leaves, for her husband, both parents and country. And
this human law was not abrogated by any other natural law, or law
of nations, or national law (except the unpublished one, with the
multiple blank lines, called "public good"). For he was not their
subject, owed no duty to them, received no protection from them [1]
or their laws, and she was under his protection. Therefore,

> if aught against my life
> Thy countrey sought of thee, it sought unjustly,
> Against the law of nature, law of nations,
> No more thy countrey, but an impious crew
> Of men conspiring to uphold thir state

By worse then hostile deeds, violating the ends
For which our countrey is a name so dear;
Not therefore to be obey'd.

That is the answer which moves from love to law to national justice. The relativism of illegal, unlimited power over the individual is turned back on itself as a definition of no community but "an impious crew." As for the religious relativism:

To please thy gods thou didst it; gods unable
To acquit themselves and prosecute their foes
But by ungodly deeds, the contradiction
Of their own deity, Gods cannot be:
Less therefore to be pleas'd, obey'd, or fear'd.

The church that has identified itself with that state can share the same definition.

There is a little transition, on a different level, of some domestic comedy, the mere he and she of it. Then Dalila makes her third argument. She does not debate, offers no virtuoso lessons in humiliation; she offers her last wile, her best and first one. She pleads folly and asks forgiveness and the chance to help undo her error. It is the secret voice of self-pity again, but now coupled with a promise that is not secret:

only what remains past cure
Bear not too sensibly, nor still insist
To afflict thy self in vain: though sight be lost,
Life yet hath many solaces, enjoy'd
Where other senses want not their delights
At home in leisure and domestic ease,
Exempt from many a care and chance to which
Eye-sight exposes daily men abroad.
I to the Lords will intercede, not doubting
Thir favourable ear, that I may fetch thee
From forth this loathsom prison-house, to abide
With me, where my redoubl'd love and care
With nursing diligence, to me glad office,
May ever tend about thee to old age
With all things grateful chear'd, and so suppli'd,
That what by me thou hast lost thou least shalt miss.

Like Manoa, she is giving him a chance to withdraw, though now

173

to the mistress-mother. It is a further chance to go back, to review his history in deed as well as thought, to withdraw the way he withdrew. The attraction is most physical, like mere undefined death, and earlier themes are recalled for comparison. The comforts of sight, which (in the lament for blindness) might have eased his grief, are available through the other senses. And here is a chance to withdraw from unsheltered exposure to the "real darkness of the body." Here is "balm," promised in a honied voice. Here is an "end" that is another "cure." Here he can sleep, as if by "deaths benumming Opium." And she concludes with her best moral horror: "That what by me thou hast lost thou least shalt miss." That comes close to pure human evil, a naked desire to have power over another, regardless. (And it makes impossible any sympathetic interpretation of Dalila as behaving so because her sincere first approach was harshly spurned; no one could conjure up this horror out of mere anger: it had to be there.)

Samson's answer begins mildly, even weakly:

> No, no, of my condition take no care;
> It fits not; thou and I long since are twain.

That lacks the firmness of a moral hero.[2] It sounds like mere miserable man, who is touched, or has remembered how he felt when an old tune sounded. And this may be the last chance to fulfill the hope of hopelessness. But he snaps back; once was enough. The sense of his folly is a protection. His weakness now, remembering how he was used in the "flower of youth and strength," serves in this extreme — if we may judge by what he says — better than heroic justice toward self. He has won all the fine big arguments in the open; but still, by some dark favor granted him, the sense of his human helplessness, which brought him to the brink of despair, now stands between him and utter defeat. He will not descend down the scale of creation to the comfortable unconsciousness of an order "Irrational and brute."

The voice having failed, the hand would try. Samson must use another "illegitimate" persuasion; if she touches him "fierce remembrance" may wake his rage to tear her "joint by joint." She may have her forgiveness, and her conscience, at a distance.

174

The comic opening of the scene begins to return to the same kind of tone. Dalila makes her final salute to the relativism of things: fame is "double-mouth'd," and she will be a heroine among her people, if not among the circumcised, celebrated in song, her tomb a shrine, and no less famous than that Hebrew heroine famous for the same kind of achievement.

> Nor shall I count it hainous to enjoy
> The public marks of honour and reward
> Conferr'd upon me, for the piety
> Which to my countrey I was judg'd to have shewn.
> At this who ever envies or repines
> I leave him to his lot, and like my own.

And so she leaves with one final snappy flip of the skirt.

Why did she come? We do not need to raise the question for the Chorus or Manoa, and perhaps not for Harapha. The first two have a natural and human motivation for coming which explains itself without question, and the drama then sees to it that there is no later need to imagine the question. But Dalila, unless we credit her with sincere arguments, had no such self-explanatory reason for coming. The moral drama needs her, of course, but that is no motivation. Her coming has to be explained by her character, which will do it, and perhaps by something in Samson.

Samson has the special mark upon him, no less distinguished among men than the early signs of his great blessing. Now it is the great curse, the enormity of his crime, not against man but God, the betrayal of God's blessing and trust; and signalized now by the great punishment, the abandonment by God, and the heroic suffering. In this way he is of course like Oedipus; and also perhaps in the sense he conveys of something *further*, some special transmission possible to human beings through the endurance of suffering which exceeds the human, and may betoken, like great blessing, an intimate link between human and divine. There is another response which Samson evokes or attracts, an ambivalence or direct hostility even from friends and father. I do not know what it is, whether a common resentment against too great a distinction, too great a blessing or curse, whether a desire for a scapegoat, or whether a curious desire to poke at the ruined mystery of something great, or whether something without a name. But Samson attracts. Finally he attracts a whole audience of Philistines.

But what of Dalila's character? Is there any destiny in it? Samson says she came out of malice, and that God sent her to "debase" him and "aggravate" his folly. (God's "motives" are, we may guess, those of the moral drama; Samson is being quite detached in this remark, accepting his due punishment; but a moral theologian would recognize the punishment and Samson's acceptance as a constructive lesson in humility.) As one looks back at Dalila's behavior, and not only as it is revealed at the end, "malice" would seem a fair diagnosis. But though that and the divine purpose are enough to satisfy Samson, the burden of our perspective requires us to press a little further. We can see, and pause to see, the peculiar forms her humiliation of him took: the undermining of justice in a relativism of weakness, a relativism of national and divine duty, the significant counter-version of Dalila's self-justice, the invitation to turn humility and helplessness into the haven of withdrawal in spiritual death. For the audience the concept of malice is neither comprehensive enough nor specific enough.

The national persuasion convinces us more as a moral symbol, which Dalila represents, than as the cause of her action. And the motivation for the return of Dalila is reinforced by, becomes a part of, the dramatizing of the character that acted in the first place. She contributes to this drama of divine justice the feminine symbol of injustice. She acts from personal will, for which "the public good" is a reciprocating justification. Her character is dominated by vanity and self-love, cut off from the natural and rational order, needing to subvert and to continue to subvert, for she suffers from the spiritual death which has lost the freedom to do good. Her love must be the love of power, including the minor loves of money, fame, and honor. She demonstrates the love of knowledge-as-power more literally than it can be demonstrated in the Garden of Eden or the desert. She associates herself with false civil and religious justice, exacting an unnatural obedience from the individual. She acts out a subversion of domestic justice by the power she gains over her husband with her weapons of words and sexual sorcery. But the sense of power is not secure; it must go back to try again, to see whether any possibility remains for further reassurance and nourishment. When she meets moral and intellectual resistance, she falls back to her greatest argument.

But Samson refuses to come to permanent terms with his guilt, to accept a remarriage of untrue minds.[3] He has already purged himself, by word and act and non-act, of the dominant image of Dalila in him. For he too shared that fatal likeness to the feminine symbol of injustice: the vanity of the warrior-athlete, his beauty of strength, that "garland briefer than a girl's."[4]

The Chorus, after a brief and human emphasis on the "strange power" of beauty and love, a reminder of the impression Dalila has maintained right up to the end, continues in a comic tone that completes the episode as it began. The themes of the Miltonic light verse are woman and domestic justice, themes which, whether personal for Milton or not, are entirely relevant, as the comic tone is relevant, for it is to emerge soon into a broader statement.

> It is not vertue, wisdom, valour, wit,
> Strength, comliness of shape, or amplest merit
> That womans love can win or long inherit;
> But what it is, hard is to say,
> Harder to hit,
> (Which way soever men refer it)
> Much like thy riddle, Samson, in one day
> Or seven, though one should musing sit.

THE GUIDING HAND

THE departure of the defeated Dalila has not left
Samson profoundly shaken, as he was when Manoa left. He has
discovered no "end" for his life or death, but he has not moved into
new error or renewed old error. The major revelation of his guilt
has not been extended or deepened, except by the small further
revelation that his love *was* an independent "motion" from self, and
not dependent upon the mission that was his "end of being." But
that further exploration of weakness now has helped. His love gave
him a sure basis for the most telling arguments; and when the
arguments of reason faltered, the weakness acknowledged and
fully understood provided a defense against the pull which had
been too strong before, and still exerted a force below the level
of argument or even justice. The margin of escape may finally
have been small — which is better for drama than for rational essays in ethical theory — but it was positive and clear. The effort
exacted from the hero was less than before; his own feelings were
less complicated; he has come through the trial more clearly the
master of himself and his condition. We have had no great tragic insights, like those evoked by Manoa, but they have not been needed.
The drama has turned; if the action has not told us this, the tone
should have made us feel it.

Harapha enters, whether on holiday excursion, or morbid pil-
grimage, whatever "wind hath blown him hither." He speaks,

178

rather over-articulately, and is answered by a remarkable piece of brevity: "The way to know were not to see but taste." Something has happened suddenly, a positive new motion in the drama. In the exchange that follows then, Samson answers the insult aimed at his external humiliation, not by patient self-justice, not by any heroic acceptance, rejection, or discrimination thus far demonstrated; he answers with a direct challenge. The dramatic surprise convinces. The terms and the timing could not have been anticipated, but have been completely prepared for. I quote the passage, for the spirit displayed and for the details:

> Therefore without feign'd shifts let be assign'd
> Some narrow place enclos'd, where sight may give thee,
> Or rather flight, no great advantage on me;
> Then put on all thy gorgeous arms, thy Helmet
> And Brigandine of brass, thy broad Habergeon,
> Vant-brass and Greves, and Gauntlet, add thy Spear
> A weavers beam, and seven-times-folded shield,
> I only with my Oak'n staff will meet thee,
> And raise such out-cries on thy clatter'd Iron,
> Which long shall not with-hold me from thy head,
> That in a little time while breath remains thee,
> Thou oft shalt wish thy self at *Gath* to boast
> Again in safety what thou wouldst have done
> To *Samson*, but shalt never see *Gath* more.

The most important fact in the speech is the return of inspiration. This could not have been prepared for, but inspiration has been mentioned enough, and now it is occurring out of some "intimate impulse" that does not contradict reason but runs ahead of it. The moral progress that led to the revelation of his helplessness, the tragic insight into the nature of his moral blindness, the articulated "hope" of withdrawal but the refusal of propositions for withdrawal, the proved acceptance that turns to use his blind helplessness — these are the grounds from which the unpredictable inspiration springs. In his challenge he has come to terms with the physical blindness; he has invented conditions that permit him to be a champion again, and in a comic scene of his own setting,

179

where the blind fool armed with a trivial weapon can arrange a redistribution of motley.

The inspiration has a further stage to go, and Harapha obligingly furnishes the bridge for Samson by charging him, as diversion, with "black enchantments." What began as private provocation, and then became a formal challenge to combat, advances to the final stage. "My trust is in the living God" — that is the natural and truthful answer to any question concerning the source of Samson's strength. That answer did not have to raise the challenge from a private affair to a trial between the champion of God and the champion of Dagon. But somehow it has happened, and the slight external chain serves chiefly to suggest the great happenings in Samson's mind and heart.

We have been tracing him on his dark paths and keeping a rough record of the turns in his journey. We can believe easily that Harapha is no temptation for Samson but a stimulant. After the hard intellectual and moral work inside, the digging in wounds and guilt, the active and strenuous passivity of not acting but not withdrawing; after the embracing of humiliation and helplessness by the free choice of inner necessity, here comes the muscular Harapha to sniff about the ruins of the old champion whose spirit, we know, is not ruined. The challenge of muscles is easy and welcome, a gift of refreshment after the torture of mind. And Samson's answer rises like a gift of lyric simplicity out of the long, torturing struggle with the inner self. He has earned the gift, but we could not have predicted it, and our tracing of the path could not have anticipated that he would move from his hope of withdrawal from the "strife" to this direct resumption. We believe that he has been inspired, as we believe that the suffering and the redemptive pattern of moral action have led him to this point.

The circle has led him from the low point of psychological retreat to this high point of psychological advance. But the moral circle has not yet completed itself back to the high point again. Harapha represents a station on the way, well on the way, but not there yet. Some review of old themes is now in order, and they are introduced both as measure of the present state and as measure of the development the themes have undergone.

First Samson must hear from the enemy a repetition of his own chief anguish, the sense of God's desertion. It comes as objective record of the facts: God has cut him off and delivered him up. There is an echo of Samson's own "To what can I be useful, wherein serve?" Harapha taunts his grinding among the slaves and asses: "As good for nothing else, no better service / With those thy boyst'rous locks." Samson has ridiculed himself as being shorn and shaven of his "precious fleece," and Harapha quips that he is not worthy of the sword, "But by the Barbers razor best subdu'd."

These are well-turned insults, and have the advantage of having been on the hero's lips already. Samson's answer is the old one of justice, and the important new addition that has appeared only with the coming of Harapha:

> All these indignities, for such they are
> From thine, these evils I deserve and more,
> Acknowledge them from God inflicted on me
> Justly, yet despair not of his final pardon.

The order of Harapha's triple "temptation," we may pause to notice, differs interestingly from Dalila's, and of course lacks the rich complexity of hers. She moved, we may say by shearing off much of the significance, from humiliating ridicule to a major attack on justice to a major test of the flesh. Harapha began, whether he intended it or not, with the physical trial, Samson's weak point with Dalila and strong point with Harapha. Then we have the ridicule and finally the question of justice. This paradigm is a thin one, for the points cross over if we look at them closely. But I think it may help indicate in another way how much less pressing Harapha's attack is. Even the direct charge of heavenly desertion is a trifle compared with Dalila's intricate web of religious self-justification and what that threatens.

The question of legality comes up, with muscular directness but not much force. Harapha is out of his element in trying to split hairs instead of skulls. What is chiefly interesting is that Milton makes the question come up again after Samson's full and penetrating reply to Dalila. It is plain that the justice of Samson's position must be clear and undoubted, with all the details accounted for, since more than human justice is involved. One use of the letter of the law perhaps needs comment. Samson says that his having married a Philistine "argu'd me no foe." His intention, we know, was to provoke, but he stands on the timing, and not without some justification. He may have known that the rascals would respond with the first hostile move, but they did not *have* to give him the "occasion" he wanted. It is a small point, and legalistic, but it anticipates the larger disregard of justice by the persuaders of Dalila. In his austere discipline of justice the hero does not overlook the small points. As for being a rebel, a larger point, Samson replies with the law of the heart (always declared illegal by conquerors but followed by patriots): "force with force / Is well ejected when the Conquer'd can." Most important, Samson invokes the higher justice:

> I was no private but a person rais'd
> With strength sufficient and command from Heav'n
> To free my Countrey.

The contest dissolves as Harapha threatens in the future and Samson threatens in the present. There is a comic inversion of Dalila's final proposal that she touch his hand. Samson threatens the warrior's loving touch, and Harapha leaves while the Chorus delightedly marks his manner:

> His Giantship is gone somewhat crest-fall'n,
> Stalking with less unconsci'nable strides,
> And lower looks, but in a sultrie chafe.

Then a new quality appears in Samson. The gap between him and the Chorus begins to demonstrate itself as a superiority in practical grasp. This is an interesting manifestation we shall have to comment on again. Samson has emerged into the world of practical action after the long descent into the darkness of self, after the "plain Heroic magnitude of mind" which has held its place against the shifting, glistening tissues of right-and-wrong challenging from without or cajoling from within. The new gap between him and the Chorus does not come from their talking about different things or on different levels of morality. They are talking about the same things, immediate, practical things. And the new gap becomes visible at the same time as the motion returning Samson to the community. Some of this can be seen more clearly if we wait a few moments, but the difference in practical grasp is already plain. The Chorus worries over the probable effects of Harapha's malice. Samson, however, can answer that general worry by three authoritative analyses. First, Harapha will say nothing, in order to avoid raising the question of a match between him and Samson. Second, the economic analysis: if his "owners" want their daily profit, they cannot make things much worse for him, "They cannot well impose, nor I sustain." Third, the kind of practical analysis possible only to someone who has moved beyond ordinary practical considerations: the worst enemy will prove his best friend, "by death to rid me hence."

This last, we must notice, recalls the hope for death first articulated in the scene with Manoa. From one point of view this may seem to contradict the inspiration and the positive hope expressed in the challenge to Harapha. Have we mistaken the motivation of that challenge, and so the temper of Samson's feelings, and so the direction and the tempo in which the drama is moving? I think not, but we are being reminded that everything does not happen at once. The movement is not all horizontal, as in the development of a simple melody; but vertical as well, in a complicated orchestration that creates its own world and can move by inner references to the created parts of that world, can move while seeming not to, and can seem to move while not moving. We have had some remarkable demonstrations of Samson progressing to low points and retreating to high, of Samson heroically not moving, and therefore moving. One of the great technical achievements of this drama is the long turning of the tide, sustained in a fascinating tension of doubt. That turning lasts for about an act and a half, from the announced hope of withdrawal from strife to the challenging of Harapha and somewhat beyond. The signs of the turning are there, but some of them seem to be going in the wrong direction, as thematic materials pull against each other, and major motions are still resisted by minor counter-motions. But the main direction has been established, though the vertical development and resistance of the dramatic line still continues. The pressures on the hero have become demonstrably less, and more nearly external. Harapha's pressure was obviously a stimulant; but so were all the pressures moral stimulants, though not obviously so. We feel the pull of the main direction, and we respond to the change in tone; but we also feel the counter-motions, for the drama still continues unresolved.

When Samson calls the "worst" of death his "best," we are reminded of the first introduction of this theme. But we cannot cancel out what has happened since. The theme itself may not have received much direct development, and Samson has found no "use" for life. The context, however, has developed and so altered the theme. We have only to compare the first introduction with this one to be aware of great differences. In fact, the reintroduction now serves that structural purpose, of comparison, as well as the continuing of unresolved tension. There is no anguish now; the remark is detached and calm. Samson's two preceding analyses have made it seem likely that the worst will not happen, but if it does it will be best. That is fact for a suffering hero; he has not changed his mind on the point, but he has tempered his feelings, and that is important. He has also, we may remember, moved from a general and undefined hope for death toward something more defined, at least by negatives, by the kinds of death he has refused to accept.

If we think ahead we may surmise that there is further definition still to come and a further stage of feeling. If we think back we see that this expression cannot be taken quite literally, even in its calm. It may be a small relapse after the big hope of the challenge, but the significance of the challenge cannot be undone simply because the hero, after a mere psychological victory, can still see no other "end" than death. The challenger of Harapha saw another "use," another "end" for his life, and certainly it was not death; for Samson had no intentions of losing a fight for such stakes. If we

look only so far ahead as the very next lines, we can see the theme
in the process of discovery, as moral intuition glimpses the small
opening, still far ahead, that will broaden into the great triumphal
avenue of the finally discovered "end":

> Yet so it may fall out, because thir end
> Is hate, not help to me, it may with mine
> Draw thir own ruin who attempt the deed.

The chorus, reassured by Samson, belatedly celebrates what
Samson has felt and we have seen. The return of consolation from
above is now formally marked, the touch of the guiding hand has
been felt. In a strange and wonderful lyric the rejoicing Chorus
anticipates the return of justice and the consequent bewildering
of presumptuous ignorance:

> Oh how comely it is and how reviving
> To the Spirits of just men long opprest!
> When God into the hands of thir deliverer
> Puts invincible might
> To quell the mighty of the Earth, th' oppressour,
> The brute and boist'rous force of violent men
> Hardy and industrious to support
> Tyrannic power, but raging to pursue
> The righteous and all such as honour Truth;
> He all thir Ammunition
> And feats of War defeats
> With plain Heroic magnitude of mind
> And celestial vigour arm'd,
> Thir Armories and Magazins contemns,
> Renders them useless, while
> With winged expedition
> Swift as the lightning glance he executes
> His errand on the wicked, who surpris'd
> Lose thir defence distracted and amaz'd.

But the Chorus, a little slow before, now has gone ahead of itself
in its enthusiasm. There is the other possibility, the more frequent
one, by which the patience of the saint delivers not others but
himself from all that "tyrannie or fortune can inflict." Though
either of these may be Samson's destiny, the Chorus believes that
his hope lies with patience. It is a reasonable guess.

The Public Officer arrives with the most external pressure of all, the command to perform at the public feast in honor of Dagon. Samson's answer summons up familiar themes for dramatic inspection. First, it is against his law, and second, it is a gratuitous indignity. The old feeling from early in the play comes back at the thought of his furnishing "sport with blind activity." And, oddly, the motive of his first marriage, an apparently finished theme, returns: "Do they not seek occasion of new quarrels?" Self-justice, religious justice, and personal indignity are all united in one remarkable piece of dramatic verse: [1]

> My self? my conscience and internal peace.
> Can they think me so broken, so debas'd
> With corporal servitude, that my mind ever
> Will condescend to such absurd commands?
> Although thir drudge, to be thir fool or jester,
> And in my midst of sorrow and heart-grief
> To show them feats and play before thir god,
> The worst of all indignities, yet on me
> Joyn'd with extream contempt? I will not come.

The Chorus and Samson go over the grounds in an interval of transition that summons up further themes for review.[2] Samson emphasizes the religious legality and also, as taken for granted, the sign of "Favour renew'd," the strength "again returning with my hair." (The two have not been linked so, except by Manoa, and then without the sense of dynamic immediacy conveyed by the return*ing*.) The Chorus represents Manoa by varying his "practical" argument to say that Samson is already using his strength in the service of the Philistines. The answer is even more practical: he works to earn his bread from the civil power. And then a subtle piece of casuistry, which works like Manoa's, by shrewdly dividing the self into parts that may more pleasantly speak for the whole: "Where the heart joins not, outward acts defile not." Samson bluntly plunges through the discrimination, and "anticipates" Aristotle: "Commands are no constraints. If I obey them, / I do it freely." And that is to prefer man's law to God's.

All this needs to be said, for it must be perfectly clear why Samson does not go and why he does go. He has answered the Officer and the Chorus "as reason was." Unheroic morality has offered other reasons — this time not to withdraw in non-action, but to go forward, to act in a withdrawal of self-deceptive surrender. If character is destiny, then Samson has reached another impasse, and by virtue of his moral and intellectual strength he has achieved a position that can be solved only by the Philistines and their mechanical contrivances. Or by what lies beyond reason and law: the inspiration of God. The terms are not definite now, as in the challenge to Harapha; Samson has only the *feeling* of "rouzing motions." But inspiration is free to go beyond heroic reasoning and patience, as it is free to exempt "From National obstriction" or from religious law. As audience we may see that Samson has earned his inspiration, while we see also that it is a gift. We understand why he goes, and thinking back, we remember that the exercise of his independent moral strength brought him to the full revelation of his guilt and human helplessness. Now the same independent strength has brought him to another impasse but another revelation.

There is no other formal solution, but we may catch something like a glimpse of an uncompleted pattern that cannot be said to support the inspiration but nevertheless acts as a kind of natural and human parallel. If Samson should flatly reject this external pressure, it would be his first refusal to accept a judgment on his folly. True, there are special circumstances here which violate religious justice; but still, the sense of personal indignity, the fierce anguish of the insulted self, which has not been purged out of existence, and will *not* be, but has been steadily mastering the raw immediacy of individual feeling into a feeling of more noble temper, as the tragic self suffers through the old self to a new self — that sense of personal indignity is revived, as argument, with a force that recalls the beginning of the play and counters, for a fierce moment, what has been a definite thematic development. (We have only to think of the calm acceptance of Harapha's external insults, which are mastered by Samson's acknowledgment of justice.) Besides, we have grown used to that rhythm of accepting judgment, for the play has insisted that we do so, and we have come to feel and expect the strength and rightness of it. But now Samson sticks to the point of reason and rejects the external consequences of his folly. It is true that he has always refused to come to permanent terms with his folly, though tempted, but he has always accepted the judgment. Now he ignores the judgment and sees this, though with some reason, as another temptation to come to permanent terms with his folly. But this temptation has at least one important difference from the others: it offers no easy promise of withdrawal, no comfortable burial as national scapegoat, no easing out of grief by Manoa's hearth or Dalila's bed. It offers the hard promise of a grief not experienced but also perhaps deserved in a logic of consequences. It offers an occasion for mastering a still-unexperienced consequence of his folly, and for pushing his personal anguish through to a victory of patience. The hero determined to go back, to try again, to suffer everything, may also go forward to suffer — if reason does not resist revelation, does not divide the self into parts in order to persuade against the hard truth of the self.

Our insight may borrow too much from the last act. But still, the pattern has been established, and we may, even here, looking only backward, feel that a created expectation, a kind of "cyclical form," would be unfulfilled if inspiration did not intervene. It is not that Milton was tying prescripts to inspiration; but even that great gift must enter a place prepared by the dramatic structure, and should assist, not violate, human reason. There has been preparation, and the inspiration has not come all at once, without lesser stages. There was the challenge to Harapha, and there was the moral intuition, that the "end" of hate might "Draw thir own ruin who attempt the deed."

The Officer, like a good angel, descends twice, and now proposes a "temptation" that is completely physical, the threat of violence, the machines that will drag Samson to the feast. As theme it echoes and varies Manoa on self-preservation and the physical trials offered by Dalila and Harapha. But now, for a moment at least, the offer has an attraction unlike theirs; it comes almost like another and rival inspiration, through human agency. Here is a chance to suffer something unexperienced, but as a champion again; a chance to fulfill the motion frustrated by Harapha; to burst through the patience of not moving by the release of a positive action; to win, at the worst, the release of death, for which he has longed. One sees and feels him respond to the flicker of possibility, as this new inspiration, the terms very definite, challenges the undefined "rouzing motions":

> I could be well content to try thir Art,
> Which to no few of them would prove pernicious.

But he refuses the rival inspiration, and in doing so takes a firm step beyond the "hope" for death.[3]

The answer summons themes for another brilliant moment during which the created parts of the dramatic world refer to each other. Nothing *happens* in a palpable way; we do not go forward or backward on the line of horizontal, physical action. But on a "vertical" line the references constitute a rich action for the mind and feelings that respond to the *form* of movement, that can see, in the "abstract," momentarily arrested relationships of movement, meanings that are not independent of the main course of physical action, but modify that course, and significantly define, even verify it. Samson's answer rejects the false hope of action or death which would lead, by illusion, to the real end of another withdrawal. He obeys the higher inspiration, and reason, for he knows that their machines can do what they threaten. Justice, again, though followed heroically, helps less in this extreme than the accepted fact of his ultimate helplessness. Even the sense of personal indignity, the unsubdued hate of ridicule which has been exercised and tempered but not eliminated by the drama, now can assist reason, inspiration, and the admitted helplessness: he will not, for a dubious gratification, be trailed like a wild beast through their streets.

Before Samson leaves the stage and the center of suffering he has occupied so long, to be seen through the different perspective of distance and report, he moves toward that distance. He jokes with what would be a facile irony if the right to say it had not been so terribly earned:

Masters commands come with a power resistless
To such as owe them absolute subjection;
And for a life who will not change his purpose?
(So mutable are all the ways of men).

It is a joke for the tragic hero; only he can afford to laugh at a common truth which no longer binds him. It exhibits again, in a repetition of reference, the gap between common morality and Samson's. It hauls up for our startled recognition two moral clichés that sounded thin when we first heard them and are positively ridiculous now: the early response of the Chorus, "O mirror of our fickle state," and the self-important recital of the lesson by Manoa, "and oh what not in man / Deceivable and vain." These are no more the lessons of the tragedy than the explanation of Samson's change of mind. The gap is unmistakable, but Samson is forcing us to see it with a clarity that hurts. Now, before he leaves, he sums up the whole history of his drama by pretending to deny it, by playing it false. In the grimly untrue we hear the true.

The Officer's hint that Samson may win favor and be set free breaks against his terrible detachment with feeble irrelevance. It is not unlike, shall we say, a compensatory offer to Othello of a retroactive increase in rank and salary, or of dream-proof sleeping pills to Macbeth. Manoa and Dalila have played that tune before to uninterested ears. Samson's detachment moves toward distance in still another way. After the departure of Harapha we noticed the sudden superiority of Samson's practical grasp. He seemed to have emerged with strange new authority into the world of practical action from the long descent into the self. Now he looks at things human, and himself in their midst, with a clarity that penetrates and understands to the last detail, but seems to see as from a great distance. He speaks as from a distance, beyond involvement, with a cold intensity of feeling that seems beyond feeling, with an energy of mind and expression raised to a great height, yet thoroughly mastered, incisive, authoritative, final, with nothing left over, no shadows, no tension. It is a quality, without name, that we have heard in other tragic heroes — in Macbeth, Lear, Othello, Hamlet, and others.

190

> Brethren farewel, your company along
> I will not wish, lest it perhaps offend them
> To see me girt with Friends; and how the sight
> Of me as of a common Enemy,
> So dreaded once, may now exasperate them
> I know not. Lords are Lordliest in thir wine;
> And the well-feasted Priest then soonest fir'd
> With zeal, if aught Religion seem concern'd:
> No less the people on thir Holy-days
> Impetuous, insolent, unquenchable.

The commanding vision of things human is accompanied by an enlargement of faculties, by a growth in the sense of spiritual power. The man who has suffered through, "In power of others, never in my own," is about to be released from bondage by accepting it through one last experience. And he communicates, like old Oedipus, the mysterious power all would touch and desire to have reflected on them, but none would dare have. As he moves from his people, and the personal gap widens, he has been moving toward them.

> Happ'n what may, of me expect to hear
> Nothing dishonourable, impure, unworthy
> Our God, our Law, my Nation, or my self.

THE RETURN OF SAMSON

THE tide has turned. Now there is no doubt. A few last counter-motions persist, but they exert no convincing pull. They ripple the surface here and there, and make a few slapping sounds to mark their own indecision before they succumb utterly to the irresistible force growing beneath them. But we are strangers, as always, to the inlet of individual human experience. We have come, and in a condensed period of time have been able to mark many of the formations revealed and partly revealed by the ebb, along with certain historical signs remaining from the flood. But the speed of the flux and the immediate details of its course we cannot know. And as the event we have waited for is finally about to happen, we are moved back from it, so that when we return it will be to experience the most revealing moment of time. (And facing the innermost revelation of tragedy we always recognize ourselves as experienced strangers.) After that we shall have some necessary leisure to recover and to make the knowledge ours. The leisure will at first be brief and intense, hardly divided from the experience itself, but then slowing and widening as it moves more quietly into the dimension of time.

Old Manoa returns "With youthful steps," encouraged by his activity and the hope he has been begetting. He has been humiliating himself, as paternal reason was, before the Philistian Lords. The details come as a belated echo of our familiar recognition that

192

Samson has now passed securely beyond this range of human consideration. The gap between Samson and the ordinary values of the world is displayed without new pressure on the hero, but as it were in retrospect. The account has an irrelevance that challenges nothing but offers a relaxed comedy of gratuitous contrast:

> Others more moderate seeming, but thir aim
> Private reward, for which both God and State
> They easily would set to sale.

But the hated Philistia is divided into three parts, of which one part is humanly decent, "More generous far and civil," though no doubt well outnumbered by the business-minded third and the inflexible, religious-revengeful third.

Time has to be occupied until the big scene. Except for the punctuation of the two shouts, nothing new can happen, but old themes can be revived as a kind of mirror between past and future. Manoa and the Chorus discuss the role of fatherhood, now that Samson has reached the helplessness of old age before his father. Time is dealt with in a leisurely way, as if this reversal of normal order had somehow suspended time. The effect is not unlike a favorite one of Puccini's, the old pathos of hopefully planning ahead while the conductor fingers the page that will change those notes to tragic. Manoa's hope continues undaunted, but the effect is different. He does not stop with his paternal delight in tending Samson, but affirms his persuasion that God will "use him further yet in some great service,"

> And since his strength with eye-sight was not lost,
> God will restore him eye-sight to his strength.

There is prophetic ambiguity, of course, in the last phrase, but that is not the cause of the difference. Manoa has expressed the same kind of hope before: "His might continues in thee not for naught." The difference, I think, is less in Manoa than in the dramatic situation, though that perhaps allows us to see Manoa in a way not quite possible before, at least not without some straining. For one thing, Samson, after strenuous efforts befitting his tragic role, has moved closer to Manoa's hopefulness. The kind of enunciation that fitted the father before but jarred on the son now fits the son too. Even if this were not true, the absence of the hero grants Manoa's words a sincerity not clear before. He speaks his mind now, such as it is; there is no question of tempting the hero to patch things up glibly. Besides, we can see that his heart is not really in the idea of withdrawal. What he said before was the natural expression of his paternal care, but like Samson he believes in "use" and "service." The gap between them has to exist, for Samson is a tragic hero; but that gap is less wide than it seemed. Granted the necessary differences, Manoa can even manage to sound like Samson:

> Not to sit idle with so great a gift
> Useless, and thence ridiculous about him.

The "universal groan" accelerates time, but there are still ironic movements to be measured out. The Chorus assumes Manoa's familiar kind of hopefulness: what if Samson's eyesight has been miraculously restored? "Nothing is hard" to God. Manoa, hearing it said by someone else, hesitates: "That were a joy presumptuous to be thought." The Chorus presses him: God has performed miracles for His people before, "what hinders now?" Manoa has been saying that himself, but it is different when it comes from outside. He reminds one of Samson hoping for a retirement from the strife, until there is a specific proposal:

> He can I know, but doubt to think he will;
> Yet Hope would fain subscribe, and tempts Belief.

I pass by the set ironies of the first exchanges with the Messenger, and Manoa's lament, which brings to the surface the death-life theme more actively than since the beginning of the play. The big scene comes, after the deliberate small delays and after the deliberate large delay which is the whole drama. The presentation is formal and complete in itself. It gains tremendously, of course, from everything that has preceded and is now released; but it is worth noting that Milton has constructed the scene so that it can stand alone, independent and complete. If it had been published separately, or had been discovered in manuscript, we should regard it

194

as an extraordinarily successful dramatic poem. One thing a conscious artist must have known before he wrote a word was how much would depend on the big scene, the only direct action in a moral drama of suffering developed through the indirect action of talk, and that talk filled with strenuous discriminations. It must have taken heroic self-confidence to choose the challenge, a mighty one, and then to endure the inevitable growth of the shadow as he approached the crucial moment with all the developed successes of the drama at stake, and quite able to fail. The technical answer — which will not explain the justified confidence of artistic genius — is to make the scene complete, to review at a final stage and on an elevated level the tragic mastery that has been nearly achieved.

We begin the scene from the distance already put between us and Samson, then approach him at the center of a new public stage, then return to him at the center of his old individual stage, and finally, perforce, step back to complete the cycle. First we have the Messenger's point of view, which effectively creates a sense of the total scene, the feeling of holiday and public triumph, beginning with sunrise and the trumpeting announcement "Through each high street." The Messenger has normal human reactions, sorrow but curious desire to see. He does not forget to describe the theater and its peculiar architecture; he repeats the important detail of Samson's intermission, as realistic fact overheard from those who stood nearer. The intoxicated mood and atmosphere of triumph ("that insulting vanity") rises to a climax with the entrance of Samson, seen as from a distance:

> The Feast and noon grew high, and Sacrifice
> Had fill'd thir hearts with mirth, high chear, & wine,
> When to thir sports they turn'd. Immediately
> Was *Samson* as a public servant brought,
> In thir state Livery clad; before him Pipes
> And Timbrels, on each side went armed guards,
> Both horse and foot before him and behind
> Archers, and Slingers, Cataphracts and Spears.
> At sight of him the people with a shout
> Rifted the Air clamouring thir god with praise,
> Who had made thir dreadful enemy thir thrall.

Then Samson is alone in the center of the stage, and we see him, as from an indeterminate distance, in his new role of public entertainer:

> He patient but undaunted where they led him,
> Came to the place, and what was set before him
> Which without help of eye, might be assay'd,
> To heave, pull, draw, or break, he still perform'd
> All with incredible, stupendious force,
> None daring to appear Antagonist.

Here finally the ridicule is faced and mastered in a total victory of patience. The internal anguish at folly, the writhing over the external indignity — they have hindered him and they have helped him, but now he is purged of his folly, for he has accepted it and the consequences entirely, followed it through to the end. He has been the Athlete of God and failed. Now he is the Fool of God and succeeds.

We see what is happening and move toward him in our knowledge. And then, at once, as he goes toward the pillars, we approach him more closely than the hard strength of the man ever permitted, perhaps more closely than his formidable weakness ever permitted.

> which when *Samson*
> Felt in his arms, with head a while enclin'd,
> And eyes fast fixt he stood, as one who pray'd,
> Or some great matter in his mind revolv'd.

This is the lover's touch he denied Dalila and was denied by Harapha. Now he has the "end" and the "use" in his arms, but it is not the old champion who is about to act. He has accepted his folly, possessed it, but not been possessed by it. He withdraws, in a gesture of wisdom learned through suffering. It is a brief gesture which would have profound significance even if the scene were an independent unit. But now we cannot fail to understand what he is doing, for the whole weight of the drama bears on the simple act, suspended as it is in a moment of complete silence on the last threshold. Even the presentation, from without, the objective reporting that carefully marks two possible interpretations of the

196

external appearance, only heightens our sense of the inwardness of the simple gesture that sums up the play. He withdraws in thought and spirit before the final redemptive act which is to end the long process of redemption. He repeats, with a difference, the passive withdrawal from his true self which asserted the feminine pride of independence as a "petty god"; the passive withdrawal which mysteriously fulfilled itself by the "act" of passivity, the surrender to Dalila. The gesture recalls and acknowledges the sense of his human weakness and helplessness which assisted him against the temptations to withdraw in self-concern. But now he renews the admitted source of strength in God and marks the separation from self. For in this act of one revived hero against a nation there must be no shadow of individual pride. High point and low point confront each other again, as the grand motion completes itself and the inspired end comes to meet him.

The released spirit trumpets the announcement as preface to the deed:

> At last with head erect thus cryed aloud,
> Hitherto, Lords, what your commands impos'd
> I have perform'd, as reason was, obeying,
> Not without wonder or delight beheld.
> Now of my own accord such other tryal
> I mean to shew you of my strength, yet greater;
> As with amaze shall strike all who behold.

The weakness of Samson, which has been defined by moral and intellectual strength, is at last granted the expression of strength. The saint's victory over himself through patience becomes, through the inspired "command from Heav'n," the champion's triumphant recovery of his "end." The accomplishment is gift, as plainly as the first gift of superhuman strength, but now the gift has been earned through human means, so that we are able to identify our-selves with Samson and the expression of his achieved recovery just as the gift turns authentically tragic, to death. That ensures our proper human relationship to the superhuman gift. To see what has happened, we have only to think of the first choral celebration of his strength. That was magnificent, and credible, but it had between us and it the distance of irrevocable history, and the very magnificence of the rhetoric consciously re-creating what no longer existed. Now all the distance is between the *inspired* Samson (with all he has come to represent) and the Philistines. He commands the knowledge and the voice of a prophet, marking for others the folly of ignorance, as he has, with the help of others, marked it for himself.

We begin to move backward from the height of the shock, our feelings expressed for us and guided through several stages. The Messenger initiates the movement by the exultation that begins to creep into his description of the result. The first choral reaction welcomes the victory, but with no notable release of feeling until after three main facts are named: Samson's fulfillment of his "work," the nature of the death (not suicide), and the dimension of the victory.

The Semichorus takes up this last item, involving national passion as it does, and releases the first and deepest wave of human feeling — hate. It is a fierce chant of triumph; all the ridicule endured by Samson is turned against the enemy in one unsparing recital of the ignorance which is folly:

> While thir hearts were jocund and sublime,
> Drunk with Idolatry, drunk with Wine,
> And fat regorg'd of Bulls and Goats,
> Chaunting thir Idol, and preferring
> Before our living Dread who dwells
> In *Silo* his bright Sanctuary:
> Among them he a spirit of phrenzie sent,
> Who hurt thir minds,
> And urg'd them on with mad desire
> To call in hast for thir destroyer;
> They only set on sport and play
> Unweetingly importun'd
> Thir own destruction to come speedy upon them.
> So fond are mortal men
> Fall'n into wrath divine,
> As thir own ruin on themselves to invite,
> Insensate left, or to sense reprobate,
> And with blindness internal struck.

This is more than "comely" and "reviving." The celebration of divine justice and of the self-destruction of evil comes as a full purge of doubts and fears.

The second Semichorus moves from the primitive to a more "civilized" range of feeling. It begins with direct exultation in the hero and a contrasting contempt for the enemy (hate is no longer appropriate). It turns finally with fuller attention to the return of the hero, celebrated now not to express human hate but hope:

> But he though blind of sight,
> Despis'd and thought extinguish't quite,
> With inward eyes illuminated
> His fierie vertue rouz'd
> From under ashes into sudden flame,
> And as an ev'ning Dragon came,
> Assailant on the perched roosts,
> And nests in order rang'd
> Of tame villatic Fowl; but as an Eagle
> His cloudless thunder bolted on thir heads.
> So vertue giv'n for lost,
> Deprest, and overthrown, as seem'd,
> Like that self-begott'n bird
> In the *Arabian* woods embost,
> That no second knows nor third,
> And lay e're while a Holocaust,
> From out her ashie womb now teem'd,
> Revives, reflourishes, then vigorous most
> When most unactive deem'd,
> And though her body die, her fame survives,
> A secular bird ages of lives.

Manoa takes us one further stage away from the height of action. The Philistines are spoken of without either hate or contempt. National joy is revised into the challenging opportunity for freedom, if Israel finds courage "to lay hold on this occasion." The expression of human hope celebrated in the return of the hero is carried toward its conclusion as the tragic experience closes the gap between the hero and his people, through the "best and happiest" realization that God was "'not parted from him, as was feard." And Manoa's optimism, so dissonant early in the play, is granted the high privilege of the purged human response to Samson's tragedy:

> Nothing is here for tears, nothing to wail
> Or knock the breast, no weakness, no contempt,
> Dispraise, or blame, nothing but well and fair,
> And what may quiet us in a death so noble.

At the height of the action there are three distinguishable sacrifices. These we may consider as ritualistic,[1] both from the perspective of a modern concept of tragedy and from the authoritative response of the audience. First, there is the regular course of sacrifice (off stage, as it were) of the Philistine festival, leading to the high point of the public enjoyment of Samson, which marks the drunken Philistine height of noon and turns the frenzied sacrificers into sacrifice. It is this second sacrifice that the first Semichorus celebrates in its ritualistic triumph, and catharsis, of hate. In that terrible chant Samson is only the instrument created by Philistine ignorance. The third sacrifice is Samson, and as the audience responds to the event the nature of the sacrifice may be seen to evolve. The first stage is the primitive release of animal fear from the lowest human depths. The second stage elevates the hero from being a mere instrument of the Philistine's brutal ignorance and hate to being a symbol of human hope and virtue. Finally, he is united to his people and their religion by the noble death which "may quiet us." There is a still further stage in the ritualizing of the sacrifice, but before I come to that I want to quote, for its relevance to Samson's case, a striking conclusion from Gertrude R. Levy's remarkable book, *The Gate of Horn*. She is considering Pythagoras after having studied certain anticipatory patterns in primitive religion:

His discipline was still the 'Way of Death,' and his ritual sacrifice; but now the animal victim existed only within the soul, a force to be liberated for creation, as the bull's blood had been poured out long ago. It did not involve a rejection of the life of the senses, but an absorption of power by their control, as it did for Plato after him.[2]

This has some bearing on Samson's sacrifice. I remind the reader of the debt Samson's redemption owes, from the beginning, to his capacity for feeling. Though he subdues the raw immediacies of feeling into a more noble temper, he does not stifle, or reject, or eradicate: he sacrifices. The powers of intellect, justice, patience — these are helped in this tragedy by the burning sense of the necessary "animal" self. I shall not review my scattered observations. I point only to the sustained theme of ridicule, over which Samson agonizes, but which assists him time and again: as at the last moment with Dalila; and with the Messenger, as the hero proceeds to the feast, not trailed through the streets "like a wild Beast," but "as reason was"; and as he performs the penultimate sacrifice by mastering, as the patient Fool of God, the final consequences of his folly.

Finally, the austere poet who could deal so sternly with the fate of the Garden of Eden allows a human dignity to ritual and place. The Samson who becomes a symbol of human hope and virtue also becomes a mere person, and there is a dead body to be cleansed and buried with proper ceremony. Decorum, both human and poetic, requires the ritual. The return of Samson to God is a return to his people, and they must, since this tragedy *is* a shared experience, not walk away numb and dumb. They need this expression of human decency and dignity, to mark the return of Samson to them and to mark their return, through the shared experience, closer to the God Whose "faithful Champion" Samson has "in the close" proved to be.

But the ritual goes beyond the bounds of simple communal decency and relationship. There is a monument, a shrine, to be built, not entirely unlike shrines built by the pagan world for its heroes (as Hercules). It is true that Samson is not to be "worshipped" as the hero of a pagan cult, or as the saint of an "idolatrous" Christian practice. Samson will serve as national inspiration to the "valiant youth"; to the Hebrew virgins (as to Christian homiletics) he will serve as moral example; what else he will mean to the virgins we are left the not-difficult task of interpreting. But still, Milton is here poetically sanctioning a shrine. Even if we knew nothing of the man beyond the compass of this poem, we should still recall with surprise that Samson's tomb resembles the one Dalila prophesied for herself, also to be visited with "annual flowers," and her acts were also to be recorded in song. Is Milton belatedly recognizing and dignifying a basic human urge? — one that could turn a grave allegedly Milton's into a ritual of shared experience for souvenir hunters!

Our best answer to the surprising extension of ritual is, I think, to be found in the decorum which maintains the inner truth of the drama. That decorum has not faltered in expressing any necessary extreme of feeling. There is no hesitation now. The hero has returned to the community, on his own terms. Heroic and ordinary morality have come together, but not quite together. The "true experience" of the tragedy still is individual, commonly available and elevating to the community, but not quite as a common, institutionalized moral property. There is no authorized identification of the two orders of morality, as in the Philistine "public good." The height of the "true experience" now can afford, without danger, some inadequate translation into the terms of the community. The "valiant youth" will not finally distort, for theirs is not the most adequate, nor the last, word. And this is equally true of the virgins and their humor of no humor:

> only bewailing
> His lot unfortunate in nuptial choice,
> From whence captivity and loss of eyes.

There is a still larger community, for whom the truth of Samson's tragic experience is individual and transcends both local place and time. It is to this community that the Chorus addresses its last word, "All is best, though we oft doubt." The tragedy has exercised human doubt fully and deeply, in order to serve the moral and intellectual purpose of spreading doubt thin.[3] Socratic catharsis of ignorance joins Aristotelian catharsis of passion in the drama of knowledge:

> His servants he with new acquist
> Of true experience from this great event
> With peace and consolation hath dismist,
> And calm of mind all passion spent.

POSTSCRIPT

I WANT to comment on some of the larger assumptions that underlie this book. Some of them I began with, others I realized only during or after the composition.

First let me try to state briefly the working hypothesis I have used for understanding Milton's solution of the dramatic problems involved in Christ's dual nature. Milton accepts the mystery of that dual nature as the kind of inscrutable fact a believer had better work *from* rather than *toward*. It is instructive to see Milton in the *Christian Doctrine* (I, v, xiv) stubbornly steering clear of the tangles of speculative possibilities. That the two natures *are* united we believe, but how they are united we are not told; and since the Scriptures tell us everything we need for saving knowledge, we may draw the practical inferences. This is an ocasion for being "lowly wise" and thinking only what concerns us and our "being," which is no minor assignment. This is what the dramatic demonstration also teaches us. For Christ has only a "normal" human curiosity about his history as it has been prophesied. What he is chiefly concerned with is not his origin in a personal sense, not the recorded personal history, but his task, his "end" of being. Like the first Adam, the second Adam has a direct assignment to an "active sphere." The mystery of his unique role he learns from intuition, from his mother, from study (of Scriptures and *all* knowledge), and from meditation. One might say that the second Adam, like all sons of God, has to think his way back to his original creation, has to *remember* it as the Platonist might say; and this he must do by uniting his beginning and his end of being in the thought of action. We enter the story with much of the work already behind the hero. The process of thought continues in the drama before us, presumably at an accelerated pace, though mostly underneath the drama, as it were: in the undramatized action of descent into the self, which is too intimate a part of the mystery of the dual nature to be dramatizable without violating Milton's sense of religious (or literary) decorum. By shifting his emphasis to the drama of choice, the necessity of imminent action in the world, Milton has been able to use richly the defining power of evil, and to postpone until all the important *human* victories have been won the emergence of the divine nature. It is plain that Milton is most interested in the *earning*, in the "By proof the undoubted Son of God," in the human part of the demonstration, in the process of learning-knowing-doing "What might be public good" which leads (through a drama of self-definition and victory) to the end of persuasion and selfless teaching.

"The fox knows many things, but the hedgehog one thing of much importance." This fragment from Archilochus — recently used as the generative insight for a brilliant book on Tolstoi by Isaiah Berlin — would make an interesting epigraph for the present drama of temptation. The Miltonic hero is a kind of hedgehog; he knows one major thing which animates, orients, protects him. But he is a Platonic hedgehog, which means being a hedgehog and knowing why, which means being a fox-protecting-the-hedgehog-who-is-still-hedgehog. For Milton wisdom and prudence are not separable; the intuition of the good is wedded to will and proved in this dramatic demonstration by the free exercise of the traditional virtues. Milton takes the ascending importance of will-faith from primitive Christianity, and links faith to the Platonic vision of the good and the inseparable unity of the virtues. He is no inventor here, but Milton's perception is fresh, immediate to self, an insight, not a learned philosophical or literary strategy. And it has the power of a major insight of a major poet.

The key for Milton is knowledge, the self-knowledge of thought tested by deed, heroic knowledge maintained against the pressing claims of immediate knowledge and action. The movement in both poems is return to the source of being and the arrival is confirmed by the acquisition of inspired knowledge. But the inspiration has been earned — at least the poetry creates an effective and persuasive illusion of this; and though that noble illusion can never be proved and must be believed, it is not therefore invulnerable to a discriminating belief. There is no private Neoplatonic ascent toward transcendent unity. The stage is here and now, the world; the demonstration is public.

In the essential movement of return, in the discursive demonstration of heroic knowledge, the poems and the protagonists have much in common. But the stages and the dramatic assignments of the heroes are of course very different. Still, when one looks at Milton's whole view of order, the differences may be described as local, the inevitable results of a true poet's masterful shaping of the artistic material and his creative obedience to the inner laws of the discovered decorum. Each hero presents a human and individual way to the same truth.

Milton's whole poetic vision is to be found in the three major poems, with some minor additions in the minor poems; but no one major poem, though *Paradise Lost* comes closest, contains the whole vision. For instance, Milton's imaginative sense of time is expressed at its fullest range in *Paradise Lost*. But the most striking achievements of the great epic sweep of time are those which give us the past. In *Paradise Regained* we have occasional flashes of present immediacy, but the dominating dimension is future, the cool future distance of decision and judgment clarifying the present. *Samson Agonistes* is full present. Or, to make another illustrative point: Christ is not tried through *all* temptation. It is not necessary to think of a traditional concept, like St. Jerome's, that the hardest temptation for the virtuous is the thought that scoundrels prosper; one could easily extend the list. But we have only to think of Samson, or even of Adam. Christ has no "facile consort" (though he has a church to found), but Satan's temptations are chiefly directed toward the Eve in man. The temptations are more complicated, subtle, and strenuous than in the garden, but they are also more restricted. The lowest level is higher (there is no commotion of passion), and the highest level is lower (there is no question of Faustian knowledge, no ascension to deity).

In the moral failures of Adam and Samson the acts approved may be formally diagnosed as positive; they will fit into the discriminating categories of moral philosophy and theology; but the causes formally proposable cannot quite satisfy; they claim to reveal the springs of human motivation, but we must surrender our questions at every point in order to be convinced. These acts, one may say without aspiring to explain them, may also be characterized as negative, as a mysterious, "stupidly" evil failure to act, as a kind of withdrawal (more than a deviation) from right. The effects are positive enough, but not so the causes. In *Paradise Regained* Milton worked the other side of the problem: a refusal to act which defines, and is positive and active. For Milton, I infer, the major temptation of man is not to act, but to withdraw down the scale of creation to the creaturely self, to the "even" order of "inferior creatures mute, / Irrational and brute"; while the major temptation of the female part of man's nature is to aspire upward, usurp transcendence, but ignorantly or impatiently, without proper self-knowledge or justice.

In *Paradise Lost* both temptations are represented. *Paradise Regained* is an extended, intensive study of Eve's temptation. Christ governs himself evenly, as the "Angelic orders." Though he is in the desert, exposed to the tempter, and with an urgent problem to solve, he is a model of elevated human intellect, disciplined will, and perfect faith. The tactical movement is withdrawal, but not to the creaturely self. A major weapon in his discipline of defense is the pious, and discriminating, maintenance of the difference between man and God. But the strategic movement is transcendence, not by the way of Eve or Satan, but by maintaining the difference between man and God while acting out the likeness of the divine image. Samson's path is more complicated, involving as it does the terrible knowledge of guilt and tragic suffering. For him the difference between man and God is less a discipline to be maintained than an agony to be suffered. The desert where he is exposed is a stage that includes his passion. In Samson Milton has found the perfect protagonist for studying man's great temptation to withdraw, a hero who discovered the way without help in pros- perous times, and now is besieged by guides who would lead him to the same end by different paths.

And so one might say that Milton divided a major dramatic theme of *Paradise Lost* (a theme ending in a tactical defeat) for specialized treatment (and strategic victory) in the other two poems. This is one way of looking at *Paradise Regained* and *Sam- son Agonistes*, as the "L'Allegro"-"Il Penseroso" of Milton's ma- turity — companion poems which are also beautifully wrought, but now embracing between them not merely a set thematic contrast but Milton's final poetic solution of a great human dilemma.

I now want to make some further comments on the relationship of the two poems, though mostly on *Samson Agonistes* when seen beside *Paradise Regained*. The tragedy has always attracted more readers than the dialectical drama, and the reasons are clear enough, but perhaps a few points can bear some brief discussion. Christ may represent pure intelligence, but he is, in my view, no Stoic athlete of apathy. He feels hunger, fervency, ambition, though he is the undisturbed master of his feeling; and he is pro- vided by the tempter not only with an opportunity for demon- strating his control but for moving under discipline toward a final definition. Let me quote, for its illustrative value, Simone Weil's comment on pure intelligence:

And just as danger, exposure to suffering are healthy and neces- sary elements in the sphere of action, so are they unhealthy in- fluences in the exercise of the intelligence. A fear, even a passing one, always provokes either a weakening or a tautening, depending on the degree of courage, and that is all that is required to damage the extremely delicate and fragile instrument of precision that constitutes our intelligence.[1]

This is not far from Milton's view at its most austere; the demon- stration is implicit throughout *Paradise Regained* and explicit during the storm and on the tower. It is a way to truth for the perfect religious hero of unbruised intelligence, though Milton insists on danger and exposure to the sphere of action. If it were the only way, we should have a *Paradise Lost* of immeasurably smaller dimensions, and no *Samson Agonistes*.

Samson, no perfect man but a tragic hero, is granted a fuller endowment of feeling. He is able, by character, and by the context of the given dramatic materials, to use emotions not available to the situation of *Paradise Regained*. His intelligence is remarkable, but it is no "delicate and fragile instrument" or it would not have sustained the shock of his fall and the stresses of his recovery. For the unfallen hero temperance (in the largest Platonic sense) may be the most helpful virtue, under intelligence; for the hero already fallen temperance has been broken, and though it may mend it cannot be his chief assistance; but justice can be, and may provide special insights for the guilty. Christ's victory is the clear victory of pure intelligence; his resignation is what he begins with and triumphantly maintains; his "weakness" proves itself stronger than what the world mistakes for strength. Samson's victory is tragic and complex: it involves the passionate pull of the world yet a purging of earthly hopes and fears; and it creates a convincing sense of the insignificance of the individual protagonist's life, but at the same time a heightened vitality and power and clarity of vision. Resignation is what Samson painfully and heroically achieves. His "weakness" also proves to be true spiritual strength, but it is also real weakness, and a source of complicated anguish that leads him to the impassable limits where weakness, first unconsciously and then consciously discovered, can serve him better than even intelligence and justice.

Pure intelligence does not move. It stands like a still center and defines the world of flux unerringly, so that things move around the center and find their place in relation to it: which creates the illusion of movement and finally reveals the true center. But since pure intelligence must discover itself and prepare to enter the world of action while standing still, must choose its action and move toward its essential revelation simultaneously, we have the preconditions of movement necessary for a dramatic poem, though only a Milton could trust himself to write it. (Surely no other poem in the language so boldly proclaims the artist's pride in his genius; or maintains the drama of humility with so much virtuosity of length and depth; or masters and subdues with such perfection of decorum the style to the essential subject, a technical achievement of unparalleled difficulty!) The smallest mistake would be fatal for Christ; and this fact, along with his positive need to decide and the wealth of concrete opposition introduced into the universal of the poem by the inventive antagonist, provides enough tension for a Milton to keep the poem moving.

But in the tragic hero a wide margin of active error can be supported, and the opposition is not only external but internal. The pressure of despair is not in the antagonist but in the protagonist. The descent into the self is not only a mythic or ritualistic withdrawal, it is tormented exploration of the dark depths of the soul. The external temptations explore, test, re-enact the internal temptations. The purge of the comic fully occurs in the hero, and not merely in the villains, or in moments of folly (as in *Paradise Lost*). Truth is tested with pressing severity, exposed to a wide range of human feeling and the shocks of non-feeling, and upon a battleground not hallowed by any word of God. If there are any divine spectators, they remain silent. The fight is not lost in the careless springtime ease of the Garden of Eden, or won in the unflinching mind of the perfect man, but lost and won in the mind and heart of a self-ruined hero.

An imaginative dimension is also internalized. Pure intelligence cannot imagine evil. This lack in human experience must be supplied externally by Satan. Milton's way of compensating in the special world of the poem is by endowing Satan with a radical incapacity for imagining good. The results make brilliant drama. In Samson, of course, Milton can unite both ranges of the human faculty. But the great benefit of escape from the meshes of self is provided by the lucky fact of moral law (as Milton consistently interprets it), that external evil is bound to interfere; so the internal imagination of evil by good is presented with a concrete image external to self, and is thus enabled to purge itself of its own image. The sterilized externality of not-self may serve the undisturbed precision of pure intelligence particularly well; but it also serves, if by means more devious, the more devious processes of discrimination rooted in the ego of the feeling self.

Both heroes arrive with eyes open at a moment of inspired knowledge, a moment scrupulously earned by the long progress of a rational discipline. There are many points in common, but the discipline is fittingly individual to each hero, and so is the rational process itself. We may see this best, I think, if we consider the problem of Samson's "despair." In *Paradise Regained* Satan's despair is part of a negative process, a progressive death of mind and spirit which gradually deprives him of options. But the despair in Samson is of a different degree; in a self-ruined tragic hero it is part of the process of imaginative and experienced thought which corresponds to the clear mental operations of the perfect man.

Don Cameron Allen has perceptively studied the concept of despair as it helps shape the drama of *Paradise Lost*. My interpretation of *Samson Agonistes*, however, leads me to this point of divergence: I see Milton endowing Samson with a greater range of ordinary human feeling; allowing, as it were, a digestible ration of despair, as he allows him a kind of nuclear sensibility of the essential self which is able to feel the agony of ridicule as a "vanity" that does not dissipate force but collects it and saves. The potentially fatal ailment of despair is contained in the drama. Samson does not avoid the natural course of his spiritual sickness, but advances to meet the advancing disease; is inoculated, as it were, and achieves immunity, making despair convert itself into a necessary transition to humility.[2]

In his medical concept of the tragic purge of passion as pitting like against like, Milton presents a fascinating many-sidedness. We may see him here as strikingly modern, an understanding practitioner of the new art of psychiatry immersing his hero creatively in the destructive element. But he is also echoing a standard Renaissance medical theory — one susceptible of important metaphysical extensions, as John Donne well knew. But what of Milton the Platonist? This is not the usual way reason and temperance work in establishing the harmony of true existence. Yet the progress of Samson's purification is also clear and intellectual, granted the terms of its special discourse, and constitutes a kind of Socratic catharsis of ignorance for the hero, as well as for other participants in the drama and for the spectators. In Milton's full drama of feeling the intellectual way is not pure but is made to incorporate and dignify the immediacies of the feeling self. The demonstration is more impressive than any formal Miltonic statements praising bodies and matter.

And now a final note, perhaps by way of justifying my own labors at understanding Milton's moral art. Let me try to address myself to a crude question: What is the moral *use* of Milton's image of order? His vision is not practically available to us, in our terms, today. It could be available only by our going backward in time, reversing history in a way that is never quite possible — at least not without more consequent danger to the human spirit than any sinking but honorable floundering in a lawfully inherited and improved bog of perplexities. Still, when is a moral vision of order practically available? When a society can respond to the vision as representative of its own realizable ideals? But it is the nature of society to change; for some realities it must recognize and deal with are not, or refuse to become, moral realities. And society has a way of solving problems only after they have ceased to be moral problems. On the other hand, it is the nature of moral order to remain by comparison stable — to shift groupings, emphases, names, of course, but to persist with remarkable consistency in the imaginative availability of its basic patterns. We can see this better perhaps in poetry and myth, which draw on the deepest roots in human experience, than in philosophy, which must take many of its problems and directions from the world around it. Poetry does this too, but for all its recognized necessity of being ever new and speaking to the present, poetry in its imaginative eloquence draws only part of its power from what contemporaries have themselves felt or almost felt.

The details of Milton's imaginative vision were more available to his contemporaries (or predecessors), in the sense that there had been no sharp break in the continuity of intellectual tradition. But was the vision practically or imaginatively more available? It is to be doubted whether the Restoration, with its new and therefore aggressive consciousness, could have felt anything like the need we may honorably feel of seeing how a vision of wholeness can be not only undertaken by a poet but carried through with imaginative perfection of parts and whole. In fact, is exact congruence between vision and audience ever possible? Is the problem not like the one Milton presents in *Samson Agonistes*? — where we have a complete and corrupt identification of Dalila and the moral order of the community; but a crucial gap preserved between Samson and the community, in order to provide the true audience of fit readers with what is permanently available, though making great demands upon us, and no complete gift exactly convertible: a vision and not a program.

The reason for this may be that the moral order is first, and perhaps last, individual. And if the group is no simple sum of its parts, with nothing unaccounted for and nothing left over, one may regret this, but not unreservedly. Victories of a group have already shifted their basis and much of their purpose before the last details of the triumph have been registered; and failure is only failure, though heroic, but never tragic. Milton's return to the individual is not escape but return to the imaginative source of being, a kind of pruning of what did not grow right, as he had hoped and thought it would. The later Milton is less interested in speckled time running back to the age of gold than in the individual returning to the root. Yet the cycle of Milton's concern is not characterized by the thinnness, bitterness, negativeness of disillusion, but by richness and creativeness. The simplicities returned to are no longer enthusiastic intellectual assertion (however beautiful), the statements of a parochial or inexperienced faith; the belief embraced is not the last alternative of a beaten man; but it is the belief of an experienced man, beaten in the right ways and with the right attitudes toward the facts of human defeat.

The models of heroic and tragic victory which he created do

not have to be exactly imitable to affect us. Moral patterns are not like machine tools, nor are we to be stamped out in permanent perfection. We cannot live as the heroes of these poems; but if we cannot be moved by the issues, then we lack — not the moral history, or even education, or belief — but moral imagination. Whatever may be unavailable to us, divided as we are within ourselves and among ourselves; and however more formidable appear to us, and in fact are, the external forces of separation and disunity; the spectacle of imaginatively realized heroic and individual independence, founded on an immovable religious dependence, a binding faith which disciplines and frees — it is a vision that makes intelligent hope available.

The immediate future of the world may belong to those who can command the hope of the world. And some version of the old virtue of *communitas*, called "humanity" or whatever, would seem to have a growing lead. Perhaps the new public morality will revolutionize the old individual morality, or perhaps only the surfaces will, as often, change. But we may well think, as individuals, of the losses to be expected when a public morality sets the example, is the model of aspiration for individual morality; when the hope that cannot be imagined at home will be officially realized abroad. We have no modern Miltons, but our writers are not indifferent to the old problems just under the surface of the new. The most distinguished exploration of the self in modern English poetry is T. S. Eliot's *Four Quartets*. And the individual struggling with and running from himself is a major theme of Robert Penn Warren, who for the past decade or so has been writing the best fiction and some of the best poetry in English. Milton never put his hope in a commonwealth better than the best individuals who composed it.

Notes and Index

NOTES

Some Problems and Solutions

[1] See the excellent formulation of Milton's "almost impossible poetic task" by Don Cameron Allen, *The Harmonious Vision* (Baltimore: Johns Hopkins Press, 1954), pp. 116–17.

[2] Cf. Allen, pp. 112ff and especially, "It is fear, cold fear, rather than uncertainty that is the major quality of the evil mind of *Paradise Regained.* . . . we must not fail to notice that Christ tempts Satan, if Satan can be tempted, both to anger and fright." For a patronizing version of a romantic tradition of criticism most subtly argued by Tillyard, see W. Menzies, "Milton: The Last Poems," *Essays and Studies by Members of the English Association,* XXIV (1938), 104: "Milton has put too much of himself into Satan's character. . . . The fervent partisan cannot, though he would, undo the poet's work. . . . This greatest perhaps of all poets was in truth a very simple soul. Much as he talked of badness he did not really know it well. The creation of an Iago would be a task quite beyond him."

[3] Mircea Eliade, *The Myth of the Eternal Return,* tr. W. R. Trask (New York: Pantheon, 1954), p. 20.

[4] See the *Christian Doctrine,* I, 8; Ephesians, 6, 12; Origen, *De Principiis,* III, ii. See the excellent survey of the tradition of temptation in Elizabeth M. Pope, *Paradise Regained, the Tradition and the Poem* (Baltimore: Johns Hopkins Press, 1947). This is a valuable and necessary book for recovering the intellectual and moral tradition back of the poem. For the most part my method is to translate for the modern reader the moral issues into what I hope are their still-recognizable forms, and to deal with the poem as a work less of an age than for all time. I have absolutely no quarrel with, but only admiration for, Pope's scrupulous effort to read the poem in terms of Renaissance theological traditions. My work is indebted to hers, but neither builds on it directly nor aspires to supplant it.

[5] See in this connection Frank Kermode, "Milton's Hero," *R.E.S.,* IV (1953), 317–30.

[6] See Pope, pp. 32ff, for a full discussion. As I assess in retrospect my own interpretation of the issue I find that it differs chiefly in details and emphasis

217

from those of Pope, Allen, or Woodhouse in "Theme and Pattern in *Paradise Regained*," *University of Toronto Quarterly*, XXV (1956), 167–82. Like Woodhouse, I too see growth and progress in Christ and a kind of romantic short circuit between Satan's mind and will. Christ does not go in for "disguises" but neither does he try, against the interests of the poem, to reduce dramatic tension. There is a difference, I think, between seeing Satan's doubt as a dramatic issue, in the working out of which we can be interested, and solving that doubt by a peremptory intellectual discrimination that may leave the reader with more curiosity over the progressive symptoms than with genuine dramatic interest. The working out of my own interpretation has perhaps less in common with Woodhouse's finally than with Bush's brief and penetrating sense of the collaboration between the literary and the intellectual: "a measure of tension is given by Satan's ignorance of his adversary's true character and by Christ's own lack of entire certainty." (*English Literature in the Earlier Seventeenth Century* (New York: Oxford, 1945), p. 391.)

⁷ *The Epistle of Ignatius to the Philippians*, Chapter 8f. The epistle may be "spurious," but not the attitude expressed.

⁸ Columbia *Milton*, III (part 1), 317–19.

⁹ *Of Patience*, Ante-Nicene, XI, Chapter 18.

¹⁰ I find overemphatic the distinction by Hanford, "*Samson Agonistes* and Milton in Old Age," *Studies in Shakespeare, Milton and Donne* (New York: Macmillan, 1925), p. 170, that the first and third temptations are "special" to Christ's mission and the second temptation universal. My underlying assumption is that Milton has maintained, in a way that resists any ordinary effort at separation, both the special and universal implications. I try to formulate the structural consequences of my view at the two places where my exposition can deal with them best — at the end of the fifth and eighth essays. As I look back I find my own view very close to Pope's: "Nowhere in the poem does he suggest openly that the Lord is laying down a law for the tempted . . . The moral lesson of *Paradise Regained* may be obvious, but every reader is left to draw it for himself" (p. 29). And close to Bush's: "His virtues may be superhuman in degree, but they are not in kind; they may be attained in some proportion by every Christian soul" (p. 391). This last reminds me of one of Hanford's points that I emphatically agree with: "By his indifference to these allurements and by his Socratic exposition of their emptiness Christ instructs all men how they may despise them" (p. 170).

¹¹ *Four Quartets*, "East Coker," III; "Little Gidding," V.

The Virtues

¹ See especially the *Charmides*; cf. the *Phaedrus*, 237–38.

² Cicero, *Tusc. Disp.*, IV, 9, 22: "Omnium autem perturbationum fontem esse dicunt intemperantiam."

³ Origen, *De Principiis*, III, 2; *City of God*, XIX, 4.

⁴ IV, xxv, Loeb edition, VIII, 93.

⁵ I am indebted to Professor Wolfson's whole treatment of Philo's ethical theory, Chapter XII of his two-volume *Philo* (Cambridge, Mass.: Harvard University Press, 1947).

⁶ *The Life of Porphyry Bishop of Gaza*, by Mark the Deacon, tr. G. F. Hill (New York: Oxford University Press, 1913), pp. 9, 13.

⁷ For Proclus see the quotation from *On the Chaldean Philosophy* in L. J. Rosán, *The Philosophy of Proclus* (New York: Cosmos, 1949), p. 208: "There-

fore it is said: 'Do not stifle your mind,' which means not to hide the desires, but rather to destroy them entirely; for that which is merely stiffled will still impart its own heat to what surrounds it." See Pfeiffer's *Meister Eckhart*, tr. C. de B. Evans (London: J. M. Watkins, 1947), I, 33, 48–49, *et. al.*

[8] "Ash-Wednesday," VI; "East Coker," III.

[9] *De Ira*, I, 9, 2. Cf. St. Augustine, *City of God*, XIII, 9, where he approves of the emotions necessary to our human infirmity. But Stoic impassibility is to be defended, he adds, if it is understood as want of the perturbations which specifically "disturb the mind and resist reason."

[10] *Two Ancient Christologies* (London: Society for Promoting Christian Knowledge, 1940), pp. 18–19.

[11] *Second Defence*, Columbia *Milton*, VIII, 131. I shall quote the prose from this edition, but modernize the spelling, and cite only volume and page, except for the *Christian Doctrine*, which I shall refer to by book and chapter.

[12] VIII, 241. I have made some small changes in the Columbia translation, chiefly the substitution of "piety" for "devotion." *Pietas* is an exact word here. Castiglione, citing Xenophon, relates piety to justice; love of God fosters true foresight in a ruler. *The Courtier*, Book IV, 32.

[13] *Republic*, IV, 427C–445B.

[14] "The Christ of *Paradise Regained* and the Renaissance Heroic Tradition," S.P., XXXV (1938), 254–77.

[15] *De Officiis*, I, 18; cf. I, 42.

[16] VIII, 9; VIII, 105; VIII, 15; VIII, 225.

[17] A notable passage from the *Gorgias* (507) seems to have impressed itself on Milton's mind: "In his relation to other men he [the temperate man] will do what is just; and in his relation to the gods he will do what is holy . . . And must he not be courageous? for the duty of a temperate man is not to follow or to avoid what he ought not, but what he ought, whether things or men or pleasures or pains, and patiently to endure what he ought."

[18] See the treatment by Kermode: cf. Tillyard, *Studies in Milton* (New York: Macmillan, 1951), pp. 101–4; *The Miltonic Setting Past and Present* (New York: Macmillan, 1949), pp. 199–201.

[19] For an excellent treatment of the seventeenth-century competition, see Cassirers' section on empiricism, Chapter III of his *Platonic Renaissance in England* (Austin: University of Texas Press, 1953). I am of course indebted to him, and not for this book only.

[20] Cited by Wolfson, *Philo*, II, 237.

[21] Quoted by Cassirer, pp. 163–65.

[22] Milton has provided us with a notable handling of the inseparable virtues when separated. In the great consult of Pandemonium Moloch demonstrates pure fortitude, which scorns all other virtues. Or rather, fortitude *is* justice; and temperance is absorbed into the courage of annihilation, or allowed the small inflexible margin "On this side nothing"; and wisdom roars in the voice of fortitude that their "proper motion" is upward and therefore as easy as their descent was "laborious" and "adverse."

Belial, defend us, speaks pure justice, or what in the environment of hell seems remarkably pure. His voice is the only one that acknowledges the omnipotence and omniscience of God; he discriminates among degrees of punishment; he recommends accepting "fate inevitable" and "Omnipotent Decree"; he accepts the justice of the law ordaining punishment and advises attempting to satisfy the sentence. The purity falters a little, one must admit, but not much, considering person, circumstances, and place. Justice makes a false bow to wisdom in the praise of "intellectual being." And hope for a new order of justice relies perhaps too much on temperance — but it is difficult, we remember, to separate those two, even under circumstances conducive to the most leisurely and enlightened definitions. Temperance will have to practice the discipline of patient waiting and the ultimate trick of self-mastery — the conforming of self in "temper and in nature," to receive as familiar the new justice of the totalitarian state of hell.

Justice, having spoken first, has already robbed temperance of its best points; but there is still left, as always, a greater purity of emphasis and concentration. Mammon can stress the discipline of freedom and "Hard liberty," the self-mastery of seeking good from self and living to self, a restricted harmony but a harmony. Mammon steals a little back from Belial, for this profession of individual dignity encroaches on justice, on a man's proper concern, and on proper subordination. The discipline of this extreme worldly puritanism will "thrive," will even achieve a kind of conspicuous greatness of transcendence not unlike some versions of magnanimity. But the last hope is, again, that of complete self-mastery, which may bring the transformation of "temper," the changing of their torments into their elements.

Incidentally, I wonder whether Milton was glancing at the high claim, and language, of Seneca, *De Ira*, II, 12: "Atque nihil est tam difficile et arduum quod non humana mens vincat et in familiaritatem perducat assidua meditatio. Nullique sunt tamferi et sui iuris affectus ut non disciplina perdomentur."

Satan's Banquet

[1] My reading of the doubts of the disciples and mother agrees with Allen's (see p. 116) and Bush's: "It is not merely Satan who misunderstands Christ's nature and purposes; even His followers look for the establishment of an earthly kingdom, even His mother's confidence is troubled" (p. 392).

[2] For citation of the Latin commonplaces on descent into the self see Kermode. I am following what I consider a more profound pattern, one more appropriate to the poem and to Milton's characteristic imagination. For the initial suggestion I am indebted to Bruno Snell, *The Discovery of the Mind*, tr. T. C. Rosenmeyer (Oxford: Blackwell, 1953). A fuller discussion must wait until the end of "The Way of Death."

[3] Watkins, in spite of many perceptive observations, falls into the trap of making the poet "wilfully intrude" into the poem. See W. B. C. Watkins, *An Anatomy of Milton's Verse* (Baton Rouge: Louisiana State University Press, 1955), especially pp. 119ff. Questions (as those rising from Belial's speech and Satan's on beauty) which can be answered significantly by the structure of the poem (whether my answers are right or not) have been more reasonably and profitably dealt with than when we assume, as we otherwise first must, a failure in the poem, and then provide an answer by reference to the poet's psyche.

[4] Not, I hasten to add, for the primary purpose of her work, which is to recover the relevant traditions back of the poem. But a gap will always remain between the tradition of ideas back of a poem and the actual expression of those ideas in the structure of the poem. It would be an error in emphasis to make the drama conform exactly to an underlying formula of moral action, even though the poem is certainly based on established traditions of knowledge, belief, and experience.

220

NOTES

[5] See Howard Schultz, "Christ and Antichrist in *Paradise Regained*," *PMLA*, LXVII (1952), 790–808. I have not tried to argue, in any point-by-point way, with Schultz's interpretation but have tried rather, by developing the main lines of my own, to offer an argument that I hope may persuade both for its conception of the intellectual and moral issues and for its effort at fidelity to the imaginative poetic structure. Similarly, I have not tried to argue with another ambitious interpretation (not allegorical), that of Dick Taylor, Jr., "Grace as a Means of Poetry: Milton's Pattern for Salvation," *Tulane Studies in English*, IV (1954), 57–90.

My interpretation and Schultz's are probably mutually exclusive, or nearly so. I think this not true of mine and Northrop Frye s — "The Typology of *Paradise Regained*," *M.P.*, LIII (1956), 227–38. For though Frye emphasizes the allegorical and mythical patterns in ways that perhaps tend to dominate the poetic patterns, or transform them into something not quite literary, his over-all control of the poem is unmistakable and authoritative.

For two other vigorous analyses of the banquet, see T. H. Banks, "The Banquet Scene in *Paradise Regained*," *PMLA*, XLV (1940), 773–76; A. H. Gilbert, "The Temptation in *Paradise Regained*," *J.E.G.P.*, XV (1916), 599–611. Hanford's old essay, "The Temptation Motive in Milton," *S.P.*, XV (1918), 176–94, is still relevant.

[6] *Othello*, II, i, and following.

[7] I agree wtih Pope (p. 78) that Christ's reply is "hypothetical," repeating Satan's terms. Woodhouse disagrees and will allow only one "ambiguity," Christ's answer on the tower.

[8] If Christ were uncertain of his identity, or if there were a failure of nerve or faith, he might have succumbed to the fallacy of the challenge and accepted the miracle as due him. In one sense this is an easier version of the earlier temptation, requiring, as it does, not the performance but the acceptance of miracle. If one gives Milton (or Satan) credit for understanding the complex perversity of the human mind in uncertainty, then one may observe that the very excess and the flaunting wrongness of the banquet might have induced an uncertain Messiah to take the challenge of his identity. An untranscendent appeal to appetite would offer little inducement to a great uncertainty. All this multiplication of fine points does not contradict, I think, the underlying simplicity of the moral rhetoric, the failure of the evil imagination to understand good. But the complexity we have been describing is, I think, in the object, Satan's dragnet of a trap, which is also an expression of Satan's mind.

A Digression on Poetry and Politics

[1] *The Education of a Christian Prince*, tr. L. K. Born (New York: Columbia University Press, 1936), p. 160.

[2] *Politics*, III, vi (179a). Cf. *The Praise of Folly*, tr. L. F. Dean (Chicago: Packard, 1946), pp. 107f.

[3] "An Apologie of Raymond Sebond," *The Essays of Montaigne*, tr. John Florio (New York: Modern Library, 1933), p. 434.

[4] There is a tradition of grudging praise for conquering virtue. See for instance Fulke Greville on the Turks, *A Treatie of Warres*, stanzas 17, 64–65; *A Treatie of Humane Learning*, stanzas 42f.

[5] See Aristotle, *Politics*, I, v (1254a); cf. *The Education of a Christian Prince*, p. 178.

⁰ Cf. *Of Reformation*, III, 38: The state ought to be "one huge Christian personage, one mighty growth and stature of an honest man, as big, and compact in virtue as in body; for look what the grounds and causes are of single happiness to one man, the same ye shall find them to a whole state, as *Aristotle* both in his ethics and politics from the principles of reason lays down."

The Kingdoms of the World

¹ As part of an interpretation emphasizing the theocentric patterns M. M. Mahood quotes — from Gladys Wade's *Thomas Traherne* (Princeton, N.J.: Princeton University Press, 1944) — Tuckney on the Cambridge Platonists: "Mind and understanding is all; heart and will little spoken of." *Poetry and Humanism* (London: Jonathan Cape, 1950), p. 222.

² *Poems of Mr. John Milton*, with J. E. Hardy (New York: Harcourt, 1951), p. 280.

³ For this suggestion, and another matter to be noted later, I am indebted to an auditor in one of my classes, Dr. Elizabeth H. Wolgast, who, with her keen argumentative skill, special learning in epistemology, and ambivalence toward Milton, put some very valuable pressure on this book during its final stages.

⁴ Northrop Frye (p. 233) sees the reference to Angelica as a kind of vestigial remain from Milton's abandoned epic romance. The point does not seem to me well grounded. Since I consider him a friend, and admire his essay and his critical powers, I'll venture further: the point, if not well grounded, seems more like speculative gossip which diverts from the proper critical tasks.

⁵ I am not sure that my reading can be reconciled with Frye's interpretation as religious allegory: "Christ rejects also the legal conception of Israel as a chosen people and is ready to usher in the new Christian conception of Israel as the body of believers" (p. 232). But perhaps Frye may kindly accommodate my interpretation as one of his levels of allegory. The biographical speculations on the political temptations are challenging here and worth considering, but I think I detect some failure in imaginative sympathy when he adopts the "demonic" view to reject Christ's rejection of the political temptations.

Milton, besides being a master of dramatic half-truths, had himself to draw on. For his emphasis on timing and ease Satan might have referred to *The Ready and Easy Way*, VI, 125: "Now is the opportunity, now the very season wherein we may obtain a free commonwealth and establish it forever in the land, without difficulty or much delay."

The Kingdom of the Mind

¹ I have no quarrel with commentators who see in the passage a reflection of Milton's personal enthusiasm for things Athenian — so long as the comment does not, like gossip, supplant a proper emphasis on great events. The speech, a necessary set passage, obeys the larger decorum of the poem. The brief statement by M. M. Mahood (p. 241) puts the issues correctly.

² Irene Samuel, "Milton on Learning and Wisdom," *PMLA*, LXIV (1949), 708–23.

³ VI, 95–98.

⁴ *De Principiis*, IV, i, 7; *Contra Celsum*, VI, 2. See in this connection G. E. von Grunebaum, *A Tenth Century Document of Arab Literary Theory and*

Criticism (Chicago: University of Chicago Press, 1950), Chapter XIV, "Descriptions of the Types of Eloquence."

⁵ Allen (p. 115) speaks of his "sacred unknowingness."

⁶ "To All the Churches of Christ."

⁷ III, 229.

⁸ Cf. Frye, p. 229: "The difficulty of the temptation for Christ is complicated by the fact that he is still, at this stage of his career, within the law. . . . The climax of the temptation corresponds to the death of Moses in the Exodus; it is the point at which Jesus passes from obedience to the law to works of faith, from the last Hebrew prophet to the founder of Christianity." This is the historical symbolism, and certainly accurate. What I have tried to express is a symbolism which is less historical than psychological, perhaps mythic (to poach on Frye's familiar preserve). My version, which I see as parallel and reconcilable to Frye's, is that the movement in Christ is from intuition, through discursive discipline (in which the law figures), back to a proved intuition and an inspiration that will no longer need the helps (either Hebrew or pagan) of the progress, though if those helps were not needed we have had much ado about nothing. One could also read this pattern as a version of the piety which is the beginning and end of wisdom. My emphasis is, I suppose, on the "humanist" side, but if I had thought of Frye's point I should have appropriated it happily. The "humanist" symbolism perhaps makes better sense of the autobiographical revelation, the heroic aspirations of human intuition, which I can fit into Frye's scheme only by a strained reference to the traditional associating of Egypt with "the world" and the frequently cited parallel of Moses rejecting the worldly kingdom of Egypt.

⁹ I cannot subscribe to W. Menzies' interpretation, that the blind Milton has already lost Greek anyway, and that, "Bare as his existence already was, it might and probably would become still barer as time went on. Life is like that. . . . In other words the invisible groundwork of *Paradise Regained* as distinguished from its avowed subject and supernatural framework is a scheme of life ideally conceived as stripped of everything superfluous. . . . Milton's whole argument for the bare life leads up to just this acute contradiction between the Hebraic and the Hellenic Spirit." (Pp. 97–99.)

¹⁰ III, 224.

¹¹ I prefer to put the emphasis on "presumption," on the dangers inherent in all claims of independence, whether of power, or glory, or knowledge. (Milton's originality here in placing the high point of human glory in the mind tempting itself has been widely and justly admired.) Woodhouse (p. 178) puts the emphasis on Christ's constant "tactic . . . to call in question the intrinsic worth of Satan's proffered gifts." He goes on, wisely, to enrich this view by inferring that Christ's "rejection" is related to the synthesis of Christian humanism, which, not without some residue of "tension," enjoins "that (as Erasmus says) things indifferent should not be pursued for their own sake but only as they conduce to the service of God, and, beyond this, that we should be *willing* to sacrifice them, and every other treasured possession, to that service." (Pp. 179f.) This is justly said and I concur, but I should want to insist also on the controlling emphasis of the dramatic structure and situation, which would mark, among other things, this high point of demonstrated knowledge and intellectual endeavor. Without its dramatic emphasis Christ's speech can have the force only of a philosophical argument (not very great), or of a sermon (eloquent to partisans but lacking the power to move by its imaginative rightness all true readers, whether believers or not).

The Way of Death

[1] Pp. 91f.

[2] F. M. Cornford, *Principium Sapientiae* (Cambridge: The University Press, 1952), p. 55. This paragraph draws freely on Cornford; I owe a general debt to the posthumous book as well as to the excellent commentaries on Plato. I am also aware of some general debts, by now not possible to identify particularly, to books by the following scholars: William F. Albright, Franz Cumont, E. R. Dodds, Henri Frankfort, Theodor H. Gaster, W. K. C. Guthrie, Jane E. Harrison, Gertrude R. Levy, Bronislaw Malinowski, George F. Moore, Gilbert Murray, Martin P. Nilsson.

[3] Cf. Allen's apt expression (p. 114): Satan "becomes an infernal poet and writes in Nature a violent version of 'Il Penseroso.'" I might add, not quite relevantly, that Satan's expression of desperate rage in action has something in common with Samson's opportunity, rejected, of action against the Philistine machines.

[4] *De Anima*, quoted from George Thomson, *Aeschylus and Athens* (London: Lawrence and Wishart Ltd., 1941), p. 124.

[5] Pope's summary is helpful here, pp. 84ff.

[6] Allen's interpretation of Satan's fear is in consequence, I think, not very different from my emphasis on the overstepping of the legitimate bounds of temptation. He sees Satan's fear "at its greatest pitch when it turns to a panic that drives him to violence. . . . in these two final acts of violence, he tosses away the elaborate plan of his great campaign and at last reveals himself as a cornered and desperate animal." (Pp. 114f.) This last is I think too strong, or too intellectual and abstract. The trap *is* clever and complex. It impresses Everyman, so that he may be still more deeply impressed by the resolution, which is swift, simple, and inevitable (a moment after it has happened).

[7] I am in general agreement with Pope that on the tower we have less a temptation than a final attempt to determine identity. However, our interpretations differ in a number of important details.

[8] See Pope's summary (pp. 83f) of the tradition against Christ's calling himself God here. Warner G. Rice, *"Paradise Regained," Michigan Academy Of Science, Arts, and Letters*, XXII (1936), 502, interprets Christ's reply as an expression of humility and "constant faith" which is "fully in accord with the central meaning of the poem."

[9] Frye (p. 237) perceptively imagines the scene as actual, not as an abstract crisis in a dialectical debate. But I cannot agree with him when he interprets the "secondary meaning" of Christ's reply as saying, "Do not continue the temptation of the Son of God."

My interpretation has much in common with that of Woodhouse (p. 181): "His injunction to stand is purely ironical: that it is possible, he never for a moment conceives. But if Satan can be ironical, so can Christ and the event. For the first and only time he complies with Satan's suggestion; but it is not in surrender to Satan: it is in obedience to God — like Samson's going to the festival of Dagon. This is Christ's supreme act of obedience and trust, and it is also the long-awaited demonstration of divinity. The poem's two themes are finally and securely united; and 'Tempt not the Lord thy God' carries a double meaning, for, in addition to its immediate application, it is Christ's first claim to participate in the Godhead. In an instant, and by the same event, Satan receives his answer and Christ achieves full knowledge of himself."

To see this as Christ's "claim," however, is to abandon much of the force

224

of the disciplined demonstration — as well as to abandon Milton's own passionate religious and moral belief, and his own disciplined unwillingness to pry into God's maintained mysteries. These are points Woodhouse must have thought of, but I do not see how he has taken them into account. And I do not see how or why, in his interpretation, "full knowledge" is achieved now. Is it the result of the assertion, the "claim"? I can hardly believe that Woodhouse means that. Is it the result of complying with Satan's suggestion? Is it the assertion of miracle (the motivation and timing clouded in mystery) which first demonstrates and then claims divinity, or vice versa? What becomes of all the careful demonstration of progress toward knowledge? Why should the method and discipline of the poem suddenly be abandoned, or reversed?

The theme of time and timing and resignation to God's time has been so constantly repeated and developed that we have some license to interpret the timing here. The God who advances to glory those who seek His and not their own may return to *being* those whom He has sent. Christ's own answer is as quietly final as the speech on God's time which provoked Satan's desire to be at the worst. But it is briefer now, and the essence of religious resignation. It is also properly learned and discursive, and, as it turns out, inspired — the complete and final uniting of the discursive return to the intuitive, the uniting of piety as the beginning and end of wisdom, knowing and worshipping God aright. If the miracle of the emergent return to deity does not find Christ calm and resigned to God's time, if he has called the time himself, a great pressure of the cumulative religious demonstration is lost.

The inspiration is parallel to Samson's rousing motions, which are *undefined*, we should notice. Samson's inspiration emerges from a solidly built discursive demonstration, but it needs to be followed and trusted in order to be proved as the inspiration of God. Samson is entirely human and tragic, he is no unique Messiah; but we may have some measure of what would be the moral loss if we conjecture that Samson knew definitely, in advance, precisely what his inspiration meant in all details. Instead of inspiration or resignation then, we should have a relation to God more like a formal contract than even legalistic Calvinism could stomach.

Dramatically, and mythically, Milton has fused in one extraordinary moment *Anagnorisis, Theophany,* and *Peripeteia.* Each of these movements is separate but simultaneous. *Anagnorisis* provides four recognizable directions. There is the special discovery-recognition by Satan; there is the implicit recognition by the hero (not dramatized but taken in stride, as it were, and reflected by Satan), the hero whose pious words as a true son become the inspired word; there is the authoritative recognition (now "By proof the undoubted Son of God") by the divine audience; there is the dramatic recognition, delayed perhaps no longer than it takes the human audience to gasp. The glory of the *Theophany* bewilders Satan with wonder; it is then ritualized by angelic ministrations, but the hero returns privately to his mother's house. The *Peripeteia* is not only an ironic reversal that unites uncommon surprise, force, and inevitability, but it resolves the whole drama in one sudden turn and changes the whole course of dramatic feeling.

[10] For a somewhat different pattern of interpretation see Allen (p. 118): "In his divine nature Christ knows his identity and foresees his course, but in his human nature the 'exalted man' is often uncertain of both." The terms of the drama give us a protagonist who has "forgotten," as Allen nicely puts it, the details of his previous history.

[11] Hughes, p. 257.

[12] One final note on the meaning of what happens on the tower. This test of "presumption" purges any suspect residue, if any remain, of those early aspirations for heroic acts — not that these constituted presumption, but they might have, and from the clear perspective of his mission that the hero finally achieves, the early hopes may be seen as lying on a dangerous border line. I forgot to comment earlier on another structural relationship between the first and last temptations. We may consider Christ's *ad hominem* insults to Satan as the unmasking of a hypocrite by a hero who is not presented as a model of apathy, but who responds with allowable human feeling to an intentional dirty trick. As a talented student of mine remarked, Christ opposes the right kind of assurance to Satan's fake display of the wrong kind of humility. This comes full circle on the tower, when Christ opposes the right kind of humility to the wrong kind of assurance.

Since completing my manuscript, I have seen the excellent critical analysis of the first encounter by Alexander Sackton, "Architectonic Structure in *Paradise Regained*," University of Texas *Studies in English*, XXXIII (1954), 37–39. Sackton also comments, with fine discrimination, on the three versions of the baptism. His interpretation of the episode on the tower is that Satan is overreaching himself and tempting not Christ but God. Sackton's approach is one Milton deserves, and richly rewards.

[13] In retrospect I think these ideas may owe something to Bergson's concept of "dynamic religion" as he expresses that concept in *The Two Sources of Morality and Religion*. But I believe I arrived at these ideas chiefly by studying Milton, who derived them from some of the same ultimate sources as Bergson. I find some confirmation in Buber's wry comment: "The image of Judaism conceived by Bergson is the conventional Christian one . . . of a God of justice who exercised justice essentially on his own people, Israel, being followed by a God of love, of love for humanity as a whole. For Bergson, therefore, Christianity represents a human conscience rather than a social conscience, a dynamic code as opposed to a static code, and the ethics of the open soul as opposed to the ethics of the closed soul. . . . It is not true that the God of the Bible has, as Simone Weil expresses it, 'never until the Exile spoken to the soul of man.' He has always spoken to the soul of the individual, even in the time of the Decalogue; to whom else, if not to the soul of the individual, can the injunction be given not to covet? . . . The Ten Commandments are not addressed to the collective 'You,' but all of them to a single 'Thou.' . . . It is not true that Israel has not accorded to spiritual inwardness its rightful place; rather, it has not contented itself with it. Its teachings contest the self-sufficiency of the soul: inward truth must become real life, otherwise it does not remain truth. . . . real relationship to God cannot be achieved on earth if real relationship to the world and man are lacking. Both love of the Creator and love of that which he has created are finally one and the same. In order to achieve this unity, man must indeed accept creation from God's hands, not in order to possess it, but lovingly to take part in the still uncompleted work of creation. . . . This concept of man's vocation as a co-worker with God is emphasized by Bergson as the goal of that mysticism which he glorifies and which he does not find in Judaism; it is, however, a fundamentally Jewish concept." See "The Silent Question: on Henri Bergson and Simone Weil," *The Writings of Martin Buber*, ed. Will Herberg (New York: Meridian, 1956), pp. 306–14.

The First Dark Steps

[1] My friend John Verrall, who speaks not as a musicologist but as a composer learned in the history of musical form, tells me that he can think of no example quite parallel to this before the eighteenth century, but then he can think of many. Anticipations of this kind of form were implicit in Monteverdi, toward whom the musical history seems to point. But Western musical form developed much later than did poetic form. The most interesting modern account of the relationship between Milton's poem and music is Gretchen L. Finney's "Chorus in Samson Agonistes," *PMLA*, LVIII (1943), 649–64. The history she explores is fascinating to the student of this poem, particularly if he is interested in music, and in things Italian, and in the enigmas that surround one rich episode in the history of Giovanni Milton. I am inclined to agree with her conclusion (p. 664), that in this poem Milton "asserts the complete freedom of poet from musician." But that leaves the poetic evidence for the influence of the oratorio still to be demonstrated.

[2] Woodhouse, "Samson Agonistes and Milton's Experience." *Transactions of the Royal Society of Canada*, XLIII (1949), 162f, sees Samson at the beginning as in "a state of unrelieved despair." Allen, whose study of the function of despair in *Paradise Lost* is most illuminating, does not quite convince me by his formulation of the issue in *Samson Agonistes*. As part of my objection I think of a traditional moral paradox, like Gregory the Great's, that our Adam (Job) lies strong on the dungheap who stood feebly in Paradise. Or his comment, that the devil struggles mightily against those who have been his subjects and quiet under the law, if they try to rebel. (*Moralia*, PL, LXXVI, 79, col. 606; 120, col. 657.) But these comments, like others out of traditional theology, do not provide concepts quite adequate, or quite flexible enough, for the complex workings of the drama.

A better analysis of the situation at the beginning of the play is that by W. C. Curry, "Samson Agonistes Yet Again," *Sewanee Review*, XXXII (1924), 343: "This Power has crushed the spirit of a man who has failed to measure up to harsh but just standards, and has discarded him as a broken and useless instrument. The physical death of the protagonist, imminent at any moment, is of little importance. This is where most tragedies end."

[3] It would perhaps be instructive to think through Samson's relations to the community from some of the interesting points of view developed by Martin Buber.

[4] I am indebted for my developing of this point to the initial suggestion of the student referred to before, Dr. Elizabeth H. Wolgast.

[5] It is perhaps invidious for a practitioner of intensive reading to point out the errors of hasty misreading in a great virtuoso of extensive reading. None of the misinterpretations in Bowra's essay on Samson irritates me more than his saying, "Even though he married Dalila at God's bidding, Samson knows that he is to blame for what happened afterwards." C. M. Bowra, *Inspiration and Poetry* (Cambridge: The University Press, 1951), p. 117.

A Little Onward

[1] See the end of "The Guiding Hand" for the ironic last turn of this moral.

[2] Tr. Lowe-Porter (New York: Knopf, 1935), pp. 292f. Perhaps in addition to the studies of the Hellenistic and Christian traditions back of this poem we could use a "modern" study of Milton's "Hebraism" — not an assessment of

his knowledge but of his understanding. Such a study would begin by use-fully excavating Matthew Arnold's old position.

³ Cf. the interesting parallel in Eve's speech, *Paradise Lost*, IX, 279–81.

⁴ I locate what Hanford calls the "darkest moment" here at the point of realization and somewhat before the actual expression, which is divided among (1) the thought of withdrawal from strife, (2) the drooping of the "genial spirits," (3) the terrible lyric on pain. All commentators, I think, agree in locating the low point in this section of the drama, though most identify the moment in the expression of drooping spirits. Only F. M. Krouse, *Milton's Samson and the Christian Tradition* (Princeton, N.J.: Princeton University Press, 1949), p. 128, says in a casual error that after Dalila leaves Samson "is now plunged even more deeply into hopelessness . . . at this depth of despair." But on p. 131 he returns to the more generally held opinion. (In-cidentally, besides not having mastered the poem he is dealing with, Krouse falls into additional error by trying to apply Pope's formula of the triple temp-tation to all the main movements of the poem — and he attempts this with much less penetration, and with less tact and awareness of difficulties than Pope.)

The commentators agree, then, in dating Samson's recovery from the lowest point. My contribution, I think, is to see even in the darkness the subtle movements of light preparing under the surface. Milton has packed so much solid intricacy into this drama that it is perilous to chart the main lines of movement without weighing every phrase and word. To those who may think I have been too detailed and overrefined, I must answer that where I feel I have not been adequate, I have not been detailed enough. For instance, I have not paused for close analysis of the style — this in order not to encumber the exposition any further, and at the expense of repressing a dominant personal interest. But a whole further range of meaning resides there. See, for example, my one such digression in the note on Samson's line "With corporal servitude, that my mind ever."

⁵ W. G. Rice completely misinterprets this (p. 501) and accepts Manoa's perspective. Tillyard (*Milton* (London: Chatto and Windus, 1946), p. 348) perceives the importance, but with a biographical twist that diverts the mean-ing from the poem to Milton.

⁶ I take this to be a recollection of the "breath of Heav'n" at the beginning of the poem.

A Little Further On

¹ A distinction, it may be worth recalling, that helped establish William Joyce's treason in the famous trial after World War II.

² Curry (pp. 343–46) goes too far in assuming in Samson (an assumption that cannot be demonstrated in the poem itself) "an almost overwhelming desire to yield again." Nor can I agree with Watkins' psychological inter-pretation, pp. 144–46. As *advocatus Dalilae* Allen argues wittily and percep-tively. My own case against Dalila has not met his argument that her con-trition and remorse are part of the appeal of lechery. I am inclined to accept this, but to see the pattern not in terms of despair but as part of the larger argument of justice, with everything genuine in her desire still an expression of usurping power. (One can support this view of Miltonic temptation by the examples of Eve and the two Satans.) Dalila's self-control, I should add, is like that of the Satan tempting Christ. At one point Allen's "chivalrous indulgence" does go too far, I think — in calling Dalila's offer of "nursing

diligence" a "selfless proposal." But the scene is a rich one. I should hate to have any reader think I had solved all his problems for him.

³ I have borrowed the turn from a former student, Warren Tallman.

⁴ Hanford (p. 176) says that Dalila's visit, "however doubtfully motivated in itself, is essential to the idea of the drama." Most commentators ignore the problem of motivation or are satisfied by an assumption of curiosity on Dalila's part. Hanford here seems willing to be satisfied by the "idea" of the drama. Bush (p. 394) says, "her appearance is an obvious dramatic necessity, both as a reminder of Samson's former weakness and as a test of his recovery." Woodhouse (pp. 165f) makes substantially the same point, but sees the primary function of the scene as demonstrating "by her powerlessness to reassert her sway the completeness of Samson's repentance." The result of this kind of emphasis, I think, is to lead criticism into too narrow a solution of literary problems. As I said in my prefatory remarks, Milton's moral art suffers not inconsiderable losses from too swift or peremptory a translation. When we reduce the poem to its moral paradigm, we not only sacrifice "subtleties," which some admirers might be willing to spare, but we damage by distortion the paradigm itself. To see only Dalila's "powerlessness" here, and to miss the development of Samson's powerlessness-humility, is to read selectively the chart of Samson's moral progress.

The Guiding Hand

¹ On this passage and the one beginning "My self? my conscience and internal peace," I have made some remarks which I should like to repeat from "A Note on Meter," *Kenyon Review*, XVIII (1956), 455. What is metrically most interesting about the passage is that it is individual and assertive in effect, and seems to put a very great strain upon the meter, as if the strength of the personal passion were tearing at the bonds of the impersonal form. But in fact, with minor exceptions, the natural emphasis of the words and the meter coincides. The apparent conflict, strengthened by some actual conflict, requires that we look twice in order to discover how much of the real emphasis derives from the metrical regularity, from the coincidence of angry, personal accent and the impersonal accent of the meter. One may also see a special kind of deception in the regularity. At three places we have lines that advertise their regularity: "To make them sport with blind activity . . . Will condescend to such absurd commands . . . To show them feats and play before thir god." The effect, most notable in the first of these lines, is the familiar slow withering of satiric focus. But what chiefly accounts for the apparent difference of the line is not a different relation between metrical and natural emphasis, but a difference in tempo, and, incidentally, the rhetorical and rhythmical placing of the line in the whole passage, with what that does for the reciprocal effect of line on passage and passage on line.

In retrospect I want to call attention to the controlled shaking of Samson's wrath in exact time with the meter in this line:

$$x \quad / \quad x \ / \ x \ / \quad x \ / \quad x \ /$$
"With corporal servitude, that my mind ever . . ."

Note the difference if the style of using the meter here permitted the otherwise allowable variation: $x \ / \ x \ / \ x \ / \ x \ x \ / \ /$. This metrical variation in the last two feet, which in most metrical styles would heighten the emphasis, here would markedly decrease the emphasis by making it more common and general, less specific to Samson and his agonized sense of self blind among ene-mies. But the meter requires and sanctions the dislocation of stressing *my* more than *mind*. I have just read Mr. Ransom's essay "The Strange Music of Eng-lish Verse," *Kenyon Review*, XVIII (1956), and am struck by part of the parallel between this case and his perceptive analysis of "my long scythe whispering" (pp. 466–68). I completely agree that when the reader declines to accept the normal prose emphasis he "will have weighed the force of the meaning he has abandoned." I think Mr. Ransom implies, what I believe, that the reader's new perspective and sense of "undeveloped" possibilities will not have cancelled out the abandoned meaning, but will *feel* its negative pull in the new equilibrium of meaning. Samson has been laboring his mind heroical-ly, and at the same time exercising but mastering the raw immediacies of feeling rooted in the essential self. He has insisted on conduct "as reason was," but he is about to follow inspiration beyond the point of reason. This is the last flare-up of the self before he accepts the role as Fool of God. The *my* stressed more than *mind* rehearses one familiar truth of Samson's tragic error; but in doing so seems to deny (falsely) the essential role of the mind; and seems to create a distorting, belated emphasis on the necessary role of the feeling self in the history of Samson's tragic redemption; but asserts a com-plicated "dramatic truth" about what is to happen.

[2] Hanford (p. 177), following a somewhat different scheme of the issues, makes the good point that the Chorus is expressing "the old implication" that Samson "cannot regard himself as a being set apart."

[3] I am tempted to associate this rival inspiration with the intuition derived from human sources that characterized Christ's aspiration for "heroic acts." And perhaps one should relate to both of these cases Dalila's being possessed-persuaded by the idea of public good.

The Return of Samson

[1] For some interesting comments, from a Burkean point of view, on ritualis-tic death in *Samson Agonistes*, see Kenneth Burke, *A Rhetoric of Motives* (New York: Prentice-Hall, 1950), pp. 3–10, 16–17, 19.

[2] (London: Faber and Faber, 1948), p. 308. If Levy's point drawn as it is from an insight of modern anthropology, seems too sophisticated to explain a seventeenth-century poem, I can defend it from some of Milton's own cul-tural background. As a humanist he never completely subscribes to one ex-treme biblical (and Stoic and Neoplatonic) view, that the will and passions are to be not mastered but entirely rooted out. As Cassirer justly says (*The Platonic Renaissance in England*, p. 107): "Erasmus sees the goal of Chris-tianity, not in the suppression and destruction of the human will, but in the education, the 'discipline of the will.'" Or as my lord Ottaviano says in Cas-tiglione's *The Book of the Courtier* (Book IV, 18): "I did not say that tem-perance wholly removes and uproots the passions from the human mind, nor would it be well to do this, for even the passions contain some elements of good; but it reduces to the sway of reason that which is perverse in our pas-sions and recusant to right. Therefore it is not well to extirpate the passions altogether; for this would be like making an edict that no man must drink wine, in order to be rid of drunkenness. . . . Thus, when moderated by temperance, the passions are helpful to virtue, like the wrath that aids strength, hatred of evil-doers aids justice, and likewise the other virtues are aided by

the passions; which, if they were wholly removed, would leave the reason very weak and languid. . . . Nor is this less true of justice."

³ I think I have been remembering here some notable words of F. H. Bradley (*Essays on Truth and Reality*, (Oxford: Clarendon Press, 1914), pp. 17f): "But in philosophy, so far as philosophy succeeds . . . doubt here is not smothered or expelled but itself is assimilated and used up. . . . A scepticism that has tried to be thorough tends, we may say, to weaken doubt by spreading it and making it more general. The doubt, if really it is intellectual and not a mere disease of the will, loses strength and loses terror by losing its contrast."

One final note on the gap between individual and social morality. For all Martin Buber's heroic and admirable modern effort to relate the religious ethos to the body politic, his underlying moral position is founded on the morality of the individual soul. He uses the theological resources imaginatively, but some of his bridgework one may sympathize with more than one may approve. His political hero is willingly "bound" to the body politic, and cannot remain aloof, though he does not abandon himself blindly "to any of its movements, rather confronting each movement watchfully and carefully that it does not miss truth and loyalty." His great goal is to change the crowd into individuals. "And if he does not achieve much he has time, he has God's own time." See *Between Man and Man*, tr. R. G. Smith (Boston: Beacon Press, 1955), pp. 64f.

Postscript

¹ *The Need for Roots*, tr. Arthur Wills (New York: Putnam, 1952), p. 27.

² Origen (*De Principiis*, III, iv, 2) posits the probability that it is better for the soul to be under the mastery of the flesh than under the power of its own will, for then conversion may be easier when the soul is "filled with those very evils which it suffers." I have drawn heavily upon Origen to elucidate Milton's thought; for in spite of Milton's self-consciously Protestant rejection of the Hellenizing spirit in biblical commentary, his own humanistic education often brings him close to Origen.

INDEX